A SOLDIER'S PROMISE

THE HEROIC TRUE STORY OF AN AMERICAN SOLDIER AND AN IRAQI BOY

by First Sergeant Daniel Hendrex
with Wes Smith

SIMON SPOTLIGHT ENTERTAINMENT
New York London Toronto Sydney

Certain names and details appearing in the book have been changed.

The views expressed in the writing are those of the writer and not the Army, DOD (Department of Defense), or the United States.

SSE

SIMON SPOTLIGHT ENTERTAINMENT
An imprint of Simon & Schuster
1230 Avenue of the Americas, New York, New York 10020

SIMON SPOTLIGHT ENTERTAINMENT and related logo are trademarks of Simon & Schuster, Inc.
Designed by Steve Kennedy
Manufactured in the United States of America
First Edition 10 9 8 7 6 5 4 3 2 1
Library of Congress Cataloging-in-Publication Data
Hendrex, Daniel.
A soldier's promise : the heroic true story of an American soldier and an Iraqi boy / by Daniel Hendrex.
p. cm.

ISBN: 1-4391-6521-1 ISBN-13: 978-1-4391-6521-8

1. Iraq War, 2003—Personal narratives, American. 2. Hendrex, Daniel.
3. Iraq War, 2003—Refugees—United States. I. Title.
DS79.76.H464 2006
956.704'4092—dc22
2006007587

A
SOLDIER'S
PROMISE

This book is dedicated to the unsung heroes
of all conflicts—the military family. Spouses, children,
parents, and extended family have to endure the
loneliness, painful separation, and grueling reality of
"not knowing." Christina, my wife, bore the weight
of raising a newborn, helping Steve-O, and handling our
personal affairs while I was deployed to Operation Iraqi
Freedom for twenty-five of the last thirty-six
months. Christina's sacrifice and the many spouses
and families in the same situation will never be forgotten.

Christina, Sydney, and Steve-O . . .
I am eternally grateful and I love you.

CONTENTS

PREFACE

Any soldier who has experienced the relentless onslaught of machine-gun fire, the punishing rain of shrapnel, or the tragedy of losing a fellow soldier will tell you that there is nothing any of us want more than peace. We fight willingly, but we understand the cost.

As soldiers, we do not choose the wars or conflicts in which we fight. We take an oath and pledge to go anywhere, anytime our nation calls. We do not fight for some greater political cause. In battle, we rarely think of the global significance of our mission. We fight for the soldier standing next to us suffering the same hardships. Every day, our primary objective is simply to do our jobs and get one another back alive.

With every sunrise in Iraq, we faced our mortality. Mortar and rocket-propelled grenade attacks, improvised explosive devices, suicide bombers, mujahideen, corrupt police, foreign fighters, Al Qaeda, and innocent civilians used as weapons— these are the threats we confronted every day.

After the overthrow of Saddam Hussein, my unit, Dragon Company, was dispatched to Husaybah, on the Syrian border, just as the insurgency began to emerge as a threat. We quickly realized that it had become the primary entry point for mercenaries, zealots, and veteran foreign fighters responsible for increasing resistance throughout the country.

Husaybah was the most dangerous assignment of my military

career. It required absolute focus and constant improvisation. The soldiers of Dragon Company responded to the challenges with courage and tenacity. We worked to provide security for people who often seemed intent on killing us.

In the beginning, I had a one-dimensional view of the Iraqi people. But then along came a slight, cross-eyed Iraqi boy who gave us a deeper understanding. We came to trust him and then to consider him one of our own. This boy named Jamil, later nicknamed "Steve-O," saved our lives more times than we could ever count. In return, I made a promise to protect him at all costs.

—Daniel Hendrex, February 14, 2006
The end of my second tour in Iraq

1

KIA ON THE FRONT PAGE

It was two a.m. We were at the city's edge. It had taken us twenty-four hours just to reach this point. We hadn't had a shower in more than a week. We hadn't slept in almost forty-eight hours. Inside the tight confines of the tank's turret, we were soaked with sweat. The stench of cordite, hydraulic fluid, oil, and fuel filled our nostrils and permeated our uniforms. The turbine engine in our M1A2 Abrams armored tank idled in a low rumble as Sergeant Wilkening, the gunner, completed final checks and preparations to fire. The sergeant, a live wire from Seattle who was always ready for a fight, scanned the foliage and outlying buildings for any threatening activity through the gunner's thermal imaging system. I keyed my CVC, a helmet with built-in communications, and informed Lieutenant Wilkins, my new platoon leader, of my location and my intentions.

The moon offered zero illumination, but the distant flashes provided glimpses of what was to come. The infantry had breeched the city's defenses. They were trying to set a stronghold so they could then begin the tedious and dangerous task of driving out the enemy, building by building, room by room, step by step. Our mission was to obliterate any heavy resistance. Radio communication in urban environments was intermittent at best. The buildings, tight alleyways, and dead space played havoc with the technology. The lack of radio contact was maddening as we prepared to move our seventy-ton vehicle into the enemy's heavily fortified position amid sporadic gunfire, thundering explosions, and a thick fog of battlefield smoke.

"White One, this is White Four. We have cleared the last minefield, and we are moving in from the north. White Three, follow me."

We were the first heavy armor to enter the city, and we drew a lot of attention. Machine-gun and small-arms fire flashed from surrounding buildings and echoed in the alleyways. It was deafening. Pure chaos. Muzzle flashes seemed to come from every window, nook, and cranny. Both soldiers and insurgents darted in and out of the shadows. Civilians screamed for help.

Staff Sergeant Smith, my lanky tank commander, who was always coolheaded whether he was lining up an approach shot on the fairway or bearing down on an enemy stronghold in battle, positioned his tank, White Three, in the southern sector. I pushed our tank eastward. We were armed with the most lethal direct fire weapon system in the U.S. Army's arsenal, yet our hands were tied because we had no radio contact with our infantry. Sgt. Wilkening yelled, "I have hot spots everywhere, but I can't tell who is who!"

Then, suddenly, Wilkening found his mark: "Friendly soldiers, three o'clock, approximately fifty meters."

He had identified our troops through his thermal sights because their Kevlar helmets have a distinct heat signature. I jumped from the tank and signaled to them. A soldier sprinted over and gave me the most accurate situation report I'd heard all night. His company had not yet established a stronghold. They were taking heavy casualties. The three buildings to our north were still in the hands of the insurgents, who were using them as cover to fire on our troops on the south side of the road.

I relayed that we would neutralize the insurgents in those buildings so that the infantry could continue their mission. He sent word to the other infantry platoons and told them to keep out of the targeted buildings. He thanked us for the support before disappearing into the darkness. I had to smile at his display of gratitude. In barrooms and chow halls, armored soldiers and infantrymen argue constantly over which of their branches is best. But when the shit hits the fan, the boys in boots do love to see a friendly tank.

We moved into a blocking position and immediately took heavy fire. It was time to go to work.

"Gunner COAX troops, identified! Fire!"

But we were both the hunter and the hunted in this fight. No sooner had we knocked out one nest of insurgents than I saw a flash and a distinctive puff of smoke near a third-story window. A rocket-propelled grenade was coming right at us. Luckily, it missed, but behind it came a flurry of fire climaxing in a large explosion that rattled our tank. The yellow light on our MILES (Multiple Integrated Laser Engagement System) immediately began blinking and the audio system began blaring in our ears as an eerie female voice intoned, *"Catastrophic kill. Catastrophic kill."*

"You're done!" yelled the observer controller, the head referee for this mock battle. "An insurgent threw a satchel charge on your front slope and blew you up. Everyone is dead!"

Training or not, I hated to lose, especially when it was bullshit. I emphatically tried to make a case that our crew would have survived that sort of attack on a real battlefield. An explosion seeks the path of least resistance, so it is doubtful that there would have been enough downward force to do lethal damage to our heavily armored tank or the crew inside. But this wasn't the

NFL, and my argument, peppered with too many expletives for the ref's taste, sealed our fate. There were no play reviews in war games. Game over. The MOUT (Military Operations in Urban Terrain) site named Shuttgart-Gordon at the Joint Readiness Training Center in Fort Polk, Louisiana, would remain in the hands of the "enemy."

The sun was breaking over the horizon and the urban warfare training exercise was wrapping up when Lieutenant Colonel Kievenaar, my squadron commander, walked over to me. He had watched the entire battle from the water tower, which was the command center where footage from hundreds of cameras throughout this thirty-five-million-dollar mock city was fed and recorded for postbattle reviews. Lt. Col. Kievenaar and I had been stationed together several times over the course of my career, and as I shared my concerns and discussed the shortcomings of the exercise, I was approached by a civilian in a baseball cap. He had a pen and notepad in hand and was shadowed by a photographer.

"Are you the tank commander of that vehicle over there? I'd like to interview you," the reporter said.

I was still fuming and not at all thrilled to be discussing the demise of my tank and my crew. But media training is often part of such exercises. Each battle is videotaped and critiqued, and they'll sometimes ask us to do mock interviews so we get used to dealing with embedded news media. I answered all of his questions, playing along with the game and not really paying attention. Then, as we wrapped it up, I asked him what unit he was with. He squinted, looked at me impatiently, and said, "I am a reporter with *USA Today*."

"Yeah, yeah, I know. I can see the sticker on your cameraman. But you can break character now. Is this going to be used in the after-action review for commanders?"

Confused, he pulled out his wallet and handed me his business card. "Look, I don't know how to tell you this any other way. I am from *USA Today.* We're doing a story on this exercise. You are going to be on the front page of my newspaper tomorrow."

And that is how I came to die along with my tank crew on page one of the newspaper with the largest circulation in the nation even before Operation Iraqi Freedom had begun. It was a mock death in a mock battle in a mock city—and thanks to *USA Today,* I was mocked plenty about it when the story appeared on October 31, 2002. I laughed off the ribbing, jokes, and e-mails that seemed to come from every soldier I'd ever walked by in my twelve-year military career. But I also used the war game defeat as a wake-up call to ratchet up my level of preparation for what would prove to be the most challenging deployment of my life.

2

A CHILD OF WAR

SUMMER 2000

A convoy of four white Mercedes sedans came cruising out of the desert, trailing dust from Baghdad, which lay two hundred miles to the west. They'd followed the greenway created by the Euphrates River as it snaked across Iraq through the Al Anbar Province to the Syrian border. The slender, dark-haired boy from Husaybah watched from a hilltop as his father, a captain in the Republican Guard, saluted the sleek vehicles. They seemed to glow like starships in the brilliant sunlight.

When the men in Iraqi army uniforms stepped from the cars, it was difficult at first for the boy, Jamil, to determine which one was Saddam Hussein. So many of them were of the same build and sported similar facial hair. But then the other men stepped back to let their leader come forward to inspect the troops. Jamil saw his father's body stiffen as the powerful leader of their country approached. Saddam did not appear to single his father out. Instead, he appeared to be addressing the higher-ranking soldiers nearby.

Yet, on their way home that night, his father replayed the scene as one in which he and Saddam had conducted intimate conversations on important matters. Jamil reflected on the disparity between the bond that his father claimed to have with Saddam Hussein and what he had seen take place that day. He had long suspected that his father exaggerated both his ties to the president and his own standing in the Baath Party. Even at that point, he was beginning to suspect that his bullying father had little true influence beyond his men, their town, or the reach of his fists.

Husaybah lies uneasily on Iraq's western border with Syria. The outpost of 100,000 inhabitants has a sordid and violent tradition as a lawless den of smugglers and prostitutes, ruled through the centuries by contentious tribes. Two Sunni Muslim tribes—the Mahalowis and the Salmanis—control cross-border trade at the sprawling marketplace inside the town's landmark arched gates. Their bitter rivalry and the bloody infighting kept even Saddam Hussein from meddling much in the affairs of the cutthroats who rule the Sunni stronghold.

Husaybah was the birthplace and home of ten-year-old Jamil, the oldest of six siblings, including two sisters (Inaya and Nada) and three brothers (Imad, Kadar, and Hassan). Their mother, Tahira, doted on the children and did her best to serve as a buffer between them and their father, Nassir. As the eldest, Jamil was positioned as the favored child, yet he was most often the target of his father's anger. In his role as a captain in the Republican Guard, the Iraqi armed forces, Nassir had grown hardened and unforgiving through decades of relentless war, first with Iran and later with Kuwait and the American-led coalition that came to its aid and drove the Iraqi forces out.

Nassir was a soldier in the army of a dictator who posed as a benevolent father while torturing and preying upon his own people. The military itself was largely ruled by violence and intimidation that seeped into the daily lives of all Iraqis. Jamil bore the scars of that brutish existence at an early age. Home from battle, his father once accused him of stealing a coin from his sack purse. Jamil, then eight years old, pleaded his innocence, but only after his father held a spoon over a flame and pressed it into the back of the boy's hand. Jamil screamed and called for his mother, but she dared not help. It was not allowed. Her interference would only have brought more suffering down upon them.

A few months later, Jamil neglected to close the gate on a sheep pen shared by several families, and his own uncle knocked him to the ground and kicked him in the head, crushing a muscle and causing one of his eyes to cross. Tahira took her son to the Husaybah hospital, where a visiting Japanese surgeon from an international medical volunteer group repaired the damaged muscle in a long and painful procedure. While still healing, Jamil drew his father's wrath once again. Nassir lashed out, knocking the sutures loose and undoing the surgeon's work. Such brutal treatment left Tahira fearful for all of her children, but especially for Jamil.

After the terrorist attacks on the United States on September 11, 2001, Nassir grew more volatile than ever. The Republican Guard was put on alert for an American invasion. Saddam was defiant, but the rank-and-file soldiers had learned in Kuwait that they were ill equipped to fight more modern armies. As the threat of invasion grew, Nassir's dark moods intensified.

His wife and children did their best to protect one another while staying out of his reach. They were a close-knit group of strong-willed characters. Inaya was as tall as Jamil and equally spirited. He loved playing pranks on her, but she was no pushover. One day, as Inaya prepared to go to school, she discovered that Jamil had emptied her schoolbag and claimed it as his own. When he refused to give it back, she chased him around the house, whacking him on the back of the head with his own sandal until he gave it up.

Jamil's younger brothers shared his knack for pranks and provocations. Imad, who had made a study of his father's extensive vocabulary of curse words, was notorious for tampering with Jamil's homemade pigeon roost. Jamil kept the homing pigeons in a pen he'd built from scavenged chicken wire and wood. Imad would raid the roost, trying to play with the birds but often setting some free in the process. Each time, Jamil first chased down the birds and then hunted his brother, who would fly around the house squawking and cursing fluently, provoking laughter from his pursuer and the rest of the family.

Unlike many victims of abuse, Jamil was not inclined to anger or violence himself. He'd developed a natural charm as a survival instinct, but it offered little defense against a father who seemed to resent the boy's innocent existence. Nassir pulled Jamil out of school in the third grade and forced him to work to help support the family. He was expected to buy his own food and clothing, which he paid for with earnings from a variety of jobs. He made bricks at a factory that belonged to one of his uncles, worked in a restaurant with another uncle, washed cars, and did rudimentary mechanical jobs, like fixing brakes and tires. In the open desert, he and his friends also hunted and picked *chi-nah* (mushrooms), which they sold to local markets for tidy sums. The boy's skill at earning money became one of the rare things that his father praised him for, as long as he turned the earnings over immediately.

Yet, Jamil's self-sufficiency at such a young age also led his father to expect more of him. Nassir began to treat him as one of his soldiers. He rode Jamil constantly, telling him that his days as a boy playing in the streets were about to end. When the Americans came, it would be time to put down his toys and fight as a man. He, too, would be a soldier in Saddam's army.

This confused Jamil. He was too young to be a soldier. How could he possibly fight men twice his size without getting wounded or killed?

His father seemed to want to treat him like a soldier and a man, but he still bullied him like a child. Somehow, the small cruelties Jamil suffered day to day hurt as much as the physical wounds. Fishing was the one thing he and his father could usually do together without conflict. They made a good team—Nassir was skilled at tossing the weighted net but could not swim, and Jamil, a natural swimmer, would retrieve the catch and free the net from any snares in the water. One day, Jamil tried his hand at tossing the net and then swam out and found he'd snared the biggest fish either of them had ever caught. It was nearly half Jamil's own length.

His father said nothing and did little to help the boy as he brought the hefty catch to the riverbank.

"You keep fishing. I'll take this home and have your mother cook it for us," said Nassir.

Jamil swelled with pride, knowing that he had provided a meal for the whole family, and he was eager to share in it. His mother was an excellent cook. In fact, she'd taught Jamil many of her culinary methods and recipes during Nassir's extended military absences. He was looking forward to watching her prepare the best catch he'd ever made, but when he got home, he found his father and several of his friends seated at the table, devouring his prize fish.

"Your father caught a very big fish," one of the friends grunted while filling his plate with another helping.

Nassir just smiled as Jamil looked to his mother, a wave of indignation rising inside him. She quickly herded him into another room.

"I caught that fish!" he whispered to her.

"I know, but don't say any more," she said. "You don't want to make your father angry."

3

A DELAYED ENTRY INTO WAR

Shortly after September 11, 2001, I was sure the Pentagon would be unleashing the heavy armor of the Third Armored Cavalry Regiment and that we'd join the push into Afghanistan in pursuit of Al Qaeda and its leader, Osama bin Laden, immediately. But instead, a few weeks after the terrorist attacks, we were sent to Tooele, Utah, to set up the defenses at the military's chemical depot there as part of Homeland Security's Operation Noble Eagle. We spent nearly three months there before returning to Fort Carson, outside Colorado Springs, where we began training for the next phase of the war.

There was no doubt that the United States would be going back to Iraq to put Saddam Hussein out of business once and for all. It was never a matter of "if" we would invade, just a question of "when." We were the only heavy-armored regiment in the army, and we anticipated leading the charge across the desert when General Tommy Franks gave the command. That seemed to be the plan when we were sent for readiness training at Fort Polk in the fall of 2002. But we were still there in January when President Bush made his intentions clear in his State of the Union Address, saying,

"A brutal dictator, with a history of reckless aggression, with ties to terrorism, with great potential wealth, will not be permitted to dominate a vital region and threaten the United States."

Our commander in chief then spoke directly to all of us in the armed forces: "Many of you are assembling in or near the Middle East, and some crucial hours may lie ahead." The message was as clear as one could expect. Little did we know just how many crucial hours we'd spend overseas—nor did we realize how many *excruciating* hours there would be before our regiment entered the fight. And after President Bush laid out his plans, we figured they'd be calling us for deployment to the Middle East any day.

We had been hearing rumblings for a month, but the rumors of our deployment shifted with the winds. We were going. We weren't going. Sometimes, that's just the way it goes in the military, but it never gets easier. The uncertainty and tension are hard on us but so much harder on our families and loved ones. The vying reports and rumors had been flying for so long that we'd become desensitized to a degree.

The call finally came on Friday, February 14, 2003. It was a crisp Colorado day. So normal. So peaceful. My wife, Christina, had gone grocery shopping. I was balancing on a ladder in the foyer, putting the finishing touches on some trim, when the phone rang. I climbed down from my shaky perch and answered it. My troop executive officer's voice came through the receiver: "Sergeant Hendrex, we just received the orders for our deployment to the CENTCOM [central command] area of operations."

The first thing I thought was, *It's about fucking time.* Tired of not knowing, I was glad to have finally received solid orders. I had been pushing my platoon for months to get them in shape for deployment. Yet, the thought of leaving my wife sent pangs through my chest. How the hell was I going to tell Christina? *Hey, honey, I may be gone for up to a year and a half or possibly killed— happy Valentine's Day from your awesome husband.*

Christina is incredibly strong and has always supported my profession one hundred percent. When she came home that day, she knew by the look on my face that I'd gotten "the call." She took it with grace. She was a rock—my rock. Still, I could tell that she was thinking the same thing I was thinking: *This is the worst Valentine's Day present ever.*

The next month was filled with the exhausting process of preparing equipment, personnel, and weapons for a trek across the world. Moving a heavy-armored regiment is every bit as difficult as it sounds. The paperwork alone is enough to drive you to madness. And the Third Cavalry doesn't pack light. We are a small, contained army of tanks, helicopters, Humvees, and our own extensive arsenal. It took the better part of a month just to get all of our equipment on boats. The demands of overseeing weapons qualifications, updating soldier personnel records, prepping vehicles and equipment for stowage and saltwater erosion, and closing out offices and soldiers' billeting kept me distracted from dwelling on the fact that my time with Christina was quickly running out.

As for the men in the platoon, I suspect they wanted to kill me at times. I pushed them as hard as I had ever pushed anyone; physical training and teamwork—those two objectives were at the forefront of everything we did. The constant message was that we work as a team, never quit, and support one another at all times, under all conditions. The mountainous terrain and high altitude tested every soldier to the limit. If one soldier fell back, his crew carried him forward. If another passed out, he, too, was picked up and carried the rest of the way. There was no quitting.

It was brutal. After running for miles, members of the platoon had to carry one of our biggest soldiers up a forty-five-degree incline for almost two hundred meters at five thousand feet above sea level. If anyone stopped, we did it again. If someone didn't pull his weight, we all did it again. In the crisp Colorado air, steam rose from piles of fresh vomit at the top of the hill. I had never been happier to see bile and snot drooling from the mouths of my men. They were ready.

Then the war started without us. It was March 30, 2003, and we were still at Fort Carson. I watched the initial push into Iraq on CNN like a civilian. Despite my years of training and firsthand combat experience, I stood there watching my first major military operation on television, as if I were not even in the army. The invasion that we thought we'd be leading had left us behind. The news stung; it was a pride issue. Instead of rolling across the desert, we were training a group of North Dakota National Guardsmen how to shoot M-16s. A lot of the gung-ho guys were depressed at missing the big show.

Everyone in the platoon seemed to fall into one of two camps: gung-ho or naive. Some wanted the deployment to happen, and others seized on any rumor that led them to believe we were staying put. I fell into the first category because I train hard and just expect to go. I figured my soldiers would have a better chance of surviving with me than without me. After all the action I'd seen in previous deployments, I felt totally disconnected from one of the biggest military actions of my career.

As we waited, on standby, things started progressing with Operation Iraqi Freedom. I posted a list of things my soldiers should pack for Iraq. It was second nature to me. Every year or two after enlisting, I was dispatched to one troubled corner of the world or another. I had been to more than thirty foreign countries courtesy of the U.S. Army. The experience I'd gained had served me well. I moved up the noncommissioned ranks from private to sergeant first class at a rapid pace. I was years ahead of the normal schedule when I made the list for the Sergeants Major Academy—the school at Fort Bliss, Texas, where you train to reach the highest rank available to a noncommissioned officer.

I was in Operation Desert Storm (the first Gulf War), and I've been involved in peacekeeping efforts in Somalia, Bosnia, Macedonia, and Kosovo. I was swept up in a new wave of heightened military activity around the world. In a relatively short period, I saw more action and gained more combat experience than soldiers twice my age.

In all the excitement, I barely had enough time to convince Christina, my whip-smart, raven-haired Italian girlfriend, to marry me. We'd met when I went to visit my cousin Sherrel at Florida State University in Tallahassee. I had just returned to Georgia from my deployment in Africa, and a visit to a college campus sounded like a great idea. My friend Sergeant Paul Stafford, who had also been in Somalia, came along for the trip. While enjoying the social scene in Tallahassee, Paul met Sandra. She had a close friend named Christina. We went out on a double date. There was a lot of verbal sparring between Christina and me, but we definitely had a spark. The next thing I knew, I was spending every free moment either on the phone with her, traveling to see her, or with her.

Three years later, Christina was working in the gracious southern town of Savannah, Georgia, when I proposed to her. I rented a suit of armor and borrowed a white horse for the occasion. Fortunately, we had some time to build the foundation of our marriage during my second three-year stint in Germany. It was like an extended honeymoon. Memories of that period have gotten me through many difficult days and nights without her. The bonds of trust and love that we formed in our travels then have given me strength time and time again.

LONG GOOD-BYES

I am good at my job. I am not good at sitting around waiting to *do* my job. But waiting was the order of the day once it was announced that we were headed back to Iraq. Even as other troops moved out for the Middle East, we waited and waited for our orders to deploy. Veteran soldiers can deal with almost any situation that calls for action, but sitting around and doing the "hurry up and wait" is the shits. It messes with your mind. "Not knowing" and "not going" are two of my least favorite states of existence.

It's hard enough when you have a definite deployment date. In fact, of all the aspects of war, the day of departure ranks in difficulty only behind dealing with a soldier's death on the battlefield. It is the time when grown men struggle to find a way to say good-bye to wives, children, parents, fiancées, girlfriends, and grandparents. The emotions are unbearable.

I've gone through it so many times, but it seems to become more difficult with each deployment. The unknowns are what drive us nuts. *How long will we be gone? Will this be the time I get hurt? Will this be the last time we see our wives, our children, our parents?* I dread these days and the images that accompany them: children looking up to parents for guidance, confused and tearful because of the fear and despair they sense; tough soldiers with swollen, red eyes trying to maintain composure; wives weeping so hard that their knees go weak and they need help to stand. I had been with the men in my troop for the past two years, and I wanted to reach out to their loved ones, not only to do what I could to ease their fears, but also to impart my pride in their military accomplishments and my own commitment to their safety.

I remember that when I was a young private heading out for the first Gulf War, my parents received a letter from my platoon leader. He assured them that he would do his best to bring me home safely. Then he added a few nice, and mostly true, things to make them proud of me. That letter always stuck with me. And it meant a great deal to my parents, too. So as a platoon sergeant, I wanted to do the same for my soldiers. Here is an example of one of the sixteen letters I wrote to every spouse or parent before we deployed:

> To Rosemary Gill,
> Good afternoon, I am SFC Hendrex, the platoon sergeant of Second Platoon, Killer Troop, Third Armored Cavalry Regiment. I am responsible for the

training, care, and welfare of your son while assigned to Second Platoon. I have been your son's platoon sergeant for just over a year and a half. In light of current events, I write you today to inform you of my pride in serving with him and his personal achievements within the platoon.

I consider Christopher Gill family. I have known your son for over eight years and have seen him grow as a person and soldier—from a young private at Fort Stewart, Georgia, to a seasoned tank commander at Fort Carson, Colorado. S.Sgt. Gill's passion and professionalism know no bounds. I was witness to this within the first week of knowing him. Private Gill was assigned to my tank, and the very next day we had a twelve-mile road march in full military gear (about forty lbs.). I told him I was going to run, and he wanted to run with me. That summer day in Georgia, he felt all the heat the South had to offer. With no acclimatization, and running an event that is designed to be walked, your son never quit. I truly saw what he was capable of. He can do anything he wants, and his never-quit mentality has taken him far. As I transferred to Fort Carson and took over a platoon, I ensured that I would get your son as a tank commander. He is a vital part of this platoon, and I am proud of everything that he has become.

Currently, we have been called to deploy to the central command area of operations (Middle East). This is a very emotional time for everyone, and the anxiety level is high. With the ever-changing land-scape of the political arena and the probability of combat operations, soldiers' and families' fears are amplified. The sacrifice we make goes unnoticed by many; being away from loved ones, not knowing the length of a deployment, being placed in harm's way, and the unknown are all sacrifices we will make. We do not take them lightly.

This is not my first deployment, and I have a very unique perspective, one based on twelve years of experience and being called to duty numerous times—the first in 1990 as a young private facing Operation Desert Storm with little to no experience, wondering "how and why." I was shaped through this and following combat deployments in Somalia, Bosnia, Macedonia, and Kosovo. My luck (depending on the perspective—you can consider it good or bad) has led me to realize that you must always be ready, train as you fight, never quit, and build a great team. For the past two years, we have done exactly that with this platoon. Your son is part of that team, and I have the utmost confidence in his abilities.

I also have extreme confidence in the abilities of our equipment. The M1A2 Abrams tank is as good as it gets—designed for firepower, speed, and survivability, and light-years ahead of anything we may possibly face. If we must go in harm's way . . . I would not want to do it on any other vehicle and pity those who would want to do us harm. Our sacrifice is great, but Second Platoon will help the enemy to make the ultimate sacrifice for their cause.

These times are filled with anxiety. The one thing that I do not fear is this platoon's ability to succeed with any given task, or your son's abilities. It puts my mind at ease that this platoon is highly capable and is full of talented and well-trained individuals. Every position is filled with competent and experienced personnel, and I am extremely proud and consider it an honor to be working with your son.

Daniel T. Hendrex

SFC, U.S. Army

2/K/3/3ACR

Several parents or spouses responded to these letters. One of the most touching came from the father of my platoon leader, Lieutenant Olric Wilkins. Normally, I wouldn't write to the family of an officer, but Lt. Wilkins is unique. He has a slight build and, with his big eyeglasses, looks more like a bookworm than an army officer. Yet, he is a leader everyone respects. He's very unassuming and low-key. He claimed that he joined the army on a bet because someone said he'd never do it. Everything about him ran contrary to expectations. He is the only black guy I've known to be a Conway Twitty fan. And he's a great leader whose men are truly fond of him. I wanted his father, a navy chaplain with the rank of colonel, to know that about his son. In return, I got an eloquent and moving e-mail that said my letter to him had given him one of the proudest days of his life.

I'm better at writing letters to my soldiers' loved ones than I am at saying good-bye to my own.

Christina and I have always kept our farewells short and to the point. We'd said good-bye so many times already, but still, the buildup of emotions was huge. There was an eight-thousand-pound elephant in the room, and it was using up all the air. Neither of us slept well the night before my departure. We just sat staring at each other, too sad to say much. Christina said she was trying to memorize every single thing about my face because she was afraid she might forget. She got teary-eyed a few times. I fought to maintain control.

We drove to Fort Carson at three in the morning so that I

could complete preparations for the eight a.m. flight out. We try to keep our good-byes private on these sad occasions. The drive was so quiet and so unlike our usual talkative rides together.

When we arrived at post, we parked and went inside the building that served as offices for Killer Troop. There were a few other soldiers around, all in uncharacteristically somber moods. Along the wall of the back room were dozens of military packs stuffed with gear waiting to go. Christina later told me that those packs reminded her that she was not alone in her grief; that so many people she knew and cared about were leaving and facing the same painful good-byes with their families. She hung out in my office for about an hour while I packed up the last of my things. We tried to joke around and lighten the mood, to relieve the aching in our chests, but it was a losing battle.

When it was time to say good-bye, I walked Christina to the car. She walked so slowly, I could tell she was trying to make the moment last. I was struggling to keep my emotions in check. I'm not afraid to cry, I just didn't want to make it any harder on her. We hugged and kissed for what we knew would be the last time in a long while. When you don't know how long you are going to be gone, it is really hard to let go. She was sitting in the car with the window rolled down when I started to back away. I got to the door and looked back with my hand on the doorknob. It was dark out, but the floodlight from the building lit my position. I knew she could see me clearly even though I could not see her. I blew a kiss to the most important person in my life as she drove away. I was relieved that I could not see her face. I didn't have the strength to look into her eyes.

We were shipping out nearly twenty-seven days after the start of Operation Iraqi Freedom. The time had finally come to put on my game face. Grab my helmet. Time to focus on getting there, doing my job, and bringing every single one of us home safely.

4

SON OF THE INSURGENCY

It was a sweltering day in May of 2003 that seemed like any other in Husaybah. Shops were open. Children were in school. The border trade was in full swing at the checkpoint bordering Syria. Jamil planned to wash cars at the gas station for a few hours and then spend the hottest part of the afternoon swimming in the river. He left home that morning as usual, following his normal path past the hospital. But as he walked on that familiar route, he felt a strange rumbling that came up from the ground and shook the bones in his chest. He feared an earthquake was beginning. Then a terrifying series of images, scenes from a war movie he'd never imagined, played out on his hometown street.

American military vehicles swarmed in like desert scorpions. Menacing camouflaged vehicles bristling with weapons sent Iraqi drivers, bicyclists, and pedestrians scrambling off the streets. Tanks and other vehicles moved on monstrous tracks instead of wheels, rumbling under the arches of Husaybah and down the street toward the police headquarters and the market. Was his town under attack? Should he run home and warn his family? Were they going to start shooting at him? Was this a new invasion? Were the Americans attacking Syria, too?

Hundreds of foreign troops poured into town from the deserts in the south and bore down on the border checkpoint. Within minutes, every corner of town seemed to be guarded by American soldiers. They filled the sky overhead with the deafening roar of their helicopters and fighter planes.

Every Iraqi Jamil saw in the streets looked panicked. No one seemed to know what was going to happen. It suddenly occurred to him that his father was gone, meeting with his friend Sayed (Sa-eed) and other former soldiers. Jamil ran home, worried about his mother and brothers and sisters. He found them safe, hiding indoors, and frightened. When his father came home, they were actually glad to see him, but then the house filled with Nassir's anti-American diatribes. He said they would fight the Americans and drive the infidels out of Husaybah.

The war was now in their backyard.

In the days that followed, the American troops dominated every street and alleyway. They set up offices in government buildings, appeared in the hallways of schools, and patrolled the marketplace in combat gear. Jamil's father spent more and more time away from the house. He would return late at night, exhausted and muttering about the Americans.

One day, Jamil found his father laughing with a small group of men outside their home. Instinctively, he turned to go the other way.

"Come here, boy!" Nassir commanded.

Jamil walked over to the men. He could feel their eyes measuring him.

"This is what those who side with the Americans have waiting for them!" said Nassir, handing his son a photograph. Jamil looked at it and then turned away. He felt sick but tried to mask his revulsion in front of his father and his men. They were laughing at his discomfort.

The photograph showed a bloodied and disfigured man, his body contorted in an unnatural pose. His facial features were distorted, swollen and discolored from blood and bruises. A sickening red puddle had formed in the dirt beneath his head. His torn gray dishdasha was stained with blood.

Nassir boasted to the others that he had shredded the man's robe while beating him with thick steel cords. Jamil could not erase the image from his mind as his father went on and on with his detailed account of the beating he'd administered. It frightened Jamil that Nassir could do such a thing, especially to another Iraqi, and a Muslim at that. How could his father nearly beat to death a fellow Muslim when he'd preached to his children that Muslims do not hurt Muslims? This was the same man who told them to hate the Americans and their coalition forces because all they wanted to do was kill Muslim people.

"I thought you told me that Muslims fought the infidels but didn't raise their hands against Muslim brothers?" the boy blurted out. "You told me that the reason for fighting the Americans was to keep them from killing Muslims."

As soon as Jamil spoke the words, he regretted it. Nassir glared at him. The other men made jokes about his manhood. Sayed, whom they all feared, did not even bother to acknowledge him. He shook his head in disgust but kept his eyes on the photograph, studying it.

When Nassir mentioned the victim's name, Jamil realized that he knew this man. He was a local shop owner, and Jamil used to see him all the time when he was in town working odd jobs. The realization made his stomach churn. This man had always been kind to him and seemed to be friendly with his father. How could his father do that to anyone, let alone an acquaintance?

As Nassir and Sayed discussed the beating, it struck Jamil that all the talk of a "war at home" and the tirades about killing Americans and their sympathizers had not been empty rants. His father and these men had joined the insurgency. That explained Nassir's intense interest in the activities of the American forces in Husaybah. It also explained why his father was always going off to talk on a new cell phone that rang day and night.

The invasion by the U.S.-led coalition and its dispatch of Saddam Hussein's government had transformed Jamil's father from a proud military man and leader in the local Baath Party into a tribal thug and underground leader of the rebel insurgency. Saddam's quick defeat and the overthrow of his regime enraged Nassir. To reassert his influence and control in the village and in their home, he became even more violent and explosive.

A few days after Nassir showed his son the photograph of the man he'd beaten, he told Jamil that it was time he joined the fight against the coalition forces in Iraq. It was time for him to become a man, his father said. "We are still at war, and you will join us in fighting the Americans. They have taken over the border check-point and set up a camp at the old train station just outside town. They cannot be allowed to simply move in and take over. This is our town. Our country!"

Tahira, as always, tried to protect Jamil and to shield him from his father's violence. She argued that at the age of only thirteen, Jamil was too young to be carrying a gun in combat. Nassir won out by threatening to beat his wife for interfering. He would kill his son if he refused to do his duty and fight. It was not her place to question his decision. Women were not allowed to do that in their family or their community.

IN THE INSURGENCY

Jamil walked along the street in silence next to his father, whose mood was dark. "This is the first step," Nassir said.

His father told him to do exactly as he was told and not to say a word—no one could be trusted, the Americans had spies every-where. It was late afternoon as they entered the courtyard of a home next to his old school. The large metal gate and high stucco walls shielded their activities from the street. Jamil felt nervous and excited as they entered. *This is not a game,* he thought. The image of the shop owner brutalized by his father flashed into his mind. Yet, he could not help but feel some pride in being accepted as a man in his father's circle.

They found eight men inside the house. Jamil saw several he knew from the community, including the menacing Sayed. There were two men whom Jamil had never seen before. He heard them speaking Arabic with unfamiliar accents. They eyed him warily, so Jamil kept his distance. He took a seat in a corner and pretended to be bored while listening to their plans for attacks on the infidel Americans. The men discussed the best places to store weapons, strategic sites for ambushes, and who was most qualified to fire mortars and rocket-propelled grenades.

"You will be responsible for getting the weapons and explosives we need," Nassir said as he handed a thick stack of cash to each of his men.

Nassir had never before had large amounts of cash around the house. Jamil realized that his father was serving as a conduit between financiers of the insurgency and the foot soldiers. Nassir was distributing the money to buy weapons and explosives and to pay for mercenaries and foreign fighters, who were coming into Iraq, primarily from Syria, but also from Jordan, Saudi Arabia, and other Middle Eastern nations, to wage a guerrilla war.

Before the overthrow of Saddam, smugglers along Husaybah's main highway traded mostly in cigarettes, gasoline, goats, and sheep. After the overthrow, they began dealing in weapons and foreign fighters. The Mahalowis and the Salmanis, who also controlled the town's police and politicians, still warred between themselves, but their primary focus had shifted. Their primary target was now the American army that occupied their town.

Jamil had been drafted into a local insurgent cell of about forty Iraqis operating under the leadership of his father and his next-door neighbor, Sayed Atta Ali, who would become a major target of U.S. intelligence agencies. The boy would also come to realize that Sayed and his father were widely feared in their own community because they were responsible for keeping local Iraqis in line with the insurgency's mission. If a male family member refused to join the insurgents, or if a family member was suspected of sympathizing, cooperating, or trading with the American soldiers in the region, these men stepped in. They raped, tortured, mutilated, and killed the offender and sometimes his family members, too.

There would be many more meetings with the insurgent cell in the weeks and months that followed. Jamil sat transfixed by the strategies and the planning but terrified at the prospect of participating. He listened as they talked about weapons caches they'd created in their homes and yards for mortars, rocket-propelled grenades, and rifles. He accompanied them on scouting trips to select ambush sites along routes used by the American troops.

The American soldiers and their menacing weaponry were all over Husaybah. Yet, Jamil's initial fear of them had given way to curiosity. They were intimidating with all of the military equipment and protection they carried. He'd seen them awkwardly trying to greet people in the marketplace, although most Iraqis were afraid to trade with them for fear of reprisals from the ever-present spies for the insurgency. Jamil had watched American soldiers reaching out to schoolchildren and adults in his neighborhood with gifts of clothing, shoes, food, soccer balls, toys, and candy. Some had even helped repair the school. It was difficult for him to reconcile the men he'd observed with the hated "Great Satan" of which his father and Sayed spoke. He had never seen them attack anyone. The American soldiers could be aggressive and threatening but only when threatened themselves. They rarely fired their weapons unless someone was firing at them.

The day Jamil had dreaded finally came. Late into a meeting of the insurgency cell, his father disappeared and came back with a battle-scarred AK-47 rifle and tossed it to him. Nearly every boy in Iraq learned to fire these rifles at a young age. But Jamil had never had one of his own. And this rifle was not for shooting games or target practice. His father expected him to kill with it. If he refused to fight, he was essentially signing his own death sentence and perhaps putting his other family members in jeopardy. If he did not join his father, Nassir might recruit his younger brothers. Jamil had gone along with the insurgent training, pretending to be as enthused as the others even while dreading the night when he would be forced to join an attack.

Now it was upon him, and there was no turning back.

5

DEATH BEFORE DISMOUNT

On April 29, 2003—twenty days after the fall of Baghdad—we pushed into Iraq. The men of Killer Troop (the Second Platoon with the Third Armored Cavalry Regiment) had spent nearly three weeks slowly broiling in the desert of Kuwait. We'd listened with growing impatience to reports of top Iraqi leaders, such as former Iraqi deputy prime minister Tariq Aziz, being hunted and captured. Finally, we'd moved across the border.

We rode inside our tank on the back of HETs (Heavy Equipment Transporters) being carried to our first destination in Iraq. I watched as a large Iraqi semitruck passed us and got my first look at several young Iraqi men. Their eyes were full of hatred as they stared at me. I lifted up my rifle and flipped the safety off. The men quickly averted their eyes.

Just on the other side of the border, an M1A1 tank sat in a heap, road wheels melted, burn marks along the turret, a mere shell of its previous form. It was left over from the fight in Baghdad. I don't know if it was left there as a reminder to everyone entering Iraq or if waste removal just wasn't high enough on the army's list of priorities. But it had one hell of an effect on me. I couldn't help but wonder about the outcome of the crew. It was the first time I began to consider my own crew's chances of survival. There is no vehicle in the army's arsenal that gives you more protection than a tank. But there was one right in front of us, all fucked up. It wasn't a great confidence booster as we started our journey into the Land of Two Rivers.

Mud huts spaced a few hundred meters off the main road dotted farmland intermittently. In the middle of nowhere, there were kids lining the road, waving, asking for food, begging for water. Dirty, no shoes—hundreds of them. We were given orders not to throw anything to them because a soldier had done it a few days earlier and a child was hit by one of our vehicles when they rushed the street.

Twenty-four hours later, we rolled over a bridge spanning the Euphrates River. The landscape changed dramatically the farther north we went. It was no longer large, open expanses of rolling desert. Tropical vegetation, palm trees, and bamboo reeds lined the riverbanks and parts of the highway. As we approached our first assembly area, the Al Taqaddum Airfield south of Baghdad, we cut along the outskirts of several cities. This was not going to be like the first Gulf War, with its tank battles in the desert. We were entering a more intimate and intense, door-to-door sort of war.

We arrived at the airfield and settled into several days of maintenance and preparation. For the Gulf War veterans, it felt like some sort of gradual reentry program, or slow torture, depending on the mood of the day. There was so much uncertainty as to just what our self-contained, versatile, high-impact fighting unit was going to be doing in Iraq now that Saddam's regime was scattered to the four winds. At that point, there were pockets of resistance around the country but no real cohesive force that could pose a long-term problem. Things seemed to change minute by minute, but we finally received an operations order to go to the Jordanian border. We were glad to have a specific mission. Then, within the hour, our orders changed again. We were directed to follow the Euphrates River north to Hīt (pronounced "Heat") instead.

We arrived on May 5, 2003. Located in the Al Anbar Province, seventy kilometers northwest of Baghdad, Hīt is a mere two kilometers long. It is sandwiched between the river and its traveling companion, Highway 12, which follows the Euphrates north to Syria. With only two major streets that intersect near the town's center, Hīt is a tight maze of narrow cobblestone and dirt paths. Most are dead ends. The one- to three-story structures and homes seem to be interconnected for blocks, like rabbit warrens in a hillside. And the population is almost one hundred percent Sunni.

Hīt was strategically important because it was home to one of the few intact, albeit shaky, bridges over the Euphrates River. Before the war, it was a city of 120,000 people, but it seemed half had fled by the time we arrived. We were the first American troops to set up there, and although it was officially designated as "friendly to American forces," it would prove increasingly hostile as the strength of the insurgency grew.

The squadron headquarters was set up in an Iraqi army training base a few kilometers north of Hīt. It sat atop a rolling desert expanse just off of Highway 12. The Iraqi base was abandoned during the initial push of the war, when local thieves had pillaged it. All tile, electrical wiring, lights, windows, doors, rebar, and anything not cemented in had been removed. Our troops moved into a two-story barracks on the south end of the camp, which offered a panoramic view of the Euphrates and the north end of Hīt. The site was called Forward Operating Base Eden, someone's poor attempt at sarcasm.

The previous Iraqi inhabitants, Saddam's army trainees, had painted images of the American and Israeli flags tied together and set ablaze on most of the buildings. There were messages scrawled everywhere depicting the United States as the tool of Israel and killer of Arabs. The barracks, obstacle course, and firing range were painted with murals depicting these two countries ripping out the heart of Iraq. The new recruits needed an enemy, and these paintings provided the motivational propaganda required. We found similar messages everywhere we went.

Within days, we had conducted our first troop operation, a raid at the local market. Our squadron's intelligence section had received information that arms were being sold to insurgents there. We were ordered to park our tanks due to the town's narrow alleys and large population. The plan was to have more soldiers on foot patrol, searching vehicles and people. This was not welcome news.

It was our first major mission in Iraq, and we were "dismounted," a term dating back to our origins as a cavalry unit. Prior to the Iraq war, the traditional tank crew credo was "Death before dismount." That matched up with another motto: "A tanker on the ground is a dead tanker." Tankers are like turtles. We don't like coming out of our shells. We were trained to fight in our tanks.

Still, we raided the market without a hitch. No weapons were found. Our intelligence section suspected that the local police chief, whose allegiance was highly suspect, may have tipped off the insurgents. I was impressed that our tank crews adapted so well to infantry tactics. We had made physical training one of our highest priorities prior to deployment, so they were up to it. Essentially, the maneuvers and strategy are the same for patrolling in a tank or on foot. There are a few obvious differences. Tank crews pack numerous HEAT (High Explosive Anti-Tank) rounds that weigh almost forty pounds apiece. They are fired from the tank's 120-millimeter main gun. Tank crews also have several machine guns and grenade launchers. Infantry soldiers have M4 rifles that fire 5.56-millimeter rounds. The tank has a 1,500-horsepower turbine engine that moves soldiers around a battlefield much faster than the standard-issue LPCs (leather personnel carriers, or boots.) And most importantly, the tank wears seventy tons of the most sophisticated armor ever developed. A soldier on foot patrol has a Kevlar helmet and flak vest. Needless to say, I preferred the tank.

Luckily, we had a soldier who was an expert in infantry tactics. Sergeant First Class McNichols was a veteran of the infantry, also known as the "light world" to the tank crews. I relied on him, and he prepared our soldiers for the difficult transition. He taught them that there are a few upsides to foot patrol. Tanks are a big target in an urban setting, and you could be pretty certain that the enemy wouldn't waste a rocket-propelled grenade on a couple of foot soldiers. It was also a little cooler to work on foot. If it was 120 degrees outside, it was generally 140 degrees inside our tanks, courtesy of all the extra heat generated by the electronics, hydraulics, and the turbine engine. It didn't help to have four sweaty soldiers sitting on top of one another. Sgt. Wilkening had a tendency to strip down to his Skivvies and pour water on himself in the tight confines of the gunner's hole. It wasn't in the manual, but it was understandable.

OCCUPATIONAL HAZARDS

Our barracks had no air-conditioning. Every time we stepped outside, it was like getting blasted by a giant blow-dryer. Our entire bodies just dried up, including our eyelids. Our eyes would get so dry, we could hear ourselves blink. And our bodies responded to the tormenting temperatures with prickly heat rash that spread throughout our pores. We had no washers and dryers at that point, so white salt stains formed like tree rings on our uniforms. You could count the rings to determine how long it had been since you tried to wash your clothes in a pail of rationed water.

The Iraqi natives couldn't fathom that we walked around in the daytime in so much clothing and gear—most of them stay inside in the hottest part of the day—so they decided that our uniforms had built-in air conditioners. If only.

If the heat didn't drive you crazy, then you might go nuts from thirst alone. There's nothing like taking a swig of 95-degree water in 120-degree heat. We grew so desperate for a cold drink of water that we finally went to see "The Iceman." Normally, we didn't do much trading with the locals because they weren't all that hospitable. But we'd forgotten to pack the snow-cone machine. We were desperate. We conducted several "ice missions" in the desert, which entailed a visit to an Iraqi icehouse run by a midget. We bought thirty large blocks of ice for a dollar a block. Although we were regular customers, the icehouse midget was always very grumpy, maybe because everyone wanted to have their picture taken with him. He particularly objected to being hoisted on our shoulders for photos. In our eagerness for souvenir pictures, we'd neglected our sensitivity training.

Other desert challenges were more difficult to overcome. At first, we had no telephones or Internet connections to contact our families. Then we were provided with what was at first designated the "Morale Phone" because it was supposed to buoy our spirits by allowing us to call our loved ones. It was quickly dubbed "The Demoralizer" instead. There was only one telephone for the entire camp, so there were soldiers standing in line to use it for hours and hours. It ran through the military phone system to Kuwait and on to the United States, where they'd connect us to a military operator at a U.S. base within the local area you were trying to call. Then we'd have to convince that operator to connect us to the number we were trying to reach. The most demoralizing part was that you had only ten minutes to use the phone and it often took that long just to make a connection. Then you had to pray that the person you were calling would pick up the phone. Often, by the time you got connected to the right number, one of the connections along the chain from Kuwait to the States would go bad, and then you'd have to start all over again—if your phone time wasn't up by then. I didn't get a call through to Christina on the phone until three months after we had deployed.

The only routine worse than standing in line for The Demoralizer was pulling shit-burning detail. Hygiene is always a primary concern since more soldiers are taken out of action by illness than for combat injuries. So field sanitation is a necessary but dreaded part of any deployment. Fifty-gallon drums were cut in half and filled with the waste produced by 130 soldiers each day. A good dose of JP-8 fuel and a splash of volatile mole gas were poured onto the shit stew to get things cooking quickly, and the odor is every bit as bad as you can imagine.

Nobody promised that our return to Iraq was going to be a party, but somehow, I had managed to block out the nastier memories of all the desert delights that awaited us. Scorpions rank near the top of the list, but even higher are the dreaded camel spiders, which are universally despised throughout all branches and ranks of the United States Armed Forces. These are the true scourge of the Middle East.

I'd learned to respect these creeping crawlers during my first deployment, when we were in the Kuwaiti desert having a rare bit of R&R. One night, one of them dropped out of the darkness. Five of us were playing Risk in a small tent. We had a droplight shining down on a wooden table with the game board set up. Someone tossed the dice, and as we all looked to see what he'd rolled, this huge camel spider dropped down onto the middle of the board, reared up on its back legs, and snapped its jaws at us.

Everything went slo-mo. All five professional fighters went bug-eyed, shot up from our chairs, and went scrambling like barnyard hens from the tent. We reconvened twenty-five yards out in the desert, where our instinctive flight left us feeling more than a little embarrassed.

"Five guys just ran from a tent because of one little spider?" I noted to my crew.

Then again, the camel spider, also known as a "sun scorpion," isn't little, nor is it really a spider. I hate those fucking things. They average about the size of a thumb with six-inch legs, and they have large outer mandibles that open sideways, exposing a second set of inner mandibles that chomp up and down. They can run as fast as 10 mph and jump amazingly high. During the Gulf War, there were "desert legend" reports of a soldier who woke up with an odd feeling in his leg. He looked down and found that a huge chunk of flesh had been eaten by a camel spider that was still going to town on him. It was commonly believed—but not true—that camel spiders inject a chemical that numbs the victim's flesh so the spider can eat without being detected. It was also rumored—but apparently not true—that they are called camel spiders because they jump up and burrow into camels' bellies and lay their eggs inside of them. Then the babies eat their way out.

Scorpions are more dangerous, but soldiers fear camel spiders more because they are so aggressive. They don't run from humans, they run at them. And they run with their dukes up, raising their two front legs in the air as they charge at you fearlessly. We caught one and put it in a jar, and it spent hours ramming full speed into the jar trying to get at us.

S.Sgt. Gill had a similar encounter a few years earlier in Kuwait. He looked down one night and saw a camel spider near his foot. With his heart in his throat, he stomped on it and grinded it into the sand. He was all excited that he'd killed one and hadn't run like a little girl. But when he got a light stick and looked for the smashed carcass, the camel spider jumped up onto the light stick and came at him. Gill dropped the chem light and jumped up on a tank turret. I've never heard a grown man scream so loud.

I take that back. There was another camel spider incident that provoked an even louder scream. We were having a platoon meeting in Hīt just as the sun was going down. Sixteen people were gathered. I had borrowed a big rubber spider from one of the maintenance guys. It looked just like a camel spider. I tied a string to it and ran it around a pole and covered it with dirt and trash near the chairs where the guys were seated.

Lt. Wilkins, who was in on the plan, was briefing the platoon when I started tugging the string so that it looked like the spider's little rubber legs were crawling. I got it right next to the foot of our big Samoan tough guy, Anitulu, and he let out a scream that sounded a lot like the famous shriek that ruined the presidential campaign of Howard Dean. Thirteen other soldiers joined in the chorus. Mayhem ensued, with two soldiers somehow ending up a hundred meters out in the desert before the lieutenant could finish his sentence.

CULTURE CLASHES

If we had misconceptions and unnecessary fears of certain desert creatures, the natives of Hīt had their own perceptions of us. We were on our first patrol mission in search of a reported weapons trading bazaar masquerading as a sheep and goat market when one of our soldiers lifted a pair of binoculars to his eyes. The local Iraqis around us had been relatively quiet up to that point, but as soon as they saw the binoculars, they started screaming and pointing at the soldier. I called over an interpreter, who informed us that the Iraqis thought that our binoculars allowed us to see through the clothing of their women. I had our man put the binoculars away but told the interpreter that he didn't need to correct the impression. Better for them to think we had X-ray vision and could see if they were hiding any weapons under their robes.

We later learned of another myth about American soldiers that spread among the Iraqis. The regiment found stockpiles of rocket-propelled grenades (RPGs) with copper wiring wrapped around the warheads. We couldn't figure out what purpose the wiring served until we took an insurgent into custody. He revealed the purpose. It seemed that so many of their RPGs missed the targeted American troops in the early days that they figured we must have had some sort of "force field" with protective devices that warded them off. The copper wiring was apparently added to somehow foil the Great Satan's force field.

The Iraqis were also concerned about our night optics. They feared the red beams used for aiming weapons in the dark. They were more terrified of those laser lights than they seemed to be of our tanks. We used that fear in our favor while operating checkpoints. Sometimes it was easier to stop a speeding car with one of those little red penlights than with a machine gun.

BOOTS MADE FOR WALKING

It quickly became apparent that our time in Iraq would not be considered a routine peacekeeping mission. In fact, there was nothing at all routine during our tour of duty. We were used to being in armored tanks with massive firepower. But after only a week in the country, we'd had to patrol on foot where we were exposed to open fire. We decided that some training in foot patrol techniques was needed—and fast. Like it or not, we were facing some serious time dismounted from our tanks and doing infantry patrols.

For someone trained to fight inside seventy tons of armor with a lethal arsenal of weapons, conducting foot patrols was like walking naked at the wrong end of a firing range. And you can imagine how the wives felt when word began to leak out that we were conducting operations without our tanks. The decision to park the tanks outside of town was made before we even knew that the Iraqis had organized resistance in Hīt. Early on, there was concern about conveying the "wrong image" to the locals with a show of such massive military firepower. But mainly, we were forced to patrol on foot because it was extremely difficult to maneuver a tank through streets and alleys designed for camels and donkey traffic—especially since the Pentagon opted not to go with the accessory package that included curb feelers.

As conventional fighting forces, we had to adapt to deal with the guerrilla tactics of the insurgents. But that is one of the great things about being in the Third Armored Cavalry—it is an extremely adaptable fighting machine. We are virtually an army unto ourselves. We have our own scouts, air support, tanks, Bradleys, military intelligence, engineers, air defense, and artillery. We are known for our ability to reconstitute ourselves in whatever form is required to take on a challenge. And that is what we did.

It's a good thing we are one highly adaptable bunch of knuckle-heads because even as we switched from tankers to infantry duty, our outfit underwent internal upheaval. It was triggered by the Pentagon's lifting of Stop-Loss. Essentially, lifting this order meant that soldiers who were at the end of their enlistment, headed for retirement, or up for new assignments were allowed to leave Iraq. We lost some key players. Lt. Wilkins, who had been my platoon leader for more than a year, was moved into a scout platoon. To complicate matters even further, the rumor mill once again kicked up reports that we could be going home soon. Some bought into that chatter, and they told their wives that we'd be home within six months. But nobody told the insurgents that the party was winding down. They began showing up in greater and greater numbers.

Over the years, I'd learned not to build up false hopes based on speculation among the rank and file. It can be a deadly mistake to let your mind wander home before your body is out of the line of fire. Ambushes, sniper fire, mortar and rocket-propelled grenade attacks appeared to indicate that the Iraqi resistance was not looking to shake hands and call it a day. Yet, it seemed like even the top brass and political leaders were buying into the hope that Iraq would settle down into a peace stabilization effort like Bosnia or Kosovo. I wasn't willing to bet my body armor on it, and it was a good thing I didn't.

On May 11, I was positioned on high ground in the desert outside Hīt with Second Lieutenant Tuttle, a lanky, redheaded platoon leader freshly matriculated from West Point, who had arrived as Lt. Wilkins's replacement. Our new leader had come just in time for a little desert war game drama. Through our binoculars, we watched the dust trails of six Bradley Fighting Vehicles maneuvering the rolling expanse of rock, wadi, and sand. They were attempting to find us, the designated "enemy," in this force-on-force training exercise.

It looked like the scouts were going to roll right by us—we could just lie low and then attack them from the rear. It was just a war game, after all, and a pretty routine one at that. But then a mushroom cloud went up fifty meters from one of the Bradleys. We heard the explosion a few seconds after we saw the massive cloud of dust.

I thought I was seeing things until the sound wave caught up with the visual sighting. We were stunned by the first explosion; the second and third got us moving a little quicker. It looked like giant meteors were crashing into the desert sand, throwing rocks, dust, and debris high into the air. The soldiers in the Bradleys weren't playing games anymore. They were scrambling for their lives. We ran back to our vehicle and got on the radio to confirm our suspicions. This was not friendly fire. Large-caliber mortars—120-millimeter or bigger—were raining down on our guys. Frantic voices were screeching on our radio net. This was the first major attack we'd experienced here: The insurgents were getting bolder and more aggressive.

The Scout Platoon linked up with us, and we verified that everyone was intact. More than a few were rattled, but no one was hurt. We were ordered to move along the major highway, headed due west of Hīt. They'd identified the likely point where insurgents had been firing the artillery on us. Lt. Col. Kievenaar, our squadron commander, figured they were on the move by now. Immediately, we were ordered to set up traffic control points along primary exit routes on the highway leading east out of Hīt.

To make things even more surreal, a huge wall of sand, dust, lightning, and wind was heading straight for our position. "Operation Desert Storm" suddenly took on a new and more immediate meaning. The sheer magnitude and width of this storm was mesmerizing. And the damn thing came churning right for us.

The idea of a massive sandblast was not appealing. As whipping sheets of sand rolled over us, turning daylight into night, everyone piled into whatever vehicle they could reach. We sat in the middle of the sandstorm for thirty minutes before it was clear enough to head out. The sun was setting, but our day was far from over. As we traveled away from the storm, S.Sgt. Gill, the platoon leader's wingman, spotted two suspicious-looking Iraqis on the side of the road, standing next to a motorcycle. They were out in the middle of nowhere and wore very nervous expressions. Gill tried his fractured phonetic Arabic: *"On-deck-ish-la?"* ("Do you have any weapons?")

The Iraqis wiped their hands together and shook their heads back and forth. Gill sensed they were up to no good. So, instinctively, he began searching the surrounding area. He found a sniper rifle and an AK-47. We joined Gill in handcuffing and detaining them. We learned to trust his insurgent ESP from that point on. Later in the deployment, he discovered a false floor in an Iraqi's cargo truck. Beneath it were more than 250 rocket-propelled grenade warheads. These RPGs were one of the insurgency's deadliest weapons, and they seemed to have an unlimited supply. They could be fired by one person without much training using a bazooka-like launcher fired from the shoulder. It didn't take a great shot with an RPG. Close enough would kill you.

Night had dropped like a blackout curtain by the time we finally arrived at our traffic control point. We prepared for it with thermal sights, night-vision goggles, chem lights, and flashlights. We had a distinct advantage at night with all of this gear, but even so, it was inherently more dangerous. Our job was to search vehicles as they came through our checkpoint. We'd let a couple vehicles go through after finding them free of weapons when a Nissan Pathfinder rolled up at high speed. Warning shots were fired. The driver stopped. We went to the doors, but the three riders refused to get out. The vehicle smelled like an Oklahoma honky-tonk, which was never a good sign in a Muslim country. We went on high alert. Locked and loaded. The Iraqis staged their version of a sit-down strike. It got pretty intense very fast. There was a lot of yelling and threatening and gesturing that communicated hostile inten- tions despite the language barriers. Finally, we had to muscle the Iraqis out of the truck.

Once we had the driver and two passengers under control, we searched the vehicle. Our day and night of wonders continued. We found a couple of bottles of booze, three locked and loaded AK-47s, and a cache of hand grenades, flares, mortars, three deto- nators, and ammo. These were former members of Saddam's army who obviously hadn't given up the fight. With the three of them safely handcuffed and tucked away, we allowed ourselves to relax. But we should have known better.

Crack! Before we could respond to the rifle fire, I heard the unforgettable whizzing of a high-caliber round rocketing inches past my grape. I joined a couple other guys in the ditch before the second round came flying at us. We scanned the surrounding darkness for the telltale flashes of rifle fire. I was so intent on try- ing to find the location of our attackers that it took me a minute or two to realize I'd dived into a ditch with our three prisoners, who didn't seem very glad to see me.

Somebody saw rifle fire coming from a factory building four hundred yards away. I was about to jump into a personnel carrier with four of our guys when I noticed 2nd Lt. Tuttle standing nearby. He wasn't officially our new platoon leader yet, but he'd been with us since the morning's training exercise, observing and getting to know us. I started to ask him if he was coming along for the factory search, but he jumped in the vehicle before I could finish my sentence. As we drove off, it hit me that, once again, I was bearing down on a hostile location without the protective armor of a tank wrapped around me. This was beginning to become a very unnerving habit.

The factory was actually a hatchery, or an egg factory. We went room to room on our search, expecting to be shot at every turn. The veins in my forehead pulsed against my helmet. All senses were on high alert, which was unfortunate given the putrid stench of ammonia and chicken shit that filled the factory. We didn't find anyone, but in those few minutes inside the hatchery, I aged a good five years.

I didn't bother to mention it to my soon-to-be new platoon leader, but I blamed this long and hectic day of major hostilities on what's called "the curse of the FNG"! It is a long tradition in the army that whenever you bring in a "Fucking New Guy," the shit hits the fan. It was 2nd Lt. Tuttle's first "unofficial" day with us, and I'd say he carried the curse with flying colors.

By the end of May, our dismount patrols were proving to be effective. The resistance was strengthening. Intelligence out of Hīt reported that members of the insurgency were paying three hundred dollars a head for dead U.S. soldiers. Our regiment was encountering hostile Iraqis almost daily and suffered its first casualty when a soldier was killed during a home raid. An engineering unit was fired upon with rocket-propelled grenades, and we'd experienced other ambushes that, I feared, were only the beginning.

We were conducting daily dismounted patrols, determined to get into a new rhythm and to get a better feel for the streets and just how treacherous they could be. We were still adjusting to an increasingly scary environment when a CBS News crew showed up, wanting to check things out in Hīt. They wanted to stroll through the town and interview the locals. Somehow, they got approval, and we were sent along to make sure that nobody died on the nightly news.

Two scout helicopters and a heavy-armored Quick Reaction Force of Bradleys and Humvees, backed by SFC "Mac" McNichols, our mortar platoon sergeant, and his mortarmen, formed a parade to provide security for the reporter and cameraman. We were the dismounted part of the reactionary force. Our job was to walk fifty meters behind the CBS crew, providing security. We had our hands full. A crowd swarmed around us. They were friendly for the most part, just curious about all of the hoopla in their streets. Even so, it was a long and exhausting three-mile hike through an Un-Easy-Bake oven, with more than three hundred rowdy Iraqis trailing us. We'd just departed from the local police station and worked our way back to our security post when the crowd got out of control.

With the CBS crew in tow, we were preparing to load our vehicles when we were hit with a rock shower courtesy of the locals. It was their opening salvo in what would prove to be an extended barrage.

JOURNAL ENTRY: MAY 29, 2003
Exhausted, dirty, tired, worn out, paranoid, angry, nervous, scared, and relieved. The last seventy-two hours have been the toughest I have seen to date. EXTREMELY lucky and

happy that there are no KIAs [killed in action] in the troop.
WIAs [wounded in action]: Lt. Wilkins, Pvt. Moyle, and
2nd Lt. Arnold.

We'd been back at Forward Operating Base Eden only a short time that evening when we got word that a rocket-propelled grenade had been fired at the Red Scout Platoon, closing down a traffic control point along Highway 12 just on the south end of Hīt. It had come out of a neighborhood designated Zone F and flew right over the platoon members' heads, exploding in the distance. At midnight, we put together a plan to clear all the homes, about one hundred of them, in Zone F until we found those responsible for the attack.

We informed local leaders and sheiks of the mission, telling them they could save everyone a lot of grief if they simply turned over the shooter. It was no surprise that they didn't come up with any suspects. This was an "urban" operation that would take us into crowded streets. That meant our tanks stayed parked at the base and we conducted cordons and searches on foot. We drove past the tanks on our way out of the gates in a light-skinned Humvee. My stomach knotted as I looked back and saw our protective steel shells get smaller and smaller as we left them in the distance.

We started at dawn. My tankless crew was slowly but surely becoming a skillful dismounted personnel security detachment. They were a sight to see. Sgt. Wilkening, my tank gunner, was a five-foot-eight-inch pit bull, in charge of the two biggest soldiers in the platoon: Specialist Moreno, at six foot two, and Specialist Anitulu, at six three. Wilkening had a bark and a bite. He also had one hell of a crew. Moreno spoke fluent Spanish, picked up basic Arabic, and became my radioman. He also served as my de facto interpreter. Anitulu was the gentle giant and the most gifted athlete I had ever seen in the military. If I had to go dismounted, I was glad to have men of their skill and size with me.

We moved into Zone F, which was one of the more affluent neighborhoods in Hīt. It is an arduous task searching one home thoroughly. Searching one hundred homes is a monumental task. We were in full gear, in a scorching daytime heat, fully aware that at any minute, a bomb could go off or a bullet could come flying. We worked from house to house, fighting exhaustion, dehydration, and hostilities from the residents we were rousing from their homes. Late in the afternoon, Staff Sergeant Berth, the Red Scout Platoon sergeant, waved me over to his observation position in a Bradley Fighting Vehicle. As I approached, he took a photograph with a small camera, laughed, and handed me a bottle of water.

"I have got to get evidence of this," he said. "Tankers on the ground. Scouts on vehicles in overwatch?"

I smiled, flipped him the bird, and left with the water. Minutes later, we arrested a couple of young guys for suspicious behavior, but we found no evidence of the rocket-propelled grenade shooters. After about seventy houses had been searched, some informants directed us to a suspect's home, but we came up empty-handed there, too. We returned to Forward Operating Base Eden completely out of juice. We were spent. Everyone hit the sack and immediately fell asleep.

My eyes had just closed when I was awakened. We had to stage an early-morning raid. This time, we turned up just a few women in a house and spotted a suspect running from the area, but once we caught him, it appeared doubtful that he was our RPG man. We wrapped it up at about ten a.m., then headed to our security post at the police station. There, the commander spoke with the police chief, who was concerned that our raids had stirred up animosities among the local population. I left Mac and his mortar crew at the police station security post and took the rest of our weary men back to Eden.

By the time we pulled into the base, all hell was breaking loose back at the police station in town. I walked into Killer Troop's tactical operations center (TOC) and found everyone gathered around the radios. They looked stunned. Over the waves came spotty situation reports from frantic voices.

"Killer X-ray, this is [static] Four. Where is that medevac bird? We have a litter urgent, and he needs attention now!"

I asked who had been injured but couldn't get an immediate answer. Unnerved, I directed my question to the TOC sergeant: "What's going on? Who is hurt?"

"It's Lieutenant Wilkins."

Now I was stunned. "Litter urgent" means that loss of life, limb, or eyesight is imminent.

"What the hell happened? We just left there."

Apparently, Lt. Wilkins walked out into a crowd outside the police station and was somehow critically wounded. I immediately got on the radio and called Thunder X-ray, our squadron headquarters, and told them that I had just returned from the police station and that I could get back there in minutes with a dismounted Quick Reaction Force.

The radio traffic was barely readable, but I knew they needed more forces to secure the police station. Squadron radioed back and told me to round up my platoon and get ready to go. The radioed reports from the scene were coming in sketchy and intermittent:

"Several police cars have been . . . securing the perimeter . . . four hand grenades were thrown."

My adrenaline was flowing along with my rage. I found S.Sgts. Smith and Gill and told them to get everybody back into gear and on the truck. When I told them about Lt. Wilkins, they didn't need any more convincing: They were angry too. This was our lieutenant, and we didn't like the fact that he was injured and we weren't there to help him. We felt responsible for his safety. We rounded up the platoon, briefed them, and moved to the squadron operations center. As I ran up the sidewalk to the entrance, several soldiers were standing outside. Word had spread that something bad had gone down and that our lieutenant was hurt. They looked at us as if we were already KIAs. Dead men walking.

Their stares only made me angrier. Fuck 'em for just standing there when we had a man down! I linked up with 2nd Lt. Tuttle, and we received a briefing. Our job was to control the crowd and get them dispersed. Nobody talked, but their eyes told me everything I needed to know. They were ready and willing to do whatever it took, tanks or no tanks.

Five hundred people had encircled the police station. Reports that several Iraqis had been shot and killed reached us. We were still on the northern edge of town when we were ordered to stop and set up a landing zone and block off Highway 12, a main route into the city. They wanted to keep more people from joining the mob.

It was maddening. We still didn't know how Lt. Wilkins was doing or even where he was at that point. He could have been bleeding to death in the crowd or being dragged through the streets. But we set up a perimeter as ordered. We heard sporadic small-arms fire but couldn't determine the location. It got hairy at our location in a hurry. Vehicles were roaring toward us and giving no signs of slowing down. We had to fire more than forty warning shots. There was a Black Hawk helicopter coming in to evacuate Lt. Wilkins. No one was allowed within a five-hundred-meter radius of that landing. If there was going to be only one secure area in Hīt on this day, it would be there.

Reports were slowly coming in on the radio. Sergeant Taft from the scout platoon rolled up in his Bradley. He'd just been at the police station, so he filled us in. After we'd left that morning, the rock throwing had escalated. Red Bradley Platoon was called in to help secure the perimeter. Lt. Wilkins was riding in the back of one of their vehicles. He had not officially switched over as their scout platoon leader at that point, but he was already on the job. When the back ramp of his truck opened, Lt. Wilkins saw Private Moyle lying in the road. He was manning a machine-gun position and covering the eastern section of the perimeter by himself. Lt. Wilkins ran over to help him. Just then, four grenades came in over a nearby wall along with a volley of rocks. Moyle and Wilkins were hit by shrapnel from the grenades. Moyle then helped the lieutenant back inside the perimeter.

Lt. Wilkins was bleeding from the face, but as it turned out, his injury was not as bad as it originally appeared. Shrapnel had sliced through his eyebrow, causing it to flap down over his eye. It had looked like he'd lost an eye, so they'd made the "litter urgent" call. To our relief, they said he would be out for just a few days but was expected to have a full recovery.

We'd just gone through forty-eight hours marked by one hellacious mix of exhaustion, fear, and anger. We evacuated the police station and then returned to our base. Even then, we couldn't hit the sack. We had to do weapons and vehicle maintenance first.

From the high ground at Base Eden as we cleaned our weapons, I could see the scout helicopters in the distance, circling the police station. Black smoke was spewing from the Hīt skyline. Our pilots overhead reported that more than twenty-eight hand grenades had been thrown into the police station, squad cars were overturned, and fires were set inside the building.

At around nine thirty p.m., as we were finishing up our final bits of maintenance, we noticed a slender figure walking toward us in the darkness. It was Lt. Wilkins. A second earlier, the platoon had seemed totally drained of energy. Now soldiers were laughing, yelling, and wrapping themselves all over their shy, unlikely leader. Guys came running from all directions. Lt. Col. Kievenaar, the squadron commander, and Captain Rozelle, the company commander, joined in the impromptu party. The happy mob damn near crushed the poor guy in a group hug.

Amazingly, the lieutenant had just a few stitches over his eye.

So the sympathy quickly turned to teasing about his good luck or bad acting. He'd been out of our platoon only a few hours when he was wounded, so that inspired a lot of comments about the dangers of breaking our protective shield. Then came a white flash, and nobody was joking anymore. It was followed by a thunderous *thump* from the direction of the river. Everyone tensed up and looked toward the light and sound. Then came an eerie, menacing whistle. Something very large was rocketing our way. I could barely get the word out as I dived for cover: *"Incoming!"*

We scrambled ass over elbow for cover. Most of us dived under the tanks. We waited and listened for the incoming round to hit. It sounded like a Volkswagen flying overhead just before it hit near the perimeter of the base. We scrambled out from under the tanks as soon as we heard the impact. We went on alert until dawn, cruising around the perimeter in full battle rattle inside the tanks, guarding the perimeter and hoping the protective shield would hold up a while longer.

MARTIAL LAW

With the continued hostilities, Lt. Col. Kievenaar informed the sheiks and imams in Hīt that martial law was in effect. If they could not control their town, we would move in with the tanks and do it for them. They were granted a forty-eight-hour reprieve to respond. In the meantime, we decided to conduct Operation Mad Mortarman, a large-scale search of the east side of the Euphrates. Our target was the party wrecker who had ended our welcome home for Lt. Wilkins.

We had a small problem. We were not allowed back into Hīt for another two days because of the forty-eight-hour grace period. Normally, we would just go over the river and into the woods to our targeted area by traveling through town. But this wasn't a stroll to Grandma's house. Instead, we had to travel up the river and look for another bridge strong enough for our heavy-duty vehicles. Unfortunately, the Iraqi Tourism Bureau in Hīt was closed for the mortar and rocket-propelled grenade season, so we had to blaze our own trails in search of a bridge that wouldn't break under our weight.

We set out with a patrol convoy of light-skinned Humvees and a cargo truck. We did practice wise traveling tips by removing the plastic doors on the Humvees. They didn't offer much protection anyway, and without them, it was easier to shoot back at whoever might be shooting at us. The Humvees were "light-skinned"—without armor—so we added sandbags as protection against mines. We also put draped netting over the passenger compartment to break up the outlines of the occupants in case of an ambush. Then we rolled out on what was to be a major exercise in frustration.

The tropical jungle that follows the flow of the Euphrates was seductive despite the dangers around us. The water moved in a glittery, translucent current through dense vegetation. Fields of bamboo reeds lined the water's edge. Ancient aqueducts made of cobblestones reached for the river but crumbled before crossing. Fishermen used sticks to push their boats up the river, casting nets and fishing with nothing more than string wrapped around a small piece of wood.

The rural, primitive scenes were from another time. But we fought off any inclination to let our guards down. Tactically, this little jaunt in the jungle was a nightmare. We were uneasy traveling in Humvees and a cargo truck on paths made for donkey carts. There were too many hiding places and ambush sites. We were also aware that drowning was a possibility. The embankments tended to crumble under the weight of military vehicles. It was particularly dangerous at night. In such rural, close quarters, we were exposed targets even for simple weapons in the hands of an enemy who knew the terrain.

We had identified three bridges as candidates for crossing.

On closer inspection, the first was nothing more than an old one-lane pontoon bridge barely big enough to accommodate a VW Bug. We pushed north to the second bridge. It was even smaller than the first. Trudging on, we reached the third bridge only to find that it was missing a key component, creating a hundred-meter gap in the middle of it. Dejected, we called off our mission and returned to Eden. Lt. Col. Kievenaar stood by the forty-eight-hour ban and told us we'd have to wait to use the bridge in Hīt. He said he'd lift the ban only if we were taking mortar fire. It was the first night the platoon slept undisturbed in a long time. We needed it.

JOURNAL ENTRY: JUNE 1, 2003
0500: Moved through the town of Hīt across the bridge to the east side of the river to conduct dismounted search of the grove areas. Cleared a cave out; full of bats, bat shit, and the remains of one human. We began clearing along the river on foot through five kilometers of dense foliage. It felt very surreal. I was standing closest to the river and looked east as more than thirty men stepped out of the dense foliage to an open area. Huge palm trees overhead and Pegasus [OH-58 helicopter] hovering above us. Very Vietnam-esque. Platoon's resiliency impresses me.

THE WILD, WILD MIDDLE EAST

Like a boxer fighting a shifty opponent, we threw every combination in our arsenal at the insurgency. We went after them on foot and in vehicles. We paired tanks with Bradleys, Bradleys with Humvees, Humvees with tanks, tanks with air support. We even went on joint missions with the local police, which wasn't exactly like sleeping with the enemy, but it was close. Lt. Col. Kievenaar had been trying to make inroads not only with the Iraqi police, but also with Hīt's sheiks and local leaders. But you never knew whom you were dealing with in this country. They'd already fired one police chief and elected another. The old one, to no one's surprise, was crooked. Someone had burned and gutted the police station for reasons we'd never been able to determine. Our presence only added another layer of intrigue to local rivalries, personal jealousies, political infighting, centuries-old tribal vendettas, and family feuds.

We wanted the police to learn to control the streets without us. We needed their experience and knowledge of the local players. Yet, our agendas were frequently at odds. Their loyalties shifted block to block, house to house, making it tough to trust any of them. And being wrong on a trust issue in Iraq would get you killed. Stupid hurts. So I kept my distance from all of them.

It didn't help our sense of security that the Hīt police had few weapons and no uniforms. We'd armed them, against our better judgment, and stationed them at checkpoints around town. I couldn't help but wonder if we were not rearming the enemy. And, of course, the communication gap added to our issues; we had a single interpreter for the entire company of 130 men. But the lack of police uniforms was probably our biggest concern at the time. How were we supposed to tell them apart from the insurgents? Apparently, their uniforms had been ordered but had not arrived yet, and getting security on the streets was our top priority. So we decided that the bad guys would be the ones in civilian clothes with AK-47s who shot at us. The ones who didn't shoot at us, they were okay. We had to watch our own backs, so we put our soldiers on rooftops, in alleyways, and in and around the station. Once they were tucked into dark corners and advantageous spots, they were hard to see. It gave us some small comfort to know they were there, but in Iraq, even small comforts were a luxury.

We conducted our first dismounted operation in that uncertain environment. The goal was to enforce the curfew between midnight and three a.m. We hit the unfamiliar streets of Hīt in darkness, positioning soldiers in armored vehicles at key checkpoints on the outskirts. Iraqi police ran the internal checkpoints throughout the city. The Hīt mayor and the police chief accompanied some of our patrols.

We set out from the police station and moved through the city. Even the humid air seemed hostile. We'd walk the night into morning, doing two loops through the central sector of Hīt and back to the police station. Minute by minute, step by step, for hours and hours and mile after mile; all of it intense, dripping in sweat.

The first night was nerve-racking; having the mayor and police chief in tow as our "guides" only made it more difficult, as we didn't put much faith in their guidance. You always had the sense that if an insurgent jumped out with a machine gun, he could be the mayor's favorite nephew or the police chief's second cousin. Fortunately, only a couple of potshots had been taken at us during our first foray, though nothing we could track down.

The second night got off to an interesting start. Instead of the mayor serving as our tour leader, we had a local cleric. While we were waiting for him to show up, an interpreter informed me that our special guest of a guide was also known as "No. 5" on our intelligence black list of known sympathizers and members of the insurgency. The Iraqis were categorized as belonging to the "black list," "gray list," or "white list." These lists are derived from different HUMINT (human intelligence), SIGINT (signal intelligence), and various other sources. The black list comprised those men known to be actively working against coalition forces; gray meant undetermined; and white indicated that a person was actively working with coalition forces. In the early days in this Sunni-dominated region, we didn't really have a white list. What a surprise.

The interpreter took the information about "Black No. 5" to

the commander. He checked it out. Then he came back and told me that it was time to enact the "keep your friends close and your enemies closer" policy. It seemed that the cleric had a huge following and his presence on our patrols might help keep thugs and others off the streets.

We decided to keep close tabs on the cleric, whom SFC McNichols dubbed "Charlie." Maybe Charlie would be our lucky charm. The second night went smoothly, except for a heart-stopping scare at the police station, when one of our highly trained Iraqi police officers misfired his weapon and scared two days of mess hall out of us.

Our third night got off to a bigger boom, and the fun never stopped on the Wild, Wild West tour. At one forty-five a.m., we were about to pull off security of the police station to begin the patrol when there was a large explosion off to the east, about three hundred meters away. The police chief assured us it was just the locals "fishing." He informed us that instead of rods and reels or even nets, Hīt's sports fishermen just tossed grenades and other explosives into the water and grabbed whatever came floating to the surface.

Huge explosions from fishing expeditions had not been on our list of things to anticipate. But we had expected a lively evening: It was a Thursday night, the Iraqi version of a Saturday night and the traditional time for weddings and other celebrations. It was also the night when, contrary to Muslim doctrine, alcohol seemed to flow freely and the locals showed their enthusiasm by firing guns and rifles in the air—a practice that tended to make us Americans more than a little jittery. Our guest tour guide, Charlie the cleric, kindly informed us that two or three men from Fallujah were setting up an ambush reception for our patrol. Then he assured us that he would go take care of it. When he returned, he stated that he'd convinced the Fallujah ambush team to take a hike. He also offered to drive ahead of our patrol to discourage anyone else who might be planning to shoot and kill us that night. So, even before we'd hit the streets, we'd had a large explosion, sporadic AK-47 fire from local celebrations, a reported ambush in waiting, and a known black lister to lead our patrol. All of this, and my cozy tank was still parked at the base.

We all had an uneasy feeling about the way things were unfolding. It looked like it would be another busy night. For added thrills, we had a military news reporter and a combat photographer tagging along to record the historic joint patrol with our forces and Iraqi police. I had a nervous flashback to my *USA Today* experience, but I shook it off. As it turned out, the Pentagon's newshounds experienced a night that could have been headlined MILITARY BLUNDERS OF THE IRAQI WAR. We got only as far as the second checkpoint, one hundred meters from the police station, when another large explosion sent us diving for cover. It felt damn close. But everyone seemed to be intact as we got up.

I glared at the police chief, yelling, "Let me guess, it's those damn fishermen again?"

We moved nervously along streets that were well lit in some places, pitch-black in others. We could see tracers flying on the other side of the river. In the distance, there was sporadic AK-47 fire. I had one nerve left, and it was being rubbed raw. We were spread out over a few hundred meters, following basic dispersion techniques. As we moved into the center of town near the mosque, everyone was on edge. We stopped near the bridge to get a situation report from our soldiers at the checkpoint. As we started to loop back into the city, a bright flash exploded in the alley behind me. Instinctively, everyone hit the ground. But there was no explosion to follow the flash, no sound at all except for the thud of our bodies hitting the ground. Then I saw the photographer standing over everyone, getting ready to take another flash shot with his camera. Before I could grab his equipment and throw it in the Euphrates, S.Sgt. Smith tore into him.

We finally made it back to the police station around two thirty in the morning and signaled our guys in the shadows and on the roofs that our patrol was calling it a night. But this being Iraq, that's when all hell broke loose.

I was sitting in a Humvee in front of the police station when I heard yet another large explosion in the distance. I was about to make another fish wisecrack when Sgt. Wilkening, who was still on the roof of a nearby building, shouted down that he'd just seen three rocket-propelled grenades flying across the sky and exploding near Highway 12. Just then, our radios came alive with traffic. *"This is Green Four. Contact, RPGs CP 6."*

Sergeant First Class West, the other tank platoon sergeant in the troop, had nearly been killed when two RPGs flew over the front slope of his tank. A third hit just short of it. Our dreams of hitting the sack after a twenty-hour day came to an abrupt end. 2nd Lt. Tuttle received orders that we were to link up with our mortar unit and conduct a raid on the old Baath Party headquarters. It was in the general vicinity of the grenade attack, and squadron intelligence said that it had been a hub of activity earlier in the night.

We were speeding in the Humvees from the police station toward the Baath headquarters when one of the helicopter scouts identified a man on the run near the attack site. We went after him, barreling through tight alleys. The helicopter scouts guided us to the suspect. We snatched him up and headed for the Baath headquarters for our raid.

We arrived at our target and started drawing together a quick plan when word came that SFC West was still under small-arms attack. Capt. Rozelle took the mortar unit to search for the source of the ambush. 2nd Lt. Tuttle and I exchanged glances. "Looks like we're on our own," I said.

With only sixteen soldiers and one Humvee, we had to get creative once again. The former Baath headquarters was two stories tall with about twenty-five rooms. There was a six-foot concrete wall around the building with about fifty meters of yard between the wall and the structure. Three cars were parked inside. We had identified at least four people in there. The iron gate to the compound was closed. Naturally.

We didn't have the time or the backup for finesse. 2nd Lt. Tuttle had a soldier get behind the wheel of the Humvee, rev the engine, spin the tires, and head for the gate at ramming speed. As battering rams go, ours was fairly advanced—and mounted with a heavy machine gun. Eight of us ran in behind the Humvee and through the crushed gate that went down with a loud clang. We fanned out in the courtyard and into the building, securing the three Iraqis who appeared at the door. S.Sgt. Smith and his four-man team were all over the back door, making sure no bad guys got out that way.

Our three-man welcome wagon had no visible weapons, but we weren't taking chances. *"ERTA-E-DICT! EM-BATA!"* ("Hands up! Get on the ground!")

They didn't put up a fight. The interpreter asked if there were any others inside, and one of them, an elder, stated there were two more people inside. Then I noticed writing in English on the front of the building: the words "Community Center" accompanied by an image of a red crescent moon, which was a symbol of the Arab Red Cross. We gathered up the other two Iraqis and secured the building. We again spoke to the elder, and he relayed what I was already suspecting. The former Baath Party headquarters had been transformed into a community center. Half was a local gathering place. The other half was a clinic. We then had him lead us on a very thorough search, and his story checked out. We'd been led on a wild-goose chase.

We wrapped things up, apologized profusely, and made plans to pay for the crushed gate. It was dawn and already heating up by the time we made our way back to the base. This night had had so many emotional ups and downs, I could barely think straight. We were soaked with sweat, smelled like raw sewage, and at the point of delirium from lack of sleep. That's when I looked at my watch and realized that it was Friday the thirteenth. Perfect, just perfect.

FROCKED

As much as I enjoyed the local sights, the sounds of mortars and fish being blown up in the night, and the joys of foot patrols in hostile neighborhoods, my time with Second Platoon, Killer Troop was cut short.

On June 26, I received notice that I had been "frocked." My promotion to first sergeant had come through. The bad news was that I was being moved out of my unit and reassigned to the Haditha Dam in the Al Anbar Province.

I spoke with Lt. Col. Kievenaar and told him the transfer would make a liar out of me. I had promised the sixteen soldiers in my platoon that I would bring them home. I was so distraught, I didn't hear his response. I almost lost it as I briefed the platoon. The looks on their faces tore me up. They couldn't believe it and neither could I. For three years, I'd been with them. I was confident in the team we'd put together. S.Sgts. Gill and Smith were perfect complements to each other and to me, too. Even with the addition of 2nd Lt. Tuttle, the operational abilities never faltered. Lt. Wilkins had been an amazing platoon leader. I respected his leadership and his toughness, and our platoon was willing to go to hell and back for him. By the end of this tour, he would earn two Purple Hearts for injuries. Yet, he never shied away from a single mission.

The pain of saying good-bye to the men I had become close to was made even tougher by the fact that the insurgency was getting stronger in Hīt. The troop was going to go through major upheaval, as S.Sgt. Smith and Sgt. Wilkening were also leaving.

There were many great soldiers left in the group, but I couldn't help but feel we were leaving them vulnerable. That feeling really hit home when the company commander, Capt. David Rozelle, lost his right foot to a land mine just before I left. It seemed like I was leaving these soldiers just when they needed me the most. I felt responsible for getting them back home safely, and the fact that I had to leave them would haunt me until the end of the deployment.

FORCED TO FIGHT

HUSAYBAH, SUMMER 2003

Jamil's stomach knotted from fear of the fight to come as much as from the garbage piled around him. He was draped in the discarded clothing and bloody bandages of the wounded and the dead. At his father's command, he had buried himself in a waste heap in an alley behind the Husaybah hospital. Used syringes, empty food cans, and torn bedding were piled around him. Dusk gave way to darkness as he sat alone wondering if he might die in the impending ambush upon the American troops in his town.

He'd worn a long-sleeved, black T-shirt as ordered, to help hide him in the darkness. But once he'd buried himself in the garbage pile, Jamil feared he'd start retching and give away his position in between the hospital and the morgue. He couldn't believe his father had placed him in such a wretched place.

He heard the low rumble of an American convoy on Highway 12 as it approached the town's entrance arches. Instinctively, he aimed his AK-47 rifle toward the street in case he was being watched by Nassir or his men. The headlights of the American vehicles danced madly in the cemetery across the street, casting eerie shadows off rows of headstones.

His stomach churned. His body shuddered with chills. He couldn't see the vehicles, but he had learned to distinguish between the sound of tracked tanks and Humvees. He feared the armored tanks the most, with their main guns that could knock down buildings. Jamil did not want to be in this fight. The Americans had night-vision equipment, and they were skilled at identifying an enemy's firing position from the flash of a weapon.

Nassir gave the call to begin the ambush. All around Jamil, insurgents in hiding opened fire. The Americans responded within a split second. Jamil burrowed into the sordid garbage pile, but the shaking of the earth beneath him and the roar of the firefight kept knocking the bloodied rags off. He had not fired his weapon and was contemplating running for better cover when the brief, violent attack ended.

The American soldiers and their vehicles roared away after the initial burst. As soon as the firing stopped, Jamil jumped up and ducked into the darkness of the alley. He heard the shouts of his father and the other insurgents but ignored them as he emptied the bullets from his rifle into his hand and threw them in the garbage. Then he sprinted home through the familiar back alleys of Husaybah, like a boy chasing the last of his childhood.

They met up at the designated site, the home of Sayed Atta Ali, the leader of the town's insurgent cells. He served as a conduit for foreign fighters and funds funneled into the region from Syria and other Middle Eastern nations. Everyone feared Sayed—with good reason. He led the attacks and ambushes on coalition soldiers and terrorized any Iraqis who sympathized or traded with them. People in Husaybah either joined the insurgency or faced his wrath.

Even before the overthrow of Saddam Hussein's dictatorship, Sayed was feared within the community. Jamil knew the stories all too well. Sayed lived next door to his family and worked closely with his father. Everyone in the neighborhood had witnessed or felt the shock waves of his violent temper. This was a man who shot one of his own brothers because he had dared to question Sayed about his womanizing. Sayed had calmly listened to his brother chastise him in front of other family members before pulling a handgun from his jacket and shooting him in the leg. He then bent down, put the gun to his brother's head, and whispered, "If you ever speak to me again of this matter, I will not be so kind."

Jamil had his own reasons to fear Sayed, who cursed and struck out at neighborhood children when he'd been drinking and popping pills. Jamil's mother was terrified of Sayed, but she'd once ordered him out of their house because he'd kicked Jamil. The boy and his brothers and sisters did their best to avoid him, especially when he was carrying a liquor bottle. Jamil had once climbed out a window at night, crawled across the yard, and stolen a full whiskey bottle that he'd seen Sayed hide behind his house. He gave it to a friend before a furious Sayed showed up at the door demanding to know if anyone there had taken his bottle. He'd stared at Jamil, who shrugged his shoulders, blinked his eyes, and walked away. As he departed, Sayed narrowed his eyes and watched. He sensed that the slightly built boy was shrewd beyond his years.

Sayed glared at Jamil when he arrived at his house after the ambush at the hospital. The other men ceased their bragging about how they'd sent the Americans running.

"Did you shoot anyone?" Nassir asked his son.

"I shot at this soldier, and he went down," Jamil lied.

His father clapped him on the back and looked at the others gathered, sweating and panting in Sayed's living room.

"I am proud of you, my son," the father said.

Sayed said nothing.

Nassir was perspiring so badly, the droplets of his sweat wet the packed sand floor at his feet. He went to a window and peered out, making certain the Americans had not followed them after the ambush. It always surprised the former Republican Guard captain how this powerful enemy, with all of its vaunted weaponry, was content simply to return fire and move on.

When he saw that the road was clear, Nassir reached into his pocket and found some coins and gave them to his son as a reward for taking part in the ambush and shooting an American.

Jamil took the coins and held them in his hand as he left the meeting and walked across the yard to his own home. He considered tossing them on the ground, but he didn't. Instead, he hid the coins in a drawer and went to bed. But he could not sleep with all that was racing through his mind.

7

CLUB PARADISE LOST

JOURNAL ENTRY: JULY 2, 2003
Welcome to Club Iraq. The dam feels like paradise compared to the rest of Iraq. The commander and I share a room with an air conditioner, a balcony overlooking the dam, electricity, hot and cold water, showers, washer, dryer, theater, refrigerator, gym.

Half the guys in my old platoon piled into two Humvees to accompany me to my new duty station. We stopped about halfway to let off some steam, firing round after round into the desert sands. I was glad to have the company and to spend just a little more time with them, but when we arrived at my new quarters, they gave me no end of grief about abandoning them for "Club Ah-Med."

After three months of miserable heat and the most arduous duty any of us had ever experienced, we found ourselves in the Iraqi version of the French Riviera. Some military units drove for hours just to swim and relax at this desert oasis. After S.Sgt. Gill and the others finished cursing my good fortune and pouring on the guilt, they stripped down to their boxer shorts and headed for the beach while I "checked in."

I was transferred to help with security at the Haditha Dam, a primary source of electricity for Baghdad and the region, just as the U.S.-controlled Coalition Provisional Authority halted all local elections and self-rule in Iraq. Increased hostilities and sabotage were anticipated as the United States put in place its own appointed mayors and administrators in towns across the country. Until an Iraqi governing council could be formed and self-rule reinstated, we were expecting growing resistance. Still, my new quarters felt like the Ritz-Carlton compared to Hīt.

The Haditha Dam, formally known as the Al Qadisayah Dam, lies on the Euphrates, just north of Haditha in the Al Anbar Province. It's an enormous thirteen-story structure (six stories below ground) that generates electricity for Baghdad, 140 miles to the southeast, and for a large portion of western Iraq. It is one of the largest structures in Iraq, and the view from on top of it was the most spectacular I had seen in the country. The view south afforded an unobstructed panorama of the unraveling path of the Euphrates, in stark contrast to the miles and miles of surrounding desert. To the north, the dam had created a beautiful lake with white and brown rock outcroppings and gorgeous light blue water that runs to a white sand beach.

I had to assume my duties as the first sergeant, the senior enlisted soldier, of Dragon Company. Dragon was the tank company for the First Squadron, known as Tiger Squadron, of the Third Armored Cavalry Regiment. The company commander, Captain Roehrman, and the executive officer, Lieutenant Sands, were also just coming on board. Together, we formed a "tripod" command leadership.

I met Lt. Sands first. He had been a scout platoon leader in Bandit Troop conducting operations in and around Al Qaim and the Syrian border. He confessed that he had asked the squadron commander, Lieutenant Colonel Dolan, if he had done something wrong to get the new assignment at the Haditha Dam. His military experiences had been similar to mine, and he wasn't happy about having to leave his team at halftime either. Immediately, I knew we would work well together.

Since he had joined the company three weeks earlier, I asked him for his observations. He confirmed my suspicions about the group: soldiers asleep on guard, dirty weapons, poor maintenance, and very green leadership. I didn't know anything about his tactical abilities, but I knew we were reading from the same sheet of music in getting the company headed in the right direction.

He was just over six feet tall and a great volleyball player, but one of the most excruciating things I ever endured in Iraq was listening to him strum his sitar. I have never seen a room clear out faster than when everyone saw Lt. Sands walking our way with his guitar backpack. Later in the deployment, I would find out he was just as good tactically as he was at everything else (minus the sitar playing, of course).

Capt. Roehrman was a West Point graduate who had been working on regimental staff at the beginning of the war. Not easily excited, very personable, deliberate in his thinking and in giving operations orders, he was as solid as they come. Very analytical, Roehrman never made a rash decision. He was definitely the moral compass of the group and never let his emotions override his decision-making process. Not one to take shortcuts, he ensured full effort was put into every plan and was always willing to listen to ideas that differed from his own.

Normally, you don't change out the company commander, first sergeant, and the executive officer all at once. But nothing was normal about my first three months in Iraq. Dragon Company's mission was to defend Iraq's number one strategic site: the Al Qadisayah Dam. It sounded like a fancy mission, but in reality, it was more like being heavily armed mall security.

Moving to Haditha was like coming out of the dark, hot desert night into the bright, cool day on Daytona Beach. It was relatively serene there at that point, but Haditha was expected to become a major target once the insurgency was strengthened with foreign fighters and their weaponry. Yet, the soldiers in Dragon Company had been lulled into complacency. They had not conducted any foot patrol operations in Iraq. Their weapons were poorly maintained. Morale was low.

Dragon had a reputation as a very good company prior to deployment; clearly, it was time for a leadership change. Due to the stagnant type of mission they'd been on and their lack of contact with what was going on outside the confines of the dam, they'd become complacent. Lt. Sands, Capt. Roehrman, and I agreed: The men of Dragon Company had lost their focus. A Groundhog Day mentality had set in. This was the first deployment for 99 percent of them, and they had not been in combat since their arrival. You can have the best-trained company in the world, but the first time you come under fire and get your nose bloodied, everything changes. Sometimes, so does the color of your shorts. I have never seen an operations plan withstand first contact. Being able to think on your feet while your life and the lives of those around you potentially hang in the balance is not an easy task.

They had some internal issues to address, but we were most concerned with their lack of combat experience. Being shielded from the violent realities of the rest of the country had made them highly vulnerable. Soldiers bond together against a common threat, but they tend to pull apart from internal conflict when they have too much free time in safe quarters.

Looking after the soldiers' care and welfare was my primary job. That meant I had to start enforcing combat standards, improving their attitudes, and preparing them for tougher times ahead. I had to light a fire under these guys, and the Fourth of July seemed like a great opportunity to do it with a bang. We had them assemble at dusk. More than one hundred people gathered on top of the dam. We borrowed a Humvee with an amazing speaker system from a military intelligence/psychological operations team. They used it to blast messages at the enemy. We put in a CD from the group Drowning Pool and raised whitecaps on the dam lake with blaring hard rock. We had their ears and were about to win them over through their stomachs. Staff Sergeant Williams, the head cook, whipped up an elaborate BBQ picnic. As the sun set over the lake, we unleashed the Fourth of July fireworks, Iraqi style.

"White Four, this is Dragon Seven. You have permission to go Red Direct!"

Four tanks and two Bradleys had been selected to light the torch. They sat idling on the east side of the dam, waiting for the final command. Inside the tank, White Four's loader hit the knee switch, and the hydraulically operated ammunition door slid open. He removed the round, approximately three and a half feet long, and slammed it into the breech, ensuring the breechblock was flush and the firing pin was aligned with the stub base of the round. The gunner was checking the computer correction factors. All the crews were going through the same procedures.

"White Four, the area has been cleared. You have permission to fire."

"This is White Four, roger."

"All elements, this is White Four. Fire at my command, in one mike!"

We had spent all day dragging an inoperable Iraqi T-55 tank, left over from the Iraqi forces that had guarded this site, across the dam and to the bottom of the east side (away from the populace). It was placed in a natural depression, and confiscated fuel was added for effect.

"All elements, ten seconds . . ." Sergeant First Class Ross, one of the tank platoon sergeants, waited with me during the final countdown: *"Three . . . two . . . one . . . FIRE!"*

Four high-explosive rounds erupted from the main guns of the tanks on the dam. The envelope, or flash, created at the end of the gun tubes was impressive in the waning light. One kilometer away, the rounds hit the stationary tank. It erupted in an all-American Middle East fireworks show. The concussions shook every window near the dam. Everyone at the top of the dam oohed and aahed, then applauded. Many of the soldiers had never seen a tank fire a main gun round. The dam security office received many phone calls that night from neighboring Iraqis who thought there had been an attack. They were relieved to hear otherwise, but their fears would be realized soon enough.

BUNKER BLOWUP

Tiger Squadron had responsibility not only for the Haditha Dam, but also for the security of a huge former Iraqi ammo dump that contained row after row and bunker after bunker of ammunition in all sizes, all shapes, and from all countries. It was about twenty-five miles east of the dam in an uninhabited desert wasteland with no vegetation for miles around. We stopped there a few days after our Fourth of July celebration as we returned to the dam from a trip to Al Asad, a regimental logistics and air base. We had picked up "Tiger Band-Aid," the squadron medics, who were headed back to the dam. I had to stop by the ammo dump to pick up a confiscated Iraqi truck. Its previous owners had been caught by the soldiers in Howitzer Battery attempting to break into the ammo, which cost them both their freedom and the keys to their truck.

After getting our new wheels, we were waiting for the security detail to let us out of the compound when a huge explosion rocked our Humvee and everything around us. Five hundred yards to my left, the roof of a bunker was blown open. Debris was thrown in all directions. It was raining down all over the desert. Through the smoke and dust, I could see a personnel carrier and an Iraqi civilian truck speeding away from it. The gate guard was catatonic. Stunned, I asked, "Is anyone inside that bunker?"

He was in shock. There was no answer, but I could tell from the sick look on his face that we needed to kick into gear. I yelled, "Are there any U.S. soldiers inside?"

He just stared at me with his mouth gaping. Then he slowly nodded up and down. I jumped out of my Humvee and ran to the one carrying the squadron medics. As I ran to it, a civilian truck with five Iraqi workers from the ammo dump went flying by. The driver and passenger were screaming in Arabic with their arms flailing as two of them in the rear of the truck tended to a severely burned man. His clothes were smoldering rags; wisps of smoke rose from what remained of his hair, and his facial features were horribly disfigured. It did not look like he was going to make it. I jumped in the back of the medics' vehicle and told them we had to get to the site of the explosion.

It was chaos around the building. Ammunition was still cooking off inside, and debris was blasting out the top. The bunker was a thick, square concrete structure with large metal bay doors. The doors were gone, and a Humvee was parked about fifty meters from the entrance. Dragon Company's Corporal Johnson pulled up in the Humvee I'd left at the front gate. Specialist Cannings, my driver, Specialist Strout, and Specialist Senneker were with him. Spec. Strout led the charge toward the bunker. I yelled at them to stop and then noticed why they were running. About thirty meters from the explosion site was a soldier flat on his back and not moving. I waved them on, following them with the medics in their Humvee.

Sporadic eruptions were still coming out of the blown-up bunker. The soldier on the ground was barely conscious and speaking incoherently. The proximity and volume of the explosions made it hard to communicate. The medics were about to begin working on him when Cpl. Johnson and Spec. Strout said, "Let's get him out of here." Just then, a large-tracked armored vehicle pulled between us and the volatile building.

The driver, Specialist Humphries, jumped out screaming: "You need to get away from here! You are way too close!"

He knew what he was talking about. Just then, there was another tremendous explosion. We were only fifty meters from the bunker. If he hadn't parked his armored vehicle in front of us, we'd have been shredded meat. As it was, we could hear the clatter of shrapnel tearing into the opposite side of his vehicle.

"I think we'll be moving now," I said.

We scooped up the soldier, Staff Sergeant Roy, who had no visible wounds. He was coming out of his daze and shrieking in panic. We moved a kilometer south before I could listen to what was troubling him so much. The staff sergeant had been in charge of two soldiers overseeing a twenty-man Iraqi work detail. They'd been clearing out brass casings inside the bunker. His soldiers were also inside when the explosion occurred. He had just stepped outside to talk on the radio of his Humvee when the blast blew him backward thirty feet. It was amazing that he had no injuries.

But two of S.Sgt. Roy's Howitzer Battery soldiers, Peterson and Creger, were not accounted for. He thought Peterson had left the bunker to fill a water can before the explosion, but he couldn't be sure. He felt certain that Specialist Creger was inside, and he was frantic about finding him. S.Sgt. Roy kept trying to move back to the bunker even though he was still shaky himself. I got the medics to hang on to him for his own safety. I told him that we would go back and look for Creger. That calmed him a bit. I knew that he would not rest until his soldier was cared for, and I didn't blame him. We headed back, not knowing for certain how we were going to get anyone out of a building that was still being rocked by explosions.

I radioed the Howitzer Battery platoon sergeant, who was known as "Smoke," but he couldn't raise anyone from headquarters, as the explosions had ripped the communications antennae off their personnel carrier, which was the tactical operations center. Smoke was collecting along with all his soldiers at the front gate. He stated on the radio that he had two soldiers from the bunker.

I was turning my Humvee toward the front gate when a third, massive explosion created a mushroom cloud more than a kilometer high. I couldn't believe what I was seeing. I had never been so close to an explosion of that magnitude. It rattled every bone and organ in my body. I had to look out the Humvee window just to see how high up it went because it was directly above us. The top of the cloud, filled with pulverized concrete, brass casings, and steel rebar, was just reaching the apex of its ascent into the stratosphere. That's when the realization hit me: All of that debris was going to be heading back down very quickly . . . on top of us!

I cut the steering wheel again, stomped on the gas, and headed for a small group of buildings one hundred meters to our right. One of them had a three-foot awning I hoped would be wide enough to fit under. The first piece of shrapnel hit us before we got under the awning. It ripped through the plastic roof tarp on the Humvee and hit Cpl. Johnson in the leg. I slammed the Humvee in alongside the building, destroying the headlight, scraping the entire side, and tearing off the mirror. I didn't care. I needed to squeeze as much of the vehicle under that awning as I could. This was going to be one hell of a debris shower.

Day turned to night in seconds. We were engulfed in dark black smoke, dirt, and dust. It seemed like there was no air to suck into our lungs. Shrapnel rained down like a Texas hailstorm. I yelled to the men with me to see if they were okay. Cpl. Johnson had a severe bruise on his calf. Everyone else was unscathed. We sat tight for what seemed like an eternity, but it was probably just ten or fifteen minutes. I radioed Smoke. Everyone was okay at his location. They'd moved farther out from the dropping debris. I double-checked to make certain he had the two men who'd been inside the bunker, Peterson and Creger, with him. He said Peterson was okay, but he didn't have Creger. He said he wasn't tracking Creger.

Where the hell was Creger? I couldn't get a status report on him. It was then that I realized we still needed to go to the bunker. There was a slim chance that he had survived, but we couldn't give up on him. I wasn't going to make my soldiers go near that volatile building with me. But I had told S.Sgt. Roy that we would get his soldier. I went around to the back of the Humvee, where my men were resting. I explained the situation. Before I even had a chance to ask them if they wanted to go, Cpl. Johnson, Spec. Strout, and Spec. Senneker were in the back of the Humvee. My driver, Spec. Cannings, hopped into the driver's seat and said, "Based on what I've seen of your parking job, do you mind if I drive now?"

We headed off, and it struck me for the first time that I'd joined up with a good group. Dragon Company had a lot of heart and guts. There may have been issues within the company, but these were men who could be counted on in the worst of situations. And this one ranked right up there. We were barreling toward the bunker, which was still on fire and erupting with explosions, when I got a radio call that Creger had been located near the highway. His situation was unclear. He did have burn injuries, but he was alive. That was great to hear, and I was very glad for the opportunity to turn around after staring into the fiery mouth of the exploding bunker. After all we'd been through, I wanted to verify his safety for myself, so we headed for the highway. On the squadron net, with the whir of helicopter blades in the background, came the scratchy voices of Nomad 15 and Nomad 32. The pilots of a pair of OH-58Ds, regimental scout helicopters, had seen the explosion from over twenty miles away, and they'd flown over to investigate.

I asked the helicopter pilots to arrange for a medevac helicopter. I didn't really know Creger's status, but I was sure that he would require medical evacuation. We arrived to find Smoke and his medics attending to Creger, who had second- and third-degree burns on his hands, back, and legs. He would live, but he needed to be evacuated. I relayed that a medevac helicopter was on the way, then had the soldiers set up an emergency landing site.

Creger relayed that he was standing in the doorway of the bunker when he saw one of the Iraqi workers light a cigarette—with a bunker full of large artillery shells, explosives, and propellant all over the floor. Creger barely had time to start running before the first fireball filled the entire place and consumed everyone in it. Most of the Iraqis were engulfed in that first explosion. Of the twenty Iraqis, the only ones who made it out alive were those five who went speeding by me in the truck.

Haditha was not as wild and woolly as Hīt had been, but it wasn't Hoboken, either. The insurgency was moving in. About a week after the bunker blew up, the mayor of Haditha and his daughter were killed and his son lost his arm when an explosion was triggered in their yard. It was clear that they were targeted because they had been cooperative with the American soldiers in the area. There were also increasing numbers of ambushes in the regimental area of operations.

The U.S.-appointed governing council had taken control of government operations in July, and Saddam's sons, Uday and Qusay, were killed in a battle in Mosul shortly after that. Those two events seemed to give rise to increasing attacks and ambushes by the insurgent guerrillas. In August, the Jordanian embassy and United Nations headquarters in Baghdad were bombed, and a car bomb in Najaf killed 125 people. Clearly, we were moving into a far more volatile and dangerous period of this operation.

In the days following the explosion at the ammo dump, we intensified our efforts to improve security at the dam. Capt. Roehrman revised the security plan, and I inspected observation posts and traffic control points. We had received intelligence reports that Saddam had a safe house in Haditha. Twenty-five Special Forces soldiers arrived to search the potential hiding place, using our quarters at the dam as their operations base. They told us that they'd detected a Syrian insurgent cell operating nearby.

The Special Forces guys tended to operate under everyone's radar, but they blipped ours when they came speeding into the base one day dressed as civilians and driving two unmarked trucks. They failed to notice that we'd tightened up security and established a traffic control point. When they showed no signs of stopping, the soldiers fired warning shots, then the tank let go of a burst of machine-gun fire that put a few rounds near the rear of one of the trucks. That got their attention.

They got out of the trucks and walked their vehicles forward. They were livid that we'd shot at them. Our guys let them know that they were lucky they weren't already in body bags. We got everyone calmed down, and our "special" guests eventually admitted that our soldiers had acted alertly and responsibly. After that, they made a point of politely identifying themselves as they came in.

We made our point. Club Iraq was now for members only.

8

COINS FOR FIGHTING

HUSAYBAH, FALL 2003

A loud knock rattled the front door. Jamil ran to the window with his brothers and sisters trailing behind. American soldiers and their vehicles filled the front yard. *They know we're the enemy! They've come for us!*

These raids had become commonplace in his neighborhood. Just as he feared, the Americans had somehow figured out that he and his father were involved in the growing insurgent activities. Husaybah had become a portal for veteran foreign fighters, mercenaries, and zealots willing to sacrifice their lives to take out American soldiers. Arms and money flowed with them. His father's guerrilla activities had increased as well; he was rarely home, but on this afternoon, he was relaxing when the Americans pounded on the door.

The soldier standing in the doorway towered over Nassir as he entered the house cautiously, his eyes sweeping the room as three more soldiers moved in behind him brandishing weapons. They were intense, taking in every detail of the house, checking floors, ceilings, from room to room. The big soldier barked something at his father in rough Arabic. He was asking about weapons. Nassir acted docile and confused. He wiped his hands together, indicating he had no weapons.

Jamil knew differently. He hoped his father wasn't convincing and that the soldiers would see through his act. The big soldier was actually standing on top of a Russian sniper rifle hidden beneath the floorboards. Jamil thought about alerting him. Maybe that would end it. His father would be taken away and the insurgent cell uncovered. Maybe Sayed would be arrested and put in prison, or even killed. As these thoughts ran through his mind, Jamil kept quiet. He did not want to endanger his mother and the other children.

Nassir shook hands with the big soldier, who then signaled for his men to move out and on to the next house in their sweep of the neighborhood. Torn, Jamil watched out the window as they walked out of the house and across the yard. He was tempted to inform them of the cache of rocket-propelled grenades that was buried in the backyard. In one sense, the boy was glad that they were leaving and his family was still safe and intact, but he could not fight off the thought that it would have given him great relief to see his father led away in handcuffs. None of them would be safe until that happened.

Later that night, Nassir took Jamil to a meeting of the insurgents, where he boasted to the other fighters that he had fooled the Americans who came to his house. Then they began planning another attack. Nassir told Jamil that he would be expected to participate in the next ambush. There would be no excuses. He had to be there. The attack was planned for that evening; mortar rounds were to be hidden in piles of trash on the main road near Jamil's former school. They were connected to a remote device— a garage door opener—that would be triggered by a man watching from a second-story window.

Jamil felt swept up in a powerful current. He didn't dare to resist taking part. His father would not let him leave, so he sat looking out a window for hours, trying to calm his fears, while the men bolstered one another's courage by disparaging the American soldiers as cowards and inept fighters. They bragged that more and more fighters were joining the insurgency each day, and they talked of spies working within and around the American encampment.

After sunset, they donned their black clothing, passed out rifles, and moved out to the school grounds. Once again, the boy found himself posted with a rifle and dreading a fight he wanted no part of. He felt disoriented and disconnected. Most of his days and nights were normal, but then he was thrown into these otherworldly situations where he was expected to fight like a man against trained and heavily armed soldiers. He'd been lucky to survive the first ambush. What if the Americans didn't keep moving this time? What if they counterattacked?

The sound of approaching American tanks roused him from his thoughts. As the convoy turned toward the school, an explosion tore through the darkness. It had been triggered too soon, missing the Humvee. The American convoy responded with a massive roar of machine-gun fire. But again, they kept moving. Jamil crouched in the dark alley as the vehicles flew past. Then he ran with darkness covering his flight. After a safe distance, he stopped to catch his breath. Maybe he could survive if this was the way it went every time, he thought. It was like a game that he would pretend to enjoy.

When he rejoined the insurgent cell members, his father clapped him on the back and handed him another handful of coins for his role in the ambush. Those coins were still jangling in Jamil's pocket a few nights later when he came home to find more than a dozen men huddled in the small courtyard between the privacy wall and the front door.

"It's good that you are here. We will need your rifle again tonight," his father said.

9

BAGHDAD AND BEYOND

JOURNAL ENTRY: AUGUST 7, 2003
Just returned from Baghdad. Very successful trip. Also got first look at Baghdad. Hopefully, my last. The highway into BIAP [Baghdad International Airport] reminded me of "Matrix Reloaded: Highway Scene." Every car that passed us could be someone waiting to shoot you. It is very draining, watching and assessing every car that passes you on the highway as "threat," "nonthreat." Interesting vicinity, BIAP, hunting/fishing palace— moats, lagoons, marbled floors, chandeliers. This war is very different for some. August heat is upon us. Word for the day: "crisp."

Five months after the invasion and liberation of Iraq, President Bush gave a television address and told the nation that "a collection of killers is trying to undermine Iraq's progress and throw the country in chaos." As he spoke, we were driving into the heart of their rebellion. We traveled from Haditha to Baghdad, passing through the most volatile regions of the Sunni Triangle formed around it by Tikrīt , Fallujah, and Ramadi. In rural areas, it was easy to find safer routes out of heavy and potentially hostile traffic. The congested thoroughfares in Baghdad didn't allow for the same margin of safety. Ambushes and sniper fire were just a few of the threats. More and more Americans were being killed by improvised explosive devices buried on roadways.

We were traveling in three unarmored vehicles with netting instead of doors. I missed my tank more than ever. The closer we got to Baghdad, the more Iraqis there were on the road. Every car, truck, and donkey cart on the road was a potential threat. Trying to track them all was like walking wide-eyed through a hailstorm. My eyeballs ached. I sweated through my helmet and my boots.

We did not relax our guard until we drove inside the security gates of the U.S. base at Baghdad International Airport. I hadn't expected it to be such an ordeal just to get there, but it gave us a very good handle on how the threat had grown throughout the center of the country. We'd come with two distinct missions. The first was to pick up supplies from headquarters. The second was to allow Lt. Sands, the company executive officer, an opportunity to see his wife, a lieutenant with the military police. Her platoon was responsible for security on the perimeter of the airport base. The U.S. military in Baghdad was headquartered at Saddam Hussein's former gold-plated hunting and fishing lodge, which was really a huge, plush palace on a man-made lagoon. Saddam and his buddies roughed it out on marble tile while most Iraqi homes had floors of packed sand, dirt, or bare concrete. The dictator and his posse didn't even have to break a sweat while hunting. Their private reserve had been stocked with a zoo's worth of wild game, and the lagoon was loaded with fish.

Our shopping list seemed woefully humble in such swank surroundings. We picked up a couple of air conditioners, several cases of nonalcoholic beer, and printers for our computers. While touring the happy hunting grounds of the deposed dictator, I spied another item that had been on our wish list at Haditha Dam. We'd been looking for a boat to use for patrolling the lake. As luck would have it, Saddam Hussein had left two of them floating in his moat: One had been claimed by the Australian Special Forces team; the other needed an engine overhaul, but it was ours for the taking. I just had to find a way to transport it to the dam. Tankers are known for our adaptability, so we crammed the sixteen-foot boat with an 85-horsepower outboard motor into the rear of our cargo truck. We drew a lot of neck-snapping stares as we cruised across the desert and back to Haditha with the boat hanging out the back of our truck.

It took nearly a month for our guys to clean out and rebuild the boat's motor, but they got it shipshape, even accessorizing with a mounted machine gun and a "fish finder," just like the pro fishermen use in tournaments. Then we held a boat christening on the lake at Haditha Dam. Our motley crew included the newly commissioned "Naval Captain" Anderson (Sergeant Anderson) wearing a pirate hat with a stuffed parrot on his shoulder. He manned the bow in a pose that might have worked for a billboard hawking Captain Morgan rum. The pirate props had been sent to us from several wives, who'd enjoyed our boat-in-the-desert saga.

For the maiden voyage, "Seaman" Ragle (formerly Private Ragle) was at the controls. A shirtless "First Mate" Moon (Sergeant Moon) was supervising in cutoff shorts with a 9-millimeter pistol tucked in his waist belt and a do-rag wrapped around his head. First Mate Moon proudly made the announcement: "We're christening the boat with the dam's finest 2003 Budweiser. Ignore the non-alcoholic label. It is a vintage brew."

He handed the bottle to the captain, who shattered it with a single blow to the machine-gun mount. They cranked the engine, which sputtered to life and propelled the crew of the *Dragon Bottom* across the lake. We had a lot of laughs in getting the boat on the water, but it was soon put to serious use. Just a week later, we redubbed it the *Drift Wood* after we had to use it to retrieve the body of a U.S. soldier who drowned in the river near the base of the dam.

We were back on the water a few weeks later as part of a special operation in Rawa, a peninsula town about sixty miles north of the dam on high ground created by the many twists and turns of the ancient Euphrates River. From a distance, in morning sunlight, the town of sixty thousand resembled a Tuscan village, or at least the closest thing Iraq had to offer. We went there searching for Sayf Al-Din Fulayyih Hasan Taha, the former Republican Guard chief of staff, referred to as the "Jack of Clubs" in the Pentagon's "personality identification playing cards," also known as "Iraq's Most Wanted Deck of Cards."

Serious players in the Pentagon had been after this particular face card for quite a while. They'd made several attempts to nab him, without success. Rawa made for a very good hiding place. One road ran into the peninsula town from the mainland. Intelligence noted that in past raids, Sayf and his entourage had escaped by boat after spotting coalition forces coming down the road. Our job was to shut off any attempt to escape by water.

I was under a camouflage net, aboard our homemade gunboat, which was hiding in the reeds, when one of the cloak-and-dagger guys delivered a baffling message in a faint whisper over the radio: *"We have been nonhostile compromised and have skinnies everywhere!"* I stared at the portable radio, wondering if it was picking up transmissions from another planet. It was two thirty in the morning, and Nightstalker, the long-range reconnaissance company, had been inserted into Rawa by rubberized Zodiac boats. Their job was to mark the targeted homes for the raiders, who were going to hit at sunrise. That seemed simple enough. But their spewed acronyms and military jargon made it difficult even for me to figure out what they were talking about on the radio. "Nonhostile compromised" apparently meant that the reconnaissance team had come around a corner and found themselves face-to-face with a friendly but nervous Iraqi. As for the "skinnies" comment, clearly someone on their team had watched *Black Hawk Down* one too many times.

Our boat was strategically tucked into a small alcove on the southern side of the Euphrates. We had a full view of both banks of the Rawa peninsula. My mission was to monitor the radio and man the *Drift Wood's* machine gun in case the Jack of Clubs hit the water. My shipmates, Anderson and Moon, were at the helm. They scanned to the north with night-vision devices, cracking jokes about the nonexistent Iraqi navy, wayward cruise ships, and nuclear submarines. But we did have a new military moniker that was not a joke, at least not an intentional one. We were dubbed the "Squadron Aquatic Quick Reaction Force." Our amphibious force also included SFC Ross and Lt. Sands in their new roles as commanders of the Zodiac rubber boat armada. They were in charge of a visiting group of National Guardsmen who were trained in Zodiac boat operations even though they were from landlocked South Dakota.

Our amphibious operation probably wouldn't go down in naval warfare history, but it was surely a first in the annals of the Third Armored Cavalry. Under cover of darkness, SFC Ross and Lt. Sands ferried the reconnaissance teams to drop-off points along the banks of Rawa. Once they'd marked the target houses, the Zodiacs were to return and "exfiltrate" the reconnaissance teams.

Unfortunately, when the squadron raiders moved in, our high-priority bad guy once again eluded capture. They did manage to nab several members of his entourage, so the noose was tightened. Less than a month later, we returned for another surprise visit to the elusive Jack of Clubs. This time, we were in Humvees guarding possible land escape routes as a team of Navy SEALs fast-roped in from Black Hawk helicopters. Once again, Jack was not home. But Dragon Company picked up a bit more experience. These raids were confidence boosters for our guys, who were beginning to feel they could handle anything Iraq threw at us—by land, by air, or by sea.

OLYMPIC EFFORTS

By the fall of 2003, the Sunni Triangle was like the red-hot end of a branding iron burning into central Iraq. U.S. soldiers had mistaken guns fired in a wedding celebration as an attack in Fallujah. They'd opened fire, killing a fourteen-year-old boy and wounding six people. The insurgency retaliated by unleashing a wave of attacks, ambushes, and bombings throughout the region. We heard reports of explosives planted in the carcasses of dead dogs left on the roadside. The American death toll hit eighty and kept climbing. All of this was coming our way, according to intelligence reports. As the guerrillas grew more organized, they were expected to target the Haditha Dam and its power-generating plants.

We felt it was important to ramp things up in our training. Dragon Company had been pulling together after a period of dissension and complacency, but there still wasn't the level of teamwork and unity that we thought would be essential for survival when the guerrillas targeted our piece of Iraq. Drills and training exercises weren't cutting it, so Capt. Roehrman and I tried a fresh approach. We put together a "Dragon Decathlon," a ten-event competition designed to pump up the competitive juices of our troops. We built the competition around tank, Humvee, and four-man foot patrol teams. The ten events tested strength and stamina, combat marksmanship with individual weapons and machine guns, and group- or crew-level tasks dealing with evacuation and tank gunnery skills. We also threw in some demanding maintenance tasks.

Since I am a certified poor loser known for "stacking" my own teams with the best people, I took myself out of the competition and opted to referee it instead. Our games played out over a three-week period. There was resistance at first. Some guys refused to buy in, like office workers snubbing management's ploy to boost company morale. But once the games got going, most couldn't quell their competitive urges. As soon as I started posting scores, the trash-talking started. They ate it up.

Sixteen four-man teams competed for first place. Sergeant First Class Callahan, nicknamed "The Old Man" because he had been in Dragon for more than six years, and his "Dixie Normous" team put a stranglehold on the lead for nearly the entire three weeks. Staff Sergeant Guetschow, the unit's freakishly strong guy, and his "Da Kids" team chased them all the way. Finally, it came down to the final event. S.Sgt. Guetschow and two of his team members had to hit a target with a .50 caliber machine gun to overtake the front-runners. No one had been able to do it. The target was an inner tube that had been placed four hundred meters from the dam, along the empty banks of the lake's north side.

S.Sgt. Guetschow took aim at what must have seemed like a black speck in the distance. The sun's mid-afternoon glare didn't help. He was the last one on his team to have a crack at it. The pressure was on. He opened fire, and fifty rounds later, the inner tube was a limp lump of rubber. It was one hell of a shot and a great ending to what turned out to be an amazing training event.

And it served us well. The next time S.Sgt. Guetschow fired his .50 caliber, it was at an insurgent in the process of launching two deadly rocket-propelled grenades at his combat patrol. Once again, the strong man stepped up!

JOURNAL ENTRY: SEPTEMBER 11, 2003
Strange! A lot going on today. Time line of events over the past month at the dam:

1. *Al Jazeera reports U.S. withdraws on west side of dam when attacked*
2. *Workers notified of a suicide bomber*
3. *Two workers making anticoalition statements*
4. *Caught two Iraqis trying to sneak up to OP [Observation Post] 1*
5. *Motorcycle probe on west side of dam*
6. *D32 hit mine at OP4*
7. *Engineers hit mine on dam road*
8. *Intelligence identifies nine workers making anticoalition statements*
9. *Three workers harassing soldier on bus*
10. *Identified two workers discussing attacks on U.S. forces*
11. *FPS workers discussing RPG attack*
12. *White truck skirting fence line*
13. *Trip flares set at OP4*

A lot of individual events that paint a very serious picture.

By the end of my second month at the "peaceful" Haditha Dam, the level of combat activity had risen dramatically. One night in late September, I stood anxiously waiting for Capt. Roehrman and the soldiers to return from Forward Operating Base Tiger, located a hundred miles to the west along Highway 12 in an old rail yard in the Al Qaim region of the Al Anbar Province. As they stepped from the vehicles, I shook hands with each of them. I was relieved that they were okay. We'd received a situation report that they had been ambushed and sustained casualties. Before they made it back, we learned that it was not a Dragon soldier injured and his injuries were not life threatening.

The violence and volume of the ambush had left them all shocked and grateful that they had walked away unscathed. Their convoy consisted of four Humvees—the first two from Dragon were led by Capt. Roehrman, the last two from Crazy Troop were led by Captain Buckeye, their commander, who had been injured in the attack. Three of the four Humvees were light-skinned, without protective armor. It had all started at around eight thirty in the morning. Sgt. Johnson, the gunner in the lead Humvee, had just noticed the lack of oncoming traffic as they moved down Iraq's primary highway. He sensed something was wrong, and he was right.

All hell broke loose. As Sgt. Johnson told his story in the darkness, I got the sense that he was reliving it. Two Iraqis had started firing from positions along the road. Johnson swung his .50 caliber machine gun in their direction. When he returned fire, the two Iraqis were joined by more than a dozen others. They were firing massive rounds from their AK-47s as the convoy moved through their curtain of lead. The ambush was well planned—four groups of four insurgents arrayed at different distances to create what is known as a "kill sac." Sgt. Johnson found his mark in group two as the ambush intensified. Four rocket-propelled grenades hurtled toward them, making that distinct and deadly whooshing sound, followed by explosions all around their vehicles.

Each soldier gave his account with the same intensity felt during the ambush. Sergeant Campos, who was driving the second Humvee, had two RPGs hit the front and rear of his vehicle simultaneously. He tried to press the gas pedal through the floor. He feared that his body armor wasn't going to offer enough protection under the barrage. From all accounts, Sergeant Graham, my clerk, who was in charge of the second Humvee, was the luckiest man in Dragon Company that day. He was stretched out across the backseat, reaching for a bottle of water, when the ambush started. The spot where he should have been sitting was riddled with bullet holes. He was also saved from being wounded because of the very unique way he was holding his rifle. A round penetrated the front stock. It would have hit someone with a normal handgrip. But Sgt.

Graham's method, which he'd often been teased about, saved him from a serious wound.

Specialist Rayo told me that he was surprised at how close the enemy set up the ambush. He recalled firing his pistol "sideways" like he was a street gang member back on the block at home. It isn't like the movies. Pistols are not reliably accurate weapons for most soldiers in combat. It would have been a miracle to hit anything in a moving vehicle at that distance. It wasn't until Sgt. Graham prompted him with a few expletives that Rayo switched to the machine gun mounted on top of the Humvee.

Inside the third vehicle, strapped to the sidewall of the back compartment, was an AT-4, our own rocket-propelled grenade launcher. It was hit by the incoming fire, which launched the warhead through the I beam and into the cab of the Humvee. It just missed Capt. Buckeye's head before striking the front windshield. Miraculously, the warhead of this lethal weapon ended up in the driver's lap, undetonated.

Capt. Buckeye was injured in the ambush, and he appeared to be losing blood rapidly. There were no medics in the convoy, so Capt. Roehrman did not order the men to stand and fight. Instead, they pushed on to Tiger Base. Luckily, the captain's wound turned out to be superficial, and everyone returned to duty. They were shaken up by the attack, but they survived to fight another day.

JOURNAL ENTRY: SEPTEMBER 24, 2003
There are no atheists in foxholes. Emotions ran the gamut after the ambush: elation, anger, mirth, helplessness. It was the first time most had been in this type of situation. All performed superbly. All happy to be alive and will never forget that day! Danger seems to creep ever closer to the dam.

Capt. Roehrman then received word from the squadron commander, Lieutenant Colonel Reilly, that we would be shifted to a new, far more volatile location. We were going to Husaybah on the border with Syria in the Al Qaim region. We were to depart by mid-October. We were immediately grateful that we'd taken advantage of Haditha's relative calm to do intensive combat training. But we didn't have to leave the dam to test the effectiveness of our training. In early October, the insurgency came knocking at Club Haditha. Machine-gun fire and RPG attacks became daily occurrences. In some ways, it was a good thing, because every insurgent attack that we walked away from helped prepare us for our next battle. We were learning to deal with this faceless enemy that blended into crowds by day and staged well-planned ambushes by night.

It became clear in those confrontations that we needed to go on the offensive. Dragon Company had fourteen of the most lethal direct fire weapon systems in the U.S. Army's arsenal. Our M1A2 Abrams main battle tanks packed seventy tons of firepower that could turn the tide in any battle. But we had to learn to set the conditions of those battles. In those final days in Haditha, we were being attacked because we went out in light-skinned Humvees. That placed the most powerful army in the world in a needlessly vulnerable position. It also put us in a reactive mode. We felt like the prey instead of the predators, even with our more powerful weaponry. It was troubling on another level as well: Every engagement that allowed insurgents to walk away after attacking coalition forces served only to strengthen their resolve. They were gaining experience at our expense. It did not bode well for our safety in this hostile country.

Before we left Haditha, I made a promise to myself. No matter what happened, if given the chance, I would not allow the enemy to ambush my men and walk away. I wasn't just tired of it, I was pissed off. According to our intelligence reports, we were heading into a situation in Husaybah that was much more volatile. Foreign fighters were pouring across the border to join a well-organized and aggressive insurgent cell there. By the time we headed out for our new assignment, I had vowed that any insurgent who attacked my soldiers was going to find himself staring down the main gun barrel of our tanks.

10

JAMIL AND THE *DA BABA*

HUSAYBAH, NOVEMBER 2003

Jamil joined the silent men sitting cross-legged on the ground as Nassir outlined the plan for his third ambush. He had to admit that his father's plan was impressive both in its strategy and its boldness. They'd already run the newly arrived American troops out of the police station and the Baath Party headquarters. They were on the defensive even with their impressive weapons.

"The agents of the Great Satan are vulnerable on our ground," Nassir said. "This is our homeland. They are lost in our streets right now, so before they have had time to get acclimated, Allah will help us destroy them."

The men in the courtyard drew strength from Nassir's words and from the thoroughness of his ambush plan. Jamil had a much different response. He had to press his hands down on his legs to keep them from trembling at the thought of being within range of the long cannons mounted on American tanks (known as the *da baba*) that were nearly as big as his family's house. It was of little comfort that this ambush was planned for a place on the northeast corner of town, within three hundred yards of their home. He and his brothers and sisters had walked past the bridge every day coming home from school. He knew every reed in the thick wadi beneath it, which was part of the Euphrates tributary system. This time of year, the marshlands were all but dry and overgrown with ten-foot bamboo reeds. He knew that while there were plenty of places to hide in the reeds, there was nothing to stop the bullets or rounds fired from the American tanks.

Jamil tried to think of an excuse to stay home, but Nassir would have none of it. He called him a coward and threatened to beat him. He would have to go. He would carry the rifle into another ambush. But he would not kill for his father. Jamil could not erase from his mind the images in the photograph his father had shown him while boasting of the beating he'd given his victim. The man's face was bloodied and battered beyond recognition. His arms were bent at strange angles. His feet and hands were bound. Black-and-blue bruises painted his flesh. Nassir told him that the man had helped the Americans. He was an informant against his own people, Nassir said. He then spit on the photograph. Jamil shuddered. He did not understand how Nassir could take pleasure, let alone pride, in the massacre of another human, a Muslim. This *is Allah's work?* he thought.

11

THROUGH THE ARCHES OF HUSAYBAH

JOURNAL ENTRY: OCTOBER 20, 2003

Husaybah has turned out to be the most dangerous place I have ever been. IEDs [improvised explosive devices], RPGs, land mines, MG [machine-gun] fire every day. After thirteen years in the army, this next one raises the hair on the back of my neck. White Platoon was on convoy escort for Forty-third Engineers, taking them to the border checkpoint, when a large IED exploded next to their tank. It is unclear at this point, but the hull of the tank had been penetrated! No serious casualties, but that invisible "S" [for "Superman"] that tankers have on their chest when inside their tank in a combat situation is now gone. All those in Dragon who complained of boredom and the repetitiveness of the dam are going to be dreaming of those days soon.

We'd often heard other soldiers compare Husaybah to Tatooine, the desert outlaw planet in *Star Wars*. If only Husaybah was that pleasant! It quickly proved to be Tatooine on Earth, a desolate place populated by a grab bag of cutthroat killers, smugglers, and warring tribal chiefs. It was the most intense place I'd ever been. Rocket-propelled grenades had rained down on Tiger Squadron with terrifying regularity. Just inside the entrance to town as you crossed over the concrete bridge, the banks of the Euphrates and surrounding marshlands were used so often as cover for attacks by the insurgents that our soldiers called that area "Ambush Wadi."

Before leaving Haditha, we'd heard reports of the hell that awaited us in this region along the Syrian border. SFC Callahan, the veteran platoon sergeant for White Platoon, had moved in ahead of us to conduct escort operations from Forward Operating Base Tiger, just outside Husaybah, to the border checkpoint, in the heart of it. In their first four days, they were attacked six times.

Foreign fighters began flowing in from Syria and other nations shortly after Saddam's fall to coalition forces. Husaybah is the primary border crossing point between Iraq and Syria. The official crossing is a narrow road guarded at one end by Syrian troops behind a red and white steel gate and at the other by Iraqi police supervised and backed up by coalition forces. That crossing provides all parties ample opportunities to be shot, blown up, or run over, either accidentally or on purpose. There were also unofficial and illegal crossing points all along the border between the two nations. Tiger Squadron had responsibility for controlling the region and part of the border and for stopping the flow of insurgents and their recruits from throughout the Middle East.

The arrival of American-led coalition forces was met with insurgent attacks featuring rocket-propelled grenades, land mines, snipers, machine-gun fire, suicide bombers, and improvised explosive devices triggered with garage door openers, cell phones, or remote controls for children's toys. Our attackers were mostly locals, who smiled and laughed with us by day and did their best to kill us by night. They were even more vicious with each other. Iraqis suspected of sympathizing with or supplying coalition forces were dragged from their homes, beaten, tortured, and never heard from again. Their wives and children and other family members were raped, beaten, and dragged off too.

Oddly enough, this historically violent and chaotic community was set up in an orderly, perfect square mile of cross-sectioned streets. We couldn't master the Arabic names of the roads, highways, and dirt trails, so someone came up with the idea of naming each of them after a men's magazine, figuring we could remember those easily enough. So we referred to the main roads in and around town as Route Hustler, Route Playboy, Route Raw, Route Penthouse, and so on. Most of them were little more than narrow dirt alleys with one- and two-story homes on either side. The squat soil-colored homes, many of which had dirt floors, were coated with layers of dust and grime. Trash adorned every yard and street corner. Raw sewage was dumped in the streets, the stench overpowering in certain pockets.

The Euphrates River frames the town's northern border and serves as a favorite route for smugglers and terrorists. The tropical vegetation along its banks provides great cover for them during their ambushes. Beyond the river to the north are cliffs rising up three hundred feet, providing views of the city and surrounding desert. The rail lines run along the city's southern borders to a train station that is still a hub of activity. The southern edge of the city overlooks a wide expanse of desert loaded with mines, IEDs, and a trench complex built by the Iraqi army to defend the city from coalition forces approaching from the south. Syria, a staging point for anti-American rebels, their weapons, and their financing, lies along the city's western edge. We quickly identified the insurgents' favorite route into Iraq, the "440 block," named for rows of governmental housing that totaled 440 units. It lies a mere four hundred meters from the Syrian border, providing a virtual rabbit hole for those who wished to scamper across the border and duck in the town's underground network of jihadist guerrillas.

JOURNAL ENTRY: NOVEMBER 10, 2003

Intelligence Report: Two separate mujahideen [freedom fighter] cells, approximately 100 men apiece, have been operating within Husaybah. They have now coordinated their efforts into one cell (150–200 men). Now there is only one safe haven within the city where U.S. forces can stay overnight. Since it is the only show in town and in need of extra protection, Dragon Company moves to and defends NLT [no later than] November 10, 2003.

A MOST DANGEROUS PLACE

We had been at the border checkpoint, our new home, for less than an hour. I was checking the perimeter defenses from a tower that stands thirty feet high. It was a clear and brisk early morning, and I was on a three-foot overhang scanning the western edge of Husaybah. The overnight temperature had dropped into the forties, so it felt like a subarctic chill to our desert-acclimated bodies. I was discussing fields of fire, identifying dominant structures, and covering the rules of engagement with the soldiers when there was a large explosion less than two hundred meters to the south. It was on a road code-named "Cherry Street," near a frequent ambush site that our forces had dubbed "RPG Alley."

That explosion was followed by a second, which violently shook the tower. It was just below us. I saw a flash from the launching point of the rocket-propelled grenade, and I spotted our attacker poking his head around a corner wall to see if he'd hit his target. Bad for him, good for us. I yelled the direction of the attack to Sergeant First Class Loredo in the tank below, and then I hit the floor in anticipation of another blast. SFC Loredo aimed the turret in the direction of RPG Alley. He then let fire a 120-millimeter High Explosive Anti-Tank main gun round. At such close range, the explosion was deafening. The tower made of brick and mortar shook violently, its third good shaking in less than a minute. The dust created from the tank fire obscured everyone's view. As it cleared and we got back on our feet, we could see that the HEAT round had made quite an impression in a wall of RPG Alley. After a dismount force was put together, we checked the alley but could not confirm casualties. I did note, however, that the insurgents never again dared to shoot at us from that alley. It seemed the strong response made an impression not only on the alley wall.

Dragon Company served as escort and security for other units traveling around Husaybah during the previous month. Tiger Squadron was camped at the old train depot in the relative safety of the desert twenty miles southeast of Husaybah. Forward Operating Base Tiger was the launching point for the squadron, and its distance from the town allowed our soldiers some relief from the daily barrage within Husaybah. Our missions there almost always ended in some type of fight, so it was good that we had somewhere to escape the threat of attack.

When we arrived in the Al Qaim region, I was surprised to learn that there had been only one attack in which our tank forces had responded by firing a main gun round at the insurgents. From what I'd seen from the tower that first day, it seemed like our enemy had a lot of respect for that kind of firepower. Yet, I was informed that there was fear of perceived collateral damage from the show of such force. Firing a main gun round in a city can be devastating to the will of the enemy, but we had to be very careful not to destroy the city's infrastructure or injure innocents.

Many soldiers do not grasp the importance of "escalation of force." If the enemy is firing a rocket-propelled grenade from within a building, it does little good to return fire with a machine gun that cannot penetrate walls. Force had to be met with even greater force. Only then would our enemy learn to respect our firepower. In the early days of our tour in Husaybah, it always felt like the deck was stacked against us. The insurgents picked the place, time, and type of attack. We were forced to react, and our patrols never seemed to be in the right place or situation to unleash the overwhelming force that we had at our disposal. It was highly frustrating to have so much unused technology and firepower at our fingertips; we felt impotent.

I shared my frustrations with Staff Sergeant Landsberger, a tank commander and veteran combat soldier, one evening as we watched the sun set over Husaybah and waited for the nightly bombardment.

"Right across the street, not fifty meters from you and me, a group of men is huddled in a circle on a dirt floor in one of those concrete shacks," I said. "They are sipping their chi tea, drawing diagrams in the sand by candlelight with a stick. They are discussing, plotting, and planning your death and mine. They can think about nothing but the glorious day that Allah will be merciful and grant their prayers. If you give them the chance, they will kill you and your men. They think about your death every day, and they will get better at hunting and killing you unless we become more aggressive."

As if right on cue, the sun dropped beneath the horizon and the local mosques broadcast their evening prayers, which we'd learned served as a prelude to the night's bombings. The music and words were eerie and unfamiliar to us, and they always put us on edge. The locals may have listened to this music as a call to prayer, but we learned to think of it as a call to battle.

DEFENDING THE BORDER

Our primary mission in Husaybah was defending and running the border checkpoint. A fence and a wall of barbed wire separated the back of the checkpoint from Syria. Vehicles poured through in an unruly, chaotic flood nearly every day. It was like the herding pen from hell.

Each vehicle had to be searched for bombs and weapons. Before the war, this was a major place of commerce, with duty-free operations, a bank, and a passport office, but security was now the primary business in town. We shared responsibility initially with some Iraqi police, who also worked at the checkpoint. Later, the Iraqi Civil Defense Corps took over.

Four buildings formed a sort of internal compound, where we had barracks, offices, and a holding cell for those taken into custody. Along the outside perimeter, there were three main thirty-foot guard towers built by the Iraqis. Our tanks were positioned to make a point, with the main guns facing the routes most likely to be used by suicide bombers. Along the southern edge of our compound, another tank was positioned to deter attacks from a large parking lot, where hundreds of Iraqis gathered every morning in hopes of crossing into Syria. There was always a steady stream of Iraqi traders moving back and forth with goods as well. It was not the sort of orderly procession of cars that you expect to see in the United States. It often took hours just to get the line going because of unruly crowds. We spent a lot of time breaking up fights between Iraqis. Many of the travelers who used the border crossing were driving vehicles packed with huge gasoline containers because there was money to be made in selling cheaper Syrian fuel at a good markup in Iraq.

The border checkpoint was a favorite target for the insurgency due to our presence and control of it. But we put out the word early on through local officials that if the insurgents made life too difficult for us at the checkpoint, we would shut it down entirely. That would have meant the end of commerce for most people in the city, and it probably would have slowed the influx of foreign fighters and helped the insurgency too. As it was, we were probably shut down almost 40 percent of the time because of direct attacks on the checkpoint.

JOURNAL ENTRY: NOVEMBER 10, 2003
First twenty-four hours at BCP [border checkpoint] so far very calm. Of course, that's if you call "calm" firing a tank round at someone firing an RPG, three mortar rounds landing short of our location, and coming under fire during mounted patrol. ODA [Operational Detachment Alpha, Special Forces] briefed us on local who acquired Russian sniper rifle with silencer, optics, and night capabilities.

I watched the tank in front of me move in and out of the streetlights and the darkness. Commanded by Lt. Sands, it was rolling along "Route Train" on the southern edge of town. I was riding in the gunner's hatch of the up-armored Humvee, and even with the winter season's cooler winds whipping around me, I was drenched in sweat. We had just taken a combat engineer team, known as "Sappers," to assess what would be required to destroy the old Baath Party headquarters on Market Street. It had been used earlier as a staging point for attacks on U.S. forces, so we had decided to aerate it. As we were returning from our inspection, a rocket-propelled grenade flew across the front slope of Lt. Sands's tank. His gunner, Sgt. Johnson, identified the attacker's position and immediately opened up with his coaxial mounted machine gun. The rest of us joined him in pouring fire at the same location. Red tracers zeroed in on the target.

"Dragon Seven, this is Dragon Five. My fire wounded him, and he has fallen back within the protection of the side alleys."

Since I was in the Humvee and had the only real dismount foot patrol force, I offered to investigate and pursue the wounded insurgent. I did not want to let him get away. Sergeant Bandel,

SFC Ross, and Sgt. Graham joined me in forming two-man teams. We quickly crossed the street and found the insurgent's ambush position behind a large pile of rocks. A large pool of blood gave it away, and a blood trail indicated he had moved off toward the city's labyrinthine maze of alleys.

It was hostile territory, so we didn't dare use flashlights for fear of attracting sniper fire. Even with night-vision goggles, it was difficult and dangerous work, and it was unwise to move out of the protective range of our tanks. With knots in our bellies, we searched the surrounding homes and alleys with no success. It was harrowing work to search for the enemy, stay alert, and track the movements of our own men. We circled back to the vehicles and reported that the amount of blood we'd seen indicated that our attacker was probably not much of a threat. Still, his quick disappearance made it likely that he was dragged off by other insurgents. We returned to our vehicles and reversed direction just in case more insurgents were lying in wait along that route.

I didn't allow myself the luxury of relaxing as I followed Lt. Sands and his tank crew; my Humvee driver turned onto Market Street and approached the bridge that spanned "Ambush Wadi."

★

His father's plan was to attack first from the cover of the wadi reeds. The police station was just two hundred yards to the west of the bridge. Members of the cell were to hide themselves in and around the dilapidated one-story buildings along the edge of the wadi. There was a shuttered school, an auto repair shop, and an abandoned garage surrounded by heaps of garbage and rusting machinery. A small cemetery also overlooked the marsh.

They hoped to surprise the American convoy, trap the soldiers and their vehicles on the bridge, and pick them off with machine-gun fire, rockets, and rocket-propelled grenades. Those who tried to flee through town would be hit with machine-gun fire from a second ambush along the road. The most experienced fighters had responsibility for the most powerful and sophisticated weapons. Jamil was given an AK-47 and told to rain rifle fire upon the convoy and any who broke from it.

After sunset, they ran through the neighborhood and through the cemetery to the wadi. Jamil at first hid himself behind an old barrel inside a shack at the edge of the wadi. But as he heard the roar of the approaching American convoy, he panicked. He heard the distinctive sound of tank tracks on the highway. There would be no hiding from their firepower. He feared that the shack was too tempting a target. He had to get to a better hiding place.

★

The hair on the back of my neck rose as we approached the bridge. The earlier attack had put me on full alert. I wished to hell that I were in my tank instead of in the Humvee. I scanned the dense reeds of the marsh and the deep embankments that ran through it, putting my .50 caliber machine gun over the right side of the Humvee toward the wadi. Then I saw a familiar flash in the distance. I knew what it was, but there was no time to react before the wall of a building twenty feet behind us exploded and brought chunks of concrete raining down upon us.

A second flash quickly ignited in the wadi. This one had the telltale signs of a rocket-propelled grenade. It flew much slower, giving us a blessed split second to react. I pressed the butterfly trigger of my "Ma Deuce" machine gun, and the weapon's *whop, whop, whop* sent incendiary rounds and their tracers in the direction of our attackers.

I screamed into the radio hand mike to alert the others in the convoy ahead of me. They'd already crossed the bridge, and they weren't aware I was taking fire. "Contact RPGs to the north, OUT!"

★

Before Jamil could move to a better hiding place, the other insurgents opened fire on the American vehicle on the bridge. They fired rocket-propelled grenades and followed with a barrage of machine-gun fire. Blinding flashes lit up the marshlands as the Americans returned fire. The intensity of their response terrified the boy. His father had predicted the Americans would flee. Instead, they'd quickly regrouped, unleashing their own torrent of heavy fire.

There was a brief lull in which Jamil heard his father yell that one of their men was hit. The boy threw his rifle down and dived into the thick reeds of the marsh, following the muddy stream through the wadi to his favorite childhood hiding place under the bridge. The old bridge shook and vibrated from the weight of the vehicles as the firefight resumed and intensified above him. The tank that was leading the convoy had returned to assist the vehicle caught near the bridge.

★

I yelled down at my Humvee driver, ordering him to turn into the enemy fire to the north, to give the attackers a smaller target. I continued to fire the .50 caliber, and, thankfully, S.Sgt. Guetschow came roaring up and joined the counterattack with his own machine-gun fire. Lt. Sands's tank had also joined the fight.

Just as things were looking better for our side, my machine gun ran out of ammo. I yelled at my crew for another box. They couldn't react quickly enough. Enemy rounds sprayed all around me. I grabbed for the nearest weapon just as I spotted a group of our attackers inside a shack at the edge of the marsh. I yelled instructions into the radio: "They are behind the blue door! Fire a main gun into the blue door, the building next to the wadi!"

At this point, I wasn't picky about choosing a weapon. I unstrapped an AT-4 antitank weapon, which resembles a bazooka, from the top of the Humvee. Operating on instinct, I unhooked the safety, placed it on my shoulder, and aimed for the shack's blue door. Sergeant First Class Evans had identified the same target. Before we could fire, there were two more distinct flashes one hundred meters to the north, and they appeared to have a bead on my forehead. I let my legs go limp and dropped down inside the Humvee in time to hear the whoosh of the rocket-propelled grenades and their fiery smoke trails skimming just overhead. It felt close enough to crease my helmet, but the RPGs hit a wall behind us, sending off another shower of concrete.

Within seconds of the explosions, I was up and ready to fire. I'd spied the RPG triggerman, drew a bead on him, and pushed the fire button. My Humvee rocked from the blast. The AT-4's high-explosive antiarmor warhead travels at 250 feet a second, so I didn't have to wait long to see an explosion light up the alley and show the silhouettes of airborne insurgents go flying. Sparks, smoke, and debris filled the alley. What a lucky shot: a direct hit!

Sgt. Bandel tugged at my pant leg, trying to get through the ringing in my ears. "Top! Top! Are you okay? Were you hit?"

In my rage at our attackers, I'd neglected a bit of battlefield etiquette. I hadn't informed the other guys in the Humvee that I was about to fire the AT-4. When they heard it, they thought we'd been hit by a rocket-propelled grenade. I answered him by yelling, "I need more .50 caliber ammo." I then tossed the smoking AT-4 to the ground.

And then the world stopped and all the air was sucked from my lungs as a ferocious roar swept over us. Apparently, Lt. Sands had decided he'd had enough of this ambush too. He'd ordered both tanks to fire their main guns at the building with the blue door. Our vehicle was between the tanks, so we were sandwiched by the stereo blasts. It was like being hit with twin sledge-hammers. For thirty seconds, my brain rattled around so hard, I couldn't hear or feel anything. I did see the blue door come flying off its hinges and an entire section of the alley explode into dust.

The tide had definitely turned. Our attackers were on the run.

★

Jamil could not think clearly from the concussive explosions that shook the old bridge and the ground beneath it. He wrapped his arms around his knees and put his head down as the tanks, machine guns, and rifles roared above him. He briefly lost his hearing when one of the American tanks fired its main gun. Then came another deafening round, and another. It was unbearable. Round after round ripped through the reeds. He heard first one insurgent turn and flee, and then another limped, fell, and then crawled away. The only gunfire was coming from the American convoy now. No one returned fire from the wadi.

One of the American tanks let fire with another round. The heat and flash of the main gun seemed to explode inside Jamil's head. Dirt, rocks, and debris rained down on him. Whole sections of the reeds around him seemed to disintegrate. The Americans were shredding the marsh with bullets and explosives as if they wanted to destroy everything in it.

★

"Don't let them use the wadi to escape," I radioed.

We poured machine-gun fire into the marsh. Their rounds ripped through the reeds, turning them into green and brown confetti. In the middle of this mayhem, I looked to my right and saw Sgt. Bandel running out to recover the spent AT-4 tube I'd fired, with covering fire provided by Sgt. Graham. He was sprinting like a madman through a shower of bullets. They didn't realize I had used it. They thought it had just come dislodged from the Humvee. Luckily, Bandel was not killed or wounded. But for the rest of our tour, he did carry the nickname "Crazy Legs" for the mad-dash running style he displayed that night.

I ordered S.Sgt. Guetschow to unleash another main gun through the wadi. His tank was on the bridge when he fired. It shook violently as the round tore through the vegetation. I wanted anyone in that marsh dead before we sent a team in to search it. After that final round, there was no response from our attackers, but then, my ears were ringing so loudly, I wasn't the best judge. To make sure there were no more surprises in the swamp, I sent three from my crew to search the area around the bridge. It seemed highly unlikely that anyone had survived the massive amount of fire we'd poured into the marsh.

★

The barrage above him stopped, and after a brief silence, Jamil heard American soldiers shouting. Long beams of light came stabbing at him, draining the blood from his veins. He could hear soldiers moving toward the reeds, coming closer to him. He jumped up to run, but in the darkness and disorientation, he forgot where he was and cracked his head sharply on a steel support beam. He tasted blood, his legs buckled, and the world went black.

He awoke with the muddy stench of the riverbed in his nose and what felt like a band saw around his head. His hair was sticky with blood. His legs wobbled when he tried to stand. He fought off another blackout, splashing water from a dank puddle onto his face. The acrid, rotten-egg smell of the putrid water brought him back to consciousness, but he still could not move, which was a good thing. Bands of light still swept all around him. Just as he began to think capture was imminent, a commanding voice called out from atop the bridge. Suddenly, the flashlight beams halted and reversed direction; the soldiers were going back to their vehicles.

Jamil was terrified, but he felt he had to get out of there before they sprayed more bullets into the wadi. Covered in oozing muck and his own blood, he pulled himself out of the sucking mud and found a narrow animal trail through the tall reeds. He ran with a long shadow chasing him, away from the bridge and through a trail of thick weeds. He tripped and went sprawling, slapping his face in the mud, but when he looked up, he heard the engines of the American vehicles moving away toward the border crossing point on the west end of town.

★

Capt. Roehrman called off the dogs on the radio. I had to take a deep breath to calm myself and ease the adrenaline rush as he spoke. I agreed that we didn't have enough men to cover such a large area in the dense reeds north of the bridge. SFC Ross called his men back as they approached the wadi. It was too dangerous to go in there in the darkness and risk stepping on a mine or being shot by any insurgents still lying down in the weeds. We rounded everyone up and drove off, grateful that this one was over and that we'd stood and fought and lived through it.

★

Jamil waited until the American vehicles disappeared before getting up. He then ran home with his hand pressed to the bleeding wound that stretched from the back of his head to his forehead. His mother cried out when she saw the blood matted in his dark hair and streaming down his face and neck. His brothers and sisters came running, shrieking and crying at the sight of his wound.

"I'm not shot, I just hit my head!" he assured them.

His mother quickly examined the wound and sent his sister for towels and water. She cleaned it and stopped the bleeding by pressing a towel soaked in cold water against his skull. She then applied her favorite home remedy to speed healing in a wound and prevent infection, sprinkling table sugar and iodine into the gash before she bandaged it. She walked her oldest son to his bed, telling him to get to sleep before his father came home and started asking questions.

Nassir did not return until past dawn. Jamil heard him and Sayed discussing the night's ambush in the courtyard. "They must not have been American soldiers! The Americans do not fire their big tank guns in the city," his father said.

They talked about losing four men and noted that three others were left wounded at the hospital. They plotted to tell the surviving members of their own cell that they'd killed many of the enemy soldiers.

The next day, his father did not mention those killed to Jamil. He did yell at him for leaving his rifle in the wadi. Jamil fled the house before his father could hit him. He walked through the crowds at the market to the bridge where the ambush had taken place the night before. Nearby buildings bore scars from the attack. The tank's guns had blown the doors off of one structure. The reeds in the wadi were ripped and torn as if by some massive talons. American soldiers were everywhere, scouring the marsh. He saw one find a trail of blood and follow it through the reeds.

12

THE ARCHANGELS OF HUSAYBAH

JOURNAL ENTRY: NOVEMBER 13, 2003

I am sick of being the hunted. The best defense is an offense, and if you are not proactive in this country, danger seems to creep into your camp. We have briefed the mayor and police chief on Dragon's response strategy to being attacked. We will respond with weapon systems of equal or greater effect. If RPG firer hides behind a house or wall or uses it as a fortification, it will be destroyed. I will not stand by waiting to be shot, maimed, or killed. . . . Dragon will take the fight to the enemy.

The gloves were off. After the firefight on the Market Street bridge, we met every incoming mortar, rocket-propelled grenade, and bullet by unleashing counterstrikes that brought the full wrath of our arsenal down upon the enemy. The town took notice. It would have been hard not to, especially after the friendly neighborhood insurgency made the huge mistake of firing mortars into our camp from the old Baath Party headquarters in not-so-beautiful downtown Husaybah. In response, we took three tanks down there and fired five HEAT rounds into the building. It has a much better ventilation system now, but the see-through walls should greatly diminish its effectiveness as a staging point for attacks on us.

We were no longer concerned about upsetting the locals with exhibitions of our military might. Iraq is a country where people have been conditioned to respect strength, so we created combat patrols, in which we cruised through the streets in our tanks and armored vehicles to let the good Iraqis know that we were there to protect them and to remind the bad Iraqis that we were more than capable of crushing their guerrilla cells and grinding them to dust.

Within hours of our lively first combat patrol, we began to get positive feedback that continued over the next several days. Capt. Roehrman heard one particularly interesting report from a local Iraqi, who said that the insurgency leaders were telling their people that the new aggressive responses to their attacks must be coming from Polish coalition troops because American soldiers have never been so forceful. We got a lot of laughs out of being mistaken for the Polish army. But it clearly drove home a point; playing nice had not made much of an impression here. This is a nation that has been ruled by brutality for decades. The innocent civilians are still controlled by those who terrorize them daily. If the Iraqi people don't feel that they will be aggressively protected by the full military power of the American-led coalition and the new Iraqi government, they will never support it.

One local told us that our fight in the marsh had left his nearby home riddled with small-arms fire. Part of it had been destroyed. Capt. Roehrman apologized but told him that someone had been shooting at us from his neighborhood and we couldn't let that happen anymore. His response was surprising. "I'm glad you shot back. There are too many insurgents there," he told the interpreter.

TURNING THE TIDE

Our new tactics reaped other unexpected rewards. Informants came knocking with some very good information. It was as if people had been waiting to see if we were strong enough to protect them from the insurgents who had been threatening them and making their lives miserable. We'd had locals approach us in the past with information. Most demanded bundles of American dollars up front, and they didn't want to get personally involved.

But things began to change rapidly in that regard, too. Suddenly, we had a string of informants who offered to take us to weapons caches and insurgent hiding places. That shift in the local attitude resulted in a new type of activity for those of us on the Pentagon's all-expenses-paid vacation in Husaybah. Our tank company began a series of raids, most of them in the wee hours of the morning, hitting the insurgents where they lived. The raids quickly earned Dragon Company the nickname "Archangels of Husaybah"—for bringing our wrath down upon the insurgency. The citizens of Husaybah responded in ways we could not have imagined.

On November 15, 2003, our tank was positioned on high ground overlooking the "440 block" on the southwest corner of Husaybah from an observation point known as "Papa-29" that offered views of the Syrian border. This report came over the radio:

"Dragon X-ray, this is White Four Golf. You are not going to believe this, but I have two Iraqi males, approximately twenty-five years old, who walked up to my position with their hands raised above their heads and just sat down in front of the tank."

"White Four Golf, what do they want?"

"Their English is nonexistent, and my Arabic is worse. I have no idea!"

"White Four Golf, we will send a Humvee with an interpreter to your location."

We transported the walk-in Iraqis to the checkpoint and questioned them through an interpreter. They claimed to be mujahideen who were tired of fighting. They were turning themselves in. As we talked about what to do with them, one of them offered a tip to the interpreter.

"I have seen an American weapon, and I know where it is buried," he said.

The surrendering insurgent described the weapon, and it was one for which we'd been searching. Another unit had lost it in the southeast sector of Husaybah a month before. We tested our informant by asking if he would take us to it. To our surprise, he said yes. With the growing dangers, our policy was that if an informant was not willing to accompany us when we acted on his information, then we didn't believe him. It wasn't worth the risk. We weren't about to be sent into an ambush.

The missing weapon was one of our M249s, an automatic light machine gun capable of firing one thousand rounds per minute. It wasn't the sort of thing you wanted your enemy to have. Our informant volunteered that the machine gun was being kept at the home of an insurgent cell leader by the name of Qadir Mohammed Auad.

We could not pass up the opportunity to retrieve the M249 and possibly nab an insurgent leader too. Our informant noted that the insurgents were very nervous about having our machine gun, so they moved it regularly. Normally, we would have done some reconnaissance and planned the raid, but we decided to act immediately. We hit Qadir's house but found only one female and three children inside. It was considered bad etiquette for other men to enter an Iraqi home when the man of the house wasn't present, but we'd lost our good manners after the first couple of rocket-propelled grenades had flown over our heads.

Our search of the house turned up a Russian sniper rifle with night optics, armor-piercing rounds, and two grenades. It was a good find, but it wasn't our missing machine gun. We did find something else of interest in one of the woman's purses: a photograph of some known insurgents. It seemed that we were on the right track and that our informant was credible.

While the house was being searched, one of our observant "Sappers," Specialist Williams, a combat engineer, noticed a disturbed patch of ground, about eight by ten feet, in the courtyard of the home. It looked like something might be buried there. Thinking it might be the missing American machine gun, he scraped some of the dirt away, hit something, and then stood up in shock.

"What the hell? There's a torpedo buried here!" he said.

It was a bangalore torpedo, a thirteen-foot plastic tube packed with nine pounds of explosive that has been used to clear antipersonnel mines from battlefields dating back to World War II. As it was being dug out of the ground and examined, the informant came up with another possible location for the missing U.S. weapon just around the corner. The engineers were still digging around the torpedo under guard of the tanks cordoned around us. Lt. Sands and I decided to take our crews in two Humvees to the next house to continue the search. It was only a few hundred meters away.

As soon as we came through the door, we came upon an Iraqi who was behaving strangely even for a guy whose home was being raided by a group of heavily armed foreign soldiers. He was chewing white sticks that we'd learned contained drugs or stimulants. He also had an open bottle of booze when we found him. He tried to stand up and run as we entered, but he fell flat on his face.

We called over Mohammed, our most hard-nosed interpreter, who got in this character's face like a drill sergeant. It was something to behold. Mohammed's Arabic tirade was nonstop. He grabbed the bottle of booze and shoved it in the guy's face as if scolding him for being a drunk. The Iraqi wouldn't look him in the eyes, he was so ashamed. I have no idea what Mohammed said to him, but it worked. The Iraqi claimed he knew where we could find "everybody" involved in the local insurgency. Within three minutes, Mohammed had extracted from him the locations of his local cell leaders. The guy had also agreed to take us there.

The names he gave Mohammed matched up to those provided by our original informant. There in the Iraqi's sparse living room, Lt. Sands and I discussed our strategy. It was tempting to put together another raid right then and there and go after the cell leaders, but it would be risky without tank support. We couldn't pull the tanks off the house with the bangalore, especially since the more the Sappers dug, the more torpedoes they turned up. Still, this was a great opportunity. If we acted quickly, we might catch these insurgent leaders; but if we waited, they'd likely be tipped off that we were hunting for them. There were eyes watching from every window.

We radioed Capt. Roehrman and got the green light. We packed up both our original and our new informant, who seemed to be sobering up rapidly, and put them in the back of a Humvee, where they could see without being seen. As soon as we hit the first alley, the second informant pointed to an unsuspecting Iraqi on a bicycle. Mohammed the interpreter ordered the guy to halt and demanded his name.

We had our first match!

As we moved onto Market Street in clear view of the arches, a very gruff-looking man sat on the corner. Our informant let out a squawk. The guy on the street corner had been staring at us with contempt, a look that changed to one of great surprise when we popped out and cuffed him. He didn't have a clue that he'd been fingered as a fighter who had attacked U.S. soldiers at the Baath Party headquarters and at the police station in Husaybah.

It was good to have the element of surprise on our side for a change. We moved on, picking up a third insurgent, whom our informants identified as the son of an IED maker and weapons merchant who had connections with cell members in Ramadi. Our two Humvees couldn't hold any more captives by the time we headed back to what had become known as the "Torpedo House." By this time, the Sappers had uncovered more than 250 of the lethal torpedoes from the hiding place, and they were sure that they'd hit only the first couple layers. That hole turned out to be twelve feet deep and had more than 800 torpedoes stacked in it!

News of that discovery reached the highest levels of our chain of command. That amazing find, coupled with our quick action on the informants' information, which led to the immediate breakup of an entire insurgent cell, earned Dragon Company a fast reputation as a flexible, aggressive force. It really boosted our confidence too. Lt. Sands picked up the nickname "Outlaw 5," and I was dubbed "Vigilante 7." Our commanding officer also heard that back at regiment headquarters, we were being called the "Shepherds of Husaybah" for the fire-and-brimstone force that Dragon had displayed.

Now that we had a reputation, we had to live up to it. And we did. The days and nights became a blur. We ran the border checkpoint during the day and defended it by night. But we also screened the border area and put together special combat patrols and raids. It took a lot of juggling of personnel and some strong leadership within the ranks. And it wasn't all fun and games. We were constantly under fire. It was hard and exhaustive work, but it was paying off. After eight months in Iraq, we were finally taking the fight to the enemy day in and day out. There would be no rest for the weary.

13

ESCAPE PLANS

In the days and weeks after the ambush at the bridge, the American soldiers and their tanks crawled all over the town, searching for insurgents and weapons by going door to door in the neighborhoods of Husaybah. The U.S. soldiers had become much more aggressive. Someone was giving them the names of insurgents and directing them to weapons caches. They'd begun a series of raids, going through hundreds of homes, interrogating and arresting anyone suspected of aiding the insurgency.

Nassir and Sayed were more determined than ever to drive them out or die trying. Jamil decided that his only choice was to get out of Husaybah. He knew that his father would continue to make him take part in attacks on the American troops. In Nassir's view, there was nothing to live for except the glory of killing Americans. Jamil saw only certain death in that view. He'd been incredibly lucky to escape being killed or captured during the attack at the bridge. It struck Jamil that his father would not have minded sacrificing his son for the cause, as it would have brought him glory.

The boy knew that sooner or later, his father would put him in a position that would not allow him to fake his participation. He had to get out of Nassir's reach. Hundreds of Husaybah's Iraqi families, including some relatives on his mother's side, had already fled into Syria to escape the growing violence between the Americans and the insurgents. Jamil devised a plan to join them across the border, get a job working in a restaurant or washing cars, and then, when he'd made enough money, he would try to help his mother and siblings. He knew his mother would not leave his father, but he would try to get her to safety.

Nassir had spies watching the border checkpoint, but Jamil had an answer for that. He'd grown up fishing and swimming in the Euphrates. He was a strong swimmer. The river was low and the current weak. He would swim across at night, avoid the Syrian border guards, and join relatives who had already fled. The boy did not share his plan with anyone because he did not want his father to find out and stop him. He planned to send word to his mother through family members once he was safely across the border. He waited for a night with a full moon and then put his plan into action.

It was after midnight when he slipped out of the house with a few possessions in a plastic bag. The route to the river was familiar even in darkness, but fear of being caught and questioned had Jamil on edge. Every dog bark, passing vehicle, and scraping branch spooked him. Finally, he reached the river's edge. He took off his clothes, put them in the plastic bag, and tied it around his waist. Then he entered the water, walking on the bottom until he felt its coolness climb to his neck. The water's familiar odor engulfed and comforted him.

As he swam, he thought of the time that he'd escaped three bullies who'd threatened him. He knew he could not outrun the bigger boys for long, so he'd dived into the river, where their bulkier bodies were at a disadvantage. The bigger boys followed him, but they swam only a few strokes before giving up. Jamil's memories of that escape pumped more adrenaline into his blood, and it felt like he was flying through the water, the one place where he felt secure and in control. He reached the Syrian side with ease, climbed ashore, and after lying down to dry on the still-warm sands, he quickly fell asleep.

A sharp back pain awakened him abruptly. Two Syrian border guards were taking turns kicking him. They'd found him shortly after sunrise. Without a word, they yanked the boy to his feet, dragged him to their truck, and threw him in the back. Jamil was still too groggy to protest as they drove him to the border crossing. The guards did not appear to be in the mood to negotiate. They pulled him out of the vehicle and prodded him with the ends of their rifles until he crossed back into Iraq with American soldiers and Iraqi police watching him suspiciously. Exhausted and dejected, he walked home. His family was still sleeping, so he came in through the back door and collapsed in his bed.

Hours later, he woke up sore and stiff but even more resolved to get away from his father and the insurgency. As he mulled over his options, he saw the coins his father had given him for taking part in the ambushes on his nightstand.

There is enough for a one-way train ticket to Fallujah, where my uncles live, he thought.

Jamil had traveled with his mother to visit her family in Fallujah many times before the American invasion. He'd loved working in his uncle's restaurant. He could go there, apprentice himself as a cook, and save enough to help support his mother and siblings. This plan was even better than the other, he realized.

He knew the train schedule for Fallujah, so he spent the day planning and secretly packing once again. It had saddened him to leave without saying good-bye to his brothers and sisters on his previous escape attempt. So this time, he gathered them together in his bedroom that night. He told them that he was going to take the train the next morning to their grandparents in Fallujah, where he would find a job. He told them not to tell their parents of his secret plan, and he assured them that they would all be together again soon. The youngest grew teary-eyed, and his brothers wanted to come with him. He told them they needed to protect their sisters and their mother. They all agreed to keep his secret, but they were young and afraid of their father's wrath.

The next morning, Jamil felt the pressure around his neck before he saw his father's men standing behind his bench at the train station. Two huge hands encircled his neck, cutting off his air. They ordered him to keep his eyes down and to not look at them.

"Where do you think you are going, little coward?"

He had prepared a story, but they were not buying it. His father had sent them.

They'll kill me, and my body will never be found, the boy thought as they walked him out of the train station. The train to Fallujah was just pulling into the station as they walked out and crossed the street into an alley. There, behind a small green kiosk, the boy found himself surrounded by two men wearing red scarves around their faces to hide their features.

"If you try to run again from your father, we will kill you," one of them said, pressing a pistol to his temple.

After the first blow to the head, Jamil felt nothing else.

If the Americans didn't kill him, his father would. The coalition troops were no longer returning fire and moving out of range. They were counterattacking and pursuing those who fired at them. Their show of strength was having an impact. His father and Sayed boasted of what they would do to the Americans, but they ran just like the others when the wadi had been blown apart. They had sent Jamil in against this powerful enemy, and then they had run, leaving him behind to die in a fight he'd wanted no part of. They'd threatened to kill him if he didn't fight their enemy. He was dead either way—at the hands of his father or by American bullets.

He had to find a way out.

14

BORDER CATCH

Our Humvee stopped in front of a razor-sharp tangle of concertina wire blocking the road that led north to the Euphrates. My driver, Sgt. Johnson, otherwise known as "J," turned on the headlights to get a better view. Then he stepped from the vehicle to pull the razor wire back to allow us to pass through.

I spoke into the hand microphone as I watched "J" wrestling with the wire, trying to find an opening in it: "Dragon X-ray, this is Dragon Seven. I am on my way to deliver Class I to White."

"Class I" was dinner chow. This was one of those glamorous missions you don't see in the recruiting films. I was taking dinner to the tank crews screening the Syrian border on the one-mile stretch of road between the river and the border checkpoint. At least, that was the plan, but Sgt. Johnson, a brawny ex-marine and combat veteran, was getting his ass kicked by that concertina wire. He couldn't find the start or end point to unravel it from the gate.

I offered the sort of encouragement that soldiers expect from their caring first sergeants: "Hey, J, can you get the fucking wire out of the way before White Platoon dies of starvation?"

"J" knew I trusted him with my life, but he glared at me as if weighing darker options. He extended an invitation to assist him, and so we were both slicing and dicing our hands on the damn wire when more important matters intervened.

"Dragon X-ray, GSR [ground surveillance radar] has identified five males running from the 440 block to the Syrian border" came the call on our radio. *"We are moving to interdict but will need more support to cordon off the area."*

They were a kilometer south of the border checkpoint, which meant we didn't have to go through the wire to assist them. On our way to meet them, we slowed down long enough to pick up Sgt. Graham, "Crazy Legs" Bandel, and Spec. Rayo from the tactical operations center. First Lt. Sands, the executive officer, was coming in another Humvee with a crew. We were on-site in less than five minutes, with the second group right behind us.

The surveillance team had moved the tank toward the suspects in blackout drive—no lights. As soon as they were in position, Lieutenant Harms turned on the headlights and fired a long machine-gun burst to stop the men from fleeing across the border. But they didn't cooperate. Instead, they disappeared in the darkness and the particularly rugged terrain marked by deep man-made trenches and huge piles of rock and dirt. Of all the godforsaken barren places in the desert, they'd picked the one location that was perfect for high-stakes hide-and-seek. There were more than a hundred dirt and rock piles scattered around the area for a construction project south of the border checkpoint.

I ordered "J" to position his vehicle so that the fugitives couldn't flee back into Husaybah's 440 block, a favorite insurgent nest. Then we tried to pick them out by shining our tank and Humvee lights on them. No luck. Our quarry had melted into the landscape. This was not going down the way these things typically played out. Most insurgents and foreign fighters simply put down their weapons and cooperated when faced with capture. This bunch seemed determined to escape, which meant they had more to lose than most.

Our night-vision goggles weren't much help. There was just enough illumination from the lights of the city to wash out the field of view in the goggles, which were most effective in total darkness. The tank thermal sights weren't picking up any body heat signatures, which was a little creepy. Where had they gone?

We felt like blind men walking through a shooting gallery, waiting for the guns to start blazing. Luckily, Capt. Roehrman had dispatched a pair of regimental scout helicopters to give us some eyes in the air. The chopper pilots quickly located our runners, who'd dug into the dirt piles to hide themselves. The pilots guided us to their hiding places with infrared beams visible only to those of us wearing the night goggles. Even then, we walked almost on top of the fugitives before we saw them. They'd done a great job of making like moles.

This was a very disciplined and well-trained group. But the five of them offered only token resistance once their eyeballs were lined up with our rifle barrels. As we handcuffed and checked them out, our suspicions were confirmed that these were not run-of-the-mill sheepherders, or even insurgents. They were dressed in expensive tracksuits and running shoes. They had a variety pack of passports from Saudi Arabia, Yemen, Jordan, and Syria. We found plane ticket receipts that indicated they'd been traveling throughout the Middle East before coming to Syria. And they carried envelopes packed with different currencies, including some we didn't recognize.

The intelligence guys were going to piss all over themselves when we brought in this prime bunch. These were some serious players. I was feeling pretty damn good about the night's work when Lt. Harms radioed from his observation post and busted my bubble. He said Sgt. Moon was adamant that he had seen a sixth guy run off from the others in the darkness. Some doubts were expressed, but I remembered what Sgt. Moon had told me when we first met. He'd described himself as a "special para-rescue recon ranger sniper delta

SEAL." He could be a joker, but he did have good instincts in these situations. So, we began searching for his missing "muj."

We radioed the helicopter crews, and they went back to work. Sure enough, within just a couple of minutes, they beamed in on Moon's man, who was buried in a good forty yards from where the others had been hiding. "J" and Lt. Sands followed the infrared light beams through the dusty maze of dirt piles to his location. Crazy Legs, Graham, and I continued our search of the other suspects, who were sprawled on the ground in front of the Humvee lights. The more we searched them and their belongings, the more goodies we found: cell phones, more envelopes, phone lists, travel bags, knives, and even a mujahideen storybook.

As we searched this trove, three shots rang out. For a split second, everyone froze. I ran toward the gunfire, which had come from the area where they'd been searching for the sixth fugitive. When I got there, I saw a very large Middle Eastern male lying on his back in the dust. He was not moving, nor was he breathing.

"J" stood over him, looking stunned, with his rifle in his hands.

Lt. Sands called for the medics to check the Iraqi on the ground. Then "J" told me what had happened. He and Lt. Sands had moved within ten feet of the suspect's hiding place when the man had jumped up, screaming in Arabic and swinging his arms at them.

As big as "J" is, this guy was taller and bulkier. When J moved in to cuff the guy, he spotted something in the fugitive's hand. That's when the guy had started screaming "American monkey!" and swinging at him. He then spit and charged "J" while thrusting the object in his hand at him. He got close before Lt. Sands yelled, *"Fire!"*

"J" got off a three-round burst and dropped his attacker.

As I talked with "J," a medic walked up: "Hey, Top, he's dead. But good thing, because I found this clenched in his hand."

I shone my flashlight on a large brass-knuckles knife he'd taken from the hand of the dead guy.

"J" was shaken by the experience, remorseful about having to kill the guy, but glad that he had not been killed himself.

Our night's catch turned out to be a very significant one, as it attracted the immediate attention of the area's Special Forces group, ODA (Operational Detachment Alpha), and agents from the OGA (Other Governmental Agency), a common euphemism for the CIA. We never saw our captives after that night, but we heard that they were highly trained, well-funded Al Qaeda foreign fighters who were on a recruiting trip. They were to each lead their own cells of approximately thirty to forty men. The cell phones we found with them yielded some very interesting phone numbers in New York, Amsterdam, and Ramadi. We were told that several other terrorists were arrested due to the information we gathered that night in the desert. Because the men we captured were leaders and recruiters, catching them was like taking a 180-man insurgency unit out of commission.

It had been a very good week. The capture of those foreign fighters brought Dragon Company even greater recognition. News of the capture made CNN. More importantly, it gave us the sense that we were finally taking control of the situation and making a difference instead of just holding down a fort under attack. We had the sense that there'd been a shift in the momentum. Our hope was that once the Iraqi people saw that we were willing to pursue the insurgents, they would put more trust in us and in our mission.

Over the next four nights, we had our longest stretch without taking any mortar fire. No one knew if it was just the calm before the storm or the eye of the hurricane passing over. It provided us a few rare moments of contemplation. I was feeling very fortunate that we'd survived our first months in one of the most dangerous places I'd ever been.

I'm not an overtly religious guy, but I found myself repeatedly reading something that soothed me a great deal. It was a copy of Psalm 91, the "Soldier's Psalm," which has been carried into battles around the world for generations. I'd seen and read it before, but here, it had a particular resonance. Death and danger seemed to wait around every corner. We'd had only one soldier wounded in action so far, and I felt we were either extremely lucky or blessed. So I wasn't going to take any chances. I found myself reciting the psalm prior to every mission. The passage that impacted me the most went like this:

I shall not be afraid of the terror by night, nor of the arrow that flies by day,
Nor of the pestilence that walks in darkness, nor of the destruction that lays waste at noonday.
A thousand may fall at my side, and ten thousand by my right hand;
But it shall not come near me.
Only with my eyes shall I look and see the reward of the wicked.

It gave me some peace to hold that little yellow card in my hands and read those words at the end of each day in this increasingly violent place. In the face of the attacks, our willingness to respond aggressively and with all of the firepower at our disposal had led to a period of relative peacefulness. I didn't know how long it would last. Fear rode with us every minute of every day. To my chagrin, I let my own fears be known on network television.

A few days after our big catch near the border, an ABC News crew came through. They'd heard about the increasing number of foreign fighters coming across the border, and they wanted to do a tour of Husaybah. We were assigned to provide security on their visit. I didn't realize the crew was videotaping inside the Humvee as we made our way back to Market Street, following the exact route of our first ambush. As we moved toward the bridge over the wadi with the ABC crew, I turned and said, "You'd better be prepared, because something might happen here. That is known as 'Ambush Wadi,' and this is a very dangerous corner." The memories of our firefight were still very vivid.

Two days later, I called my wife, Christina, and one of the first things she said was, "You haven't been telling me the entire story about how safe it is over there, have you?"

Apparently, her parents had been sitting in their home in Florida watching television, and lo and behold, there I was with the ABC crew, riding through Husaybah and describing it as the most dangerous place I'd ever been! I hadn't exactly been lying to my wife—just telling her the PG-13 version of my stories from Iraq. I would tell her stories of funny times and interesting missions, but I'd learned through my many deployments that it didn't help your family members to tell them of the dangers and close calls while you were still far away from them and facing many more months of deployment. Describing Husaybah as the most dangerous place I'd ever been didn't mean all that much to the ABC crew. But it meant everything to the person who knew me best.

THE HUNT IS ON

Our endurance was tested in our first weeks in Husaybah, and the increased activity in the area drew the attention of our regimental commander, Lieutenant Colonel Teeples. This little border town had clearly become a major staging point for foreign fighters joining the insurgency, which was growing stronger and bolder in other regions of the country as well. In response, he decided to notch up the firepower of the Third Armored Cavalry in border regions with Syria, Jordan, and Saudi Arabia. And so on November 20, 2003, and for the ten days that followed, major American forces joined us in Operation Rifles Blitz. We swarmed the area with a massive display of military might designed to intimidate our guerrilla foes.

Every branch of the U.S. Army and a huge force of special operations commandos came pouring into Husaybah and the surrounding region. We joked that the Pentagon's parking lot must have been empty. Every conceivable weapons system was brought to bear—more tanks, Bradley vehicles, Apache helicopters, Specter gunships, Black Hawks, Kiowa recon helicopters, close air support, and Paladins. We were joined by elements of the 82nd Infantry, a battalion of the 101st Airborne, and the 2–5 Field Artillery. Some said it was like killing a fly with a sledgehammer, but it sure felt good to have all that backup.

In those ten days, our forces searched 7,000 homes and took in 348 captives. We uncovered many caches of mortars, mines, and other explosives. The insurgency pulled in and maintained a very low profile with all of the military heat in town. The U.S. military's muscle flexing gave many more Iraqis the confidence to assist us against the insurgents. Suddenly, we had a lot of willing informants showing up at our gates.

The informant who had led us to the eight hundred bangalore torpedoes was among the first to reappear. He offered to show us the location of another cache of mortar rounds and the home of a weapons merchant who specialized in making deadly remote-controlled improvised explosive devices. And then came "Barney Fife," the nickname given to an informant who worked as a doorman at the Husaybah police station. He walked up to the gate of the border checkpoint, stated his name and position, and offered the less-than-shocking news that the local police were corrupt. But he also said he would tell us who the bad cops were and where they lived—for a price. He offered up information on a group of mujahideen fighters, IED makers, and weapons dealers operating in northeast Husaybah. Barney said they were involved in planning and conducting attacks on coalition forces with RPGs and mortars. Barney also said these guys could lead us to other foreign fighters, their weapons, and financiers.

After the interpreter collected all the information, we checked the names against our "black list" and the records of our counterparts in intelligence operations. The Special Forces guys always had great intelligence. Of the eleven names that Barney had given up, we had several hits. He had also drawn a very descriptive map. He agreed to accompany us on the raids—again, for a fee.

We planned to hit six target homes at once, searching for eleven suspects all within a 500-meter span in the neighborhood behind the police station and near Ambush Wadi. We wouldn't have been able to conduct a raid of this scope normally because we were stretched so thin with all of our responsibilities along the border. But Lieutenant Colonel Reilly, the squadron commander, chipped in with a Sapper platoon and a few more tanks from another squadron for extra support. Capt. Roehrman laid out the foundation of the plan, and over several hours, we refined it until we felt comfortable with its simplicity and the likelihood for success.

It was important to be able to hit all the targets at once because we'd learned that as soon as our forces moved into an area or neighborhood, the insurgents spread the alarm via phones and cell phones that served as their early-warning system. We'd learned this early on after staging raids on homes that had obviously just been vacated.

Just as we were making final preparations for this major raid, Capt. Roehrman contracted a severe intestinal virus that made him so violently ill, he couldn't stand up. He was hospitalized and put on an IV to keep his fluid levels up. We couldn't wait for our leader to recuperate, so 1st Lt. Sands and I briefed Lt. Col. Reilly on the plan. He agreed to let Dragon Company retain operational control. Another commander was brought in for the operation, but since he wasn't all that familiar with the area or with our plan, it was our show to conduct.

Lt. Sands coordinated the operation from Dragon X-ray at

the border checkpoint, and I led the raids on the ground. My role was simple. I had our informant, Barney Fife, in my Humvee so that I could relay, through the interpreter, the exact location of the homes. I was also the designated pointer for this operation. From the gunner's hatch of the Humvee, I stood and directed a red dot laser at the doors of each targeted house. That way, our raiders were sure that they were banging on the right doors. The Iraqis' homes were built on top of one another along tight alleys. It would have been easy to hit the wrong house otherwise. SFC Evans and S.Sgt. Guetschow led the raid teams on the first three houses. SFC Evans was a gruff Mississippian who had just come off a stint as a recruiter, so I was nervous about his combat readiness. He quickly dispelled my concerns and proved his leadership. Dragon Company really gelled as a combat unit when he teamed with the freakishly strong S.Sgt. Guetschow.

The combat engineer team, the Sappers, took the second grouping of three homes. We had three tanks positioned on the outer cordon for security. With lights off and our night-vision gear to guide us in the dark, my Humvee flew through the alleyways undetected. SFC Evans was close behind in his vehicle. The raids went more quickly and smoothly than expected. Our informant-for-hire, Barney Fife, gave directions through the interpreter and helped me identify each house. Then the raiders went into action. It was a pleasure to behold the courage and skill of our soldiers. After all, these were tankers and engineers, not special operations troops. Barney Fife may have been our ace in the hole for this raid, but three of our own men helped stack the deck against the targets of the operation.

Outside each house, the raiders would extinguish any outside lighting to darken the area. But there remained the challenge posed by the exterior walls that guarded the yards of most homes. If the raiders had to crash through the front gates of those walls, they would alert the occupants of the home before they'd gotten through the front door inside the courtyard. To overcome this problem, two of our largest noncommissioned officers, S.Sgt. Guetschow, six foot three, and Sergeant Betances, six foot two, improvised a modern-day catapult system. Their designated "catapultee" was "Baby Huey," also known as Sergeant Huegerich, a five foot six, 125-pound former standout wrestler out of Cherokee, Iowa, whose athleticism enabled him to always get perfect scores on the army physical fitness test.

The fearless Sgt. Huegerich would get a running start, jump onto the joined hands of the two other soldiers, and then get launched up and over the wall. He would land inside the courtyard, roll to his feet, unlock the gate on the outside wall, and within thirty seconds, our raiders would be securing the house from the inside. Due to the stealth and inventive technique of these guys, the occupants were usually still fast asleep until they awakened to rifles and flashlights in their faces.

Once the house was secure, we'd get photographs of the occupants on our digital cameras and then show them to Barney Fife inside the Humvee, where no one could see him. That night, we nabbed five primary targets and six alternates. The key catch was an imam, or Muslim priest, who had been responsible for distributing money from Syria to the local insurgency and its foreign fighters. Several fighters, mortarmen, and rocket-propelled grenade firers were caught. A second improvised explosive device maker was identified in our catch, and we also took in several weapons caches and a journal that had details of planned actions against our forces.

All in all, it was a very good night that led to many other similar raids. Nobody had been injured or killed. It felt as if Dragon Company had accomplished more in the past twenty days than in my previous seven months in Iraq. We found that each successful raid led to more information and brought more informants out of the woodwork. Some were motivated only by the money we were paying for good information, but there were those who simply were tired of being terrorized from within. They were showing up at the front gates in surprising numbers. Some were no help at all. Some were not to be trusted. One, in particular, would prove to be of great value.

15

CROSSING THE LINE

Jamil showed his friends Salah and Reza a military knife that he'd found and then asked them to walk to the border crossing with him because he wanted to kill an American soldier. The boys knew their friend well. They were certain he was playing one of his jokes on them—either that, or his father had finally beaten him senseless.

"Idiot, the soldiers will shoot you and kill you," said Salah.

"Allah will take care of me!" Jamil replied.

Salah and Reza exchanged looks of concern, still not believing that a boy who cried at the loss of one of his homing pigeons was capable of stabbing someone in the street. They'd expected Jamil to offer a smile or a joke to assure them that he was just teasing. Instead, he grew silent as they walked with him through the market toward the checkpoint where American soldiers worked alongside Iraqi police. The boys were not supposed to go near the border checkpoint. Their parents told them to stay away for fear of bombings, mortar attacks, or other violence there. Yet it was just the sort of chaotic place to which teenage boys were drawn. Jamil grew more animated as the three boys approached the checkpoint, as if energized by the horns honking, drivers chattering and shouting, and soldiers and police barking orders.

He described his plan to Salah and Reza as they walked, saying he planned to ask an American soldier for candy and then stab him and run into the wadi, where he would hide until darkness. As he spun his story for his friends, Jamil scanned the streets for members of the insurgency. They would kill him if they caught him this time. The men in the red scarves had made that clear at the train station. He also worried that Salah and Reza were right. He might be shot for even approaching soldiers at the border crossing. There was also the danger that his father's spies might grab him. Everyone knew that there were spies stationed around and even inside the American compound. He would have to talk quickly to convince the American soldiers that he had something of value to them.

He'd been up most of the night putting together his plan, and before he'd left that morning, he'd told his mother another story concocted in his bed. Tahira had always tried to love him enough for two parents because his father showed so little care for him. Jamil told her that he had decided to go to Syria, where he would find work and make money. Tahira agreed that Jamil had to get out of Husaybah, and she was glad that he intended to go to Syria, where he might escape the growing violence of his own country. She had hopes that she and the other children might join him one day. Their volatile homeland was no place for children. Tahira told herself that over and over, and it helped her hold back the tears until Jamil walked out that morning.

As he and his friends neared the border crossing, he had difficulty maintaining his brash pose. His trembling legs made it difficult to walk. His mouth was dry. The dust kicked up by passing vehicles stung his eyes and made him choke. More than one hundred cars were lined up. Fierce-looking soldiers stood watch with their rifles and machine guns at the ready in the three towers and along the fence line. Americans and Iraqis stood sentry on the Husaybah side.

Syrian military personnel manned the other. Helicopters swarmed overhead. Tanks and trucks roared in and out.

The boy nearly started to turn back. Images of his brothers and sisters and mother flashed through his mind, and he worried that he might never see them again. But how could he help them if he was blown to pieces in the next ambush, or the one after that? He'd nearly died in the ambush at the bridge. If the soldiers with the flashlights hadn't stopped coming, they'd have found him. It was amazing that he was not killed by the bullets they'd sprayed into the wadi. And now the Americans had become far more aggressive, and there seemed to be more of them and more of their tanks and trucks pouring through the city gates every day. They had so many powerful weapons. The heat didn't bother them. They could see at night. When they were attacked, they responded with such force that it shook the entire town. They'd done what no one had ever dreamed possible in bringing down the government of Saddam Hussein. And they'd done it so easily. They were not going to be beaten or chased from Iraq by scattered bands of men lobbing grenades and mortars from the shadows. Jamil had seen the fear in his father's eyes. He'd seen him scream at his men and beat those who wanted to flee across the border. They were scared of the Americans in spite of all their boasting.

Jamil knew that he couldn't just run into the American camp and beg to be protected. He was young, but already he knew life didn't work that way on either side of the barbed wire. He had to give them something they wanted. He had to be of use to them if they were to protect him and keep him within their camp.

He was there. He'd left Salah and Reza standing a block away. They would go no farther. They still didn't believe he was going to try to kill an American, but they found hiding places and watched quietly while Jamil walked toward a tall American soldier. As he drew near to the soldier, Jamil raised his arms.

"Arrest me!"

16

IN HARM'S WAY

JOURNAL ENTRY: DECEMBER 3, 2003
Kid's got an amazing story. Fourteen years old and his father wants him dead. Great life.

Unlike most kids who showed up at the gate, this one didn't want money or candy. He wanted to be cuffed, blindfolded, and arrested. But S.Sgt. Guetschow, who was in charge of the outbound traffic at the border checkpoint, had his hands full trying to control the long line of cars and their drivers pushing to get into Syria. At first, the soldier ignored the scrawny boy walking through the mobs, but then something in his determined stride caught his eye. The kid was moving against the flow toward the border, coming directly toward him and the fortified entrance to the American encampment. The guards were trained to regard anyone who approached our camp as a potential threat. They stopped the boy at gunpoint and called S.Sgt. Guetschow. He summoned an interpreter, who briefly questioned the boy. Then he radioed me.

I was just one hundred yards away, at the command post within the tactical operations center at the checkpoint.

"Dragon X-ray, this is the main gate" came Guetschow's voice. "We have a young Iraqi here who is telling my interpreter he has information about mujahideen and a weapons cache."

"Okay, you know the drill," I replied. "Bring him up to the operations center, and let's get his story."

"There's one hitch," S.Sgt. Guetschow said. "He won't come unless we arrest him, handcuff him, and put a hood over his head."

I'd had a long night. Our raid had led to the capture of an insurgent group we dubbed "The Dirty Dozen," and processing the captives had taken most of the night. I'd gotten just a few hours of sleep. I could smell my own breath. I hadn't shaved in twenty-four hours, and someone had fried the coffeepot again. This was the second young informant to show up in just two hours. The first one was playing games with us, so I was in no mood to waste time on a second kid looking for a handout.

Nevertheless, I sent a Humvee for him; the request to be handcuffed and hooded was a new one. I was intrigued. Most of them wanted money up front, not handcuffs and a bag over their heads. We'd had kids show up offering information in exchange for candy, soda pop, or money, but most of their information was shaky at best. Still, we'd found that the younger Iraqis were more open to talking with our interpreters than adults who'd built up hatred or fear of Americans. Kids had free run of the town for the most part. They saw a lot and were inclined to give honest answers, even if details were often sketchy.

"Okay," I told S.Sgt. Guetschow. "Do as he asks. Cuff him and bag him."

The boy was pretty sad-looking when they brought him through the gates. They'd handcuffed him with strips of plastic and put an empty sandbag over his head. Before they got him to my location, I had to check the perimeter defenses as part of my daily rounds. I left, telling an interpreter to find out what the kid's story was and then to hold him until I got back.

I returned to the TOC a half hour later. A designated safe room in the vault of a former bank, it had been remodeled by some thieves who had attempted to blow it up by chiseling through the concrete and rebar. As I entered the room where the boy was waiting, I took off my body armor and Kevlar and threw my gear on my cot. The interpreter, nicknamed "Raw Hide"—our best shot at his Arabic name of Rahid (pronounced "Raaheed")—introduced the boy as Jamil. We had to come up with another name for this potential informant because the kid who'd been in an hour earlier had a similar first name, and we didn't want to mix up the two of them. So SFC Ross dubbed this kid "Steve" and the first kid "Allen," for reasons I never really understood.

Raw Hide filled me in while I checked out our young "captive." He claimed to be fourteen, but he looked about ten. The Iraqis don't keep birth records or celebrate birthdays, so I doubt if Steve even knew how old he was. He was a good-looking kid, but he was so skinny that his white dishdasha robe and beige jacket hung on him like a collapsed tent. I could tell that he was doing everything he could to maintain his composure. His smile was forced, and I could see that one of his legs was shaking pretty badly. As happy as he tried to look, I got the sense that he was terrified.

Raw Hide gave me the basics. He said if half the kid's claims were true, this might be something to act on. We'd had several kids come forward with information on weapons caches, but the fact that he wanted to be taken captive suggested that there was more going on with this boy. It appeared that he had a plan. He wanted the locals to think we'd arrested him for something. He was trying to fool either them or us.

We weren't in the habit of taking minors into custody or away from their families. But then I learned something from the interpreter that made this particular kid much more interesting.

"He says he can identify a large mujahideen cell in the area. He knows where their weapons are hidden, and he wants to take us to them." I nodded, only half listening. "Oh, and, First Sergeant, you'll find this interesting: He lives near Ambush Wadi, and he claims the leader of the local insurgent cell is his father."

That got my attention. I looked at the boy sitting in a plastic chair against the wall. His father? He was turning against his own father in a culture where the senior male ruled every aspect of the family? It was then that I noticed some signs that the boy had been abused. His arms bore several scars, and when he looked up to meet my stare for the first time, I saw that one of his eyes was slightly crossed. It began to dawn on me that this kid hadn't come to us for a handout at all. He'd come to us for protection, to ensure his own survival. And yet, things were never as they seemed in this lawless corner of Iraq. I had to use extreme caution in assessing this kid and his motives. The insurgents were not above using young boys as stool pigeons, sending them in with promises of information that would lead our soldiers into carefully laid traps.

After speaking with him further, Raw Hide said Steve claimed his father wanted to kill him because he'd refused to join the insurgency. My mind was racing. This kid's whole situation was very odd, even for this city of cutthroats and connivers. The fact that he was willing to turn in his own father was mind-boggling. Going against your father is one of the biggest taboos in the Muslim culture, especially in a rural, tribal place like Husaybah. Either this kid really feared and hated his father, or he was part of a very elaborate setup for an ambush of some sort. Things were always murky in Al Qaim and Husaybah. There were no easy reads, neither in the landscape nor among the people. There was a smuggler's mentality here. Corruption ran deep in every aspect of life. Duplicity was considered a virtue in most circles. Locals would wave at you one day in the market and join an ambush that same night. The smiling guy at the border checkpoint one morning might be the suicide bomber on his return trip.

I looked hard at Steve. His leg was still shaking. We didn't count on having many friends among the people here. Anyone who offered assistance was regarded with great suspicion and carefully watched. Often, there was some ulterior motive: money, revenge, murderous intent. Our suspicions were frequently confirmed, our mistrust rewarded. We were doing our best to follow orders to restore peace and help start the rebuilding process. But we did it on full alert.

Capt. Roehrman returned to the tactical operations center at that point. I briefed him on our unusual new informant. We talked over our shared concerns that this kid might just be bait thrown out to lure us into a deadly ambush. We decided to talk to him a little more to get a better handle on the validity of his information.

It didn't take long for the boy to convince us. We were hesitant because of his age, but he was adamant that he wanted to help us. He said his father had buried multiple rocket-propelled grenades, explosives, and weapons in his yard in preparation for another ambush. He told the interpreter that he could lead us to a forty-man insurgency cell. I asked him to show us the weapons cache location on a satellite photo map, but he'd never seen his hometown from that perspective. We were stymied until the boy began describing landmarks and locations near his house. The interpreter figured out that he was describing the residential area near Ambush Wadi, where we'd had the firefight three weeks earlier. He didn't have to convince me that this was a lair of the insurgency. It made sense that they lived nearby because most of these Iraqis didn't have cars. They had to stage their ambushes near their homes so they could get to their hiding places quickly.

We didn't have a pinpoint location, so we still needed the boy to go with us. We also had some residual concerns about being led into a trap, but if this intelligence was as good as it sounded, we also didn't have time to waste. We had to act quickly. The fact that this kid wanted to accompany us scored him some points, but we kept in mind that the insurgents were not at all hesitant about blowing up their own people if it meant killing Americans, too.

Capt. Roehrman gave the go-ahead, and that afternoon, we set up a plan to raid the house. We waited until the border checkpoint was shut down and the Iraqi evening prayers and nightly mortar bombardment on our camp were over. We then formed a raid party with two tanks and two Humvees. First Lt. Sands was in the lead on the ground. The commander would run the show from his tank located in the outer cordon. My job was to coordinate with our squadron headquarters at Tiger Base from the border checkpoint. This was considered a high-risk mission because our young informant's house was in the neighborhood near Ambush Wadi, an area infested with insurgents who could easily hit us from the marsh and then run to their homes in a densely packed neighborhood.

Steve wore a hood over his head and a bulletproof vest as he rode, out of sight, in the back of SFC Evans's Humvee. They were seconds from rolling out of the gate of our compound when a very agitated SFC Evans came across the radio with some disturbing news that Steve had just revealed to the interpreter.

"He says his father has a suicide vest!"

That late-breaking bit of critical information from the boy infuriated SFC Evans, for good reason. We were about to send our men in there. If the father pulled the fuse on a bomb vest, they'd all die.

This kid was starting to piss me off.

"Okay, this is Dragon Seven," I radioed back. "Find out if he has any other interesting pieces of information that he would like to share with the group."

"What else are you not telling us, kid?" SFC Evans roared as he grabbed Steve by the cuff.

Raw Hide fired questions at him a mile a minute. Steve cowered from his interrogator's rage, shouting that he was only trying to protect them by letting them know about the vest. We decided to continue with the raid, with a few minor adjustments. We would send the Humvees in first because they were quieter than tanks and allowed for more of an element of surprise. We also gave orders that the father was to be shot if he made one suspicious move. We were not going to allow him to blow up our soldiers with a suicide vest.

The raid team rolled out, feeling very uneasy about this mission based on the claims of a very nervous boy underneath a hood in the back of a Humvee. Sgts. Bandel and Graham hit the squat brown house so fast, Steve's father could do nothing but throw his hands up in the air and stare into the two flashlights mounted on rifles aimed at his forehead. Even with our butchered Arabic, he understood. There was no suicide vest in sight, but there was another adult male in the house, whom we had not expected. A woman and a handful of children were also there. We took digital photographs of them all and sent the camera back to the convoy so Steve could identify his family. He identified his parents, brothers, and sisters, and he said the other man was a Syrian mujahideen who fought with his father's cell.

From what I already knew of the father, I was half hoping he'd put up a fight. He was docile but very nervous. That was usually the case with these local thugs. They tortured, raped, and murdered their own people, but when captured, their knees buckled, and on more than one occasion, their bladders gave out. His father was just a scared, short, chubby man at that point. Our soldiers often said, "Never trust fat Iraqis because if they've been eating that well, they must have been sitting at Saddam's table."

We cuffed and blindfolded the two men and put them under guard as we searched for the weapons cache Steve had said was located in an empty lot next to their house. Guards were posted around the perimeter. A helicopter hovered overhead to provide perimeter security. The neighborhood was obviously swarming with insurgents. Steve joined the search when his father and other family members were out of sight. He kept the hood over his head in case any neighbors were watching. He walked SFC Evans and his men to a spot in the vacant lot and pointed to the ground. Within a few minutes, they were pulling a large trove of rockets, hand grenades, and rocket-propelled grenades from their hiding place. The rockets, one of the most sophisticated weapons in the insurgents' arsenal, were a major discovery. It was the first time we'd found them intact. We'd been looking for them since our arrival in Husaybah.

We put Steve back in the Humvee before we brought the father and his Syrian sidekick out back to ask them about the arsenal.

"Walla, walla, walla!" was their response to every question. Translation: "I didn't have anything to do with it, I promise to Allah."

The military intelligence guys and their weapons specialists were very keen on tracking the source of those rockets. Steve's father, who had no idea that his son was with us and serving as an informant, claimed that he had no knowledge of the rockets being buried there. He said they were not his. The Syrian wasn't any more forthcoming. We had them hauled back to Tiger Base, where interrogators were already waiting to talk to them.

Once they were gone, SFC Evans spoke to Steve's mother, a small woman with a kind face. There was no doubting that this was Steve's family. The family resemblance was strong from the mother to each of her wide-eyed boys and girls. SFC Evans sympathized with this woman nervously talking to the interpreter with her children pressed around her.

Steve's mother told our interpreter that Sayed was the leader of the local insurgency and that he forced her husband to bury the weapons in the yard. We heard a lot of that from captives and their families, of course. They usually had no idea that there was a small arsenal buried in the backyard. The dog must have done it. We didn't buy it before, and we didn't buy it now from Steve's mother either. She wasn't a convincing liar. She seemed torn between wanting to help us and fearing for the safety of her children. SFC Evans could hardly blame her.

PUTTING A FACE ON THE ENEMY

Upon returning to the command center, Capt. Roehrman and I were stunned that this kid had just walked in and served up intelligence as valuable as the location of the rockets and the other weapons. The fact that he'd turned in his own father certainly gave us second thoughts. He might look like a lost puppy, but his actions were very calculated, and there was no telling what sort of training had been beaten into him. I resolved to watch him very carefully.

After briefing the commander the next morning, I learned that the Iraqi boy's name had morphed into "Steve-O" and that he'd already become like a little brother to many of the soldiers. It was amazing. This Iraqi boy had already won the affection of American soldiers who'd been under attack by his father's insurgent cell for months. I was determined to find out more about him. He asked if he could stay at the border checkpoint for a few days. He had given his mother a cover story, he said, and he felt it was too dangerous to return so quickly after the raid and detention of his father. The kid was shrewd. I arranged for the interpreter Raw Hide to hang out with me and Steve-O over the next several days so we could have some time to talk about the boy's family, what he knew about the mujahideen and their plans, and his life in general.

A few hours later, I returned to my "office," which consisted of my cot with a little desk alongside it. I was putting together a detailed operational summary describing our activities. This is tedious work for me—writing narratives and attaching the pictures, graphics, and maps that lay out the "who, what, where, when, and why" of every mission. I was looking through my computer file of photographs of people we had detained or questioned as suspected members of the insurgency when Steve-O came in with one of our guys; he spotted the face on my computer screen.

"Mujahideen!" he said.

He started jabbering, but I couldn't understand him. I told him to hang on and then called for an interpreter. Raw Hide translated: "He said he knows these people on your computer."

Jamil pointed to a face on the screen and said a name. I checked the military intelligence report. The kid was dead-on. I pulled up more operational summaries to see how much he really knew. I pointed to another photograph, this one of a major Muslim imam we'd just captured.

"Who's this?" I asked.

Jamil started rattling off a response. Our interpreter's jaw dropped.

"He says this is a holy man who moves Syrian money to the insurgency for weapons in the region."

Okay, I thought, *maybe that was too easy. Everybody should know the local holy man.* But then, Jamil had just given me more intelligence than we had in the priest's file.

"How about this guy?"

He identified him right away. I showed him a series of other mug shots, and he nailed them all. Right on target. He then offered up additional information on their backgrounds, their roles in the insurgency, their relatives, and what kind of vegetables they grew in their gardens.

I looked at the interpreter in disbelief. He asked Jamil how he knew so much about these people.

"I told you. My father took me to all their meetings. He made me fight with them!"

★ ★ ★

Dragon Company had turned a corner by becoming more aggressive, but we still lacked the sort of intimate knowledge of our enemy that can come only from having someone inside their camp—a spy, an informant, a captive willing to talk. We'd had some informants come and go, but no one as valuable as Steve-O. He not only knew the names and faces of the insurgents and their leaders, he knew everyone's role, who was good with explosives, who could fire a mortar, where the money flowed, and what the strategies were.

Other informants had given us bits and pieces and even some very big chunks that had led to major raids, weapons caches, and captures. But this kid was like finding the Rosetta stone. He seemed to grasp the whole picture. He was like a little CIA agent. He was much smarter than most of the informants who'd come walking into our camp. He said he'd identified some of his father's cohorts as Syrian by their accents. He had a very analytical mind and a very thorough understanding of the insurgency, its hierarchy, and the way it operated. That was probably even more reason not to trust him. Then again, unlike nearly every other informant we'd encountered, he had not asked for money. And he'd offered up his own father—in a tribal society where the male elders are always treated with deference.

You had to wonder about someone who would turn in his own family members, even if he'd been abused by them. Still, I wanted to protect this valuable source of information and to keep him close by. That first night, I sent him to bed, telling him he could work with the cooks for a couple days before returning to his mother. I told him that I didn't think his father or the Syrian would be back anytime soon.

Over the next few days, I'd see him kicking a soccer ball around with some of the guys, looking like a typical Iraqi schoolkid one minute, and then the next, he'd be telling me about specific meetings, details on the insurgency's infrastructure, the influx of foreign fighters from Syria, the pipeline to get them in, the money trails, and on and on and on. I was stunned at the depth of his knowledge and his memory.

I still had conflicted feelings. In fact, I worked hard at not liking him. I kept telling myself he was very manipulative and could not be trusted. One day, I saw Steve-O taking photographs with a disposable camera given to him by one of our guys. I told the soldier who'd been keeping an eye on him to make sure he didn't leave the base with either the camera or the film in it. I still thought he could be playing both sides for his own purposes. He might use photographs of the camp as insurance if the insurgents accused him of helping us. That way, he could say he'd gotten inside our compound to gather intelligence for them. He was obviously a skilled survivor, if nothing else. I did not want to underestimate him.

Normally, we didn't waste time pondering the motives of our informants. But Steve-O's were a frequent topic of debate. We were always trying to figure out what his motives were. He was very good at ingratiating himself and winning people over by making himself useful and offering information. He also tried hard to fit in with the troops, many of whom weren't much older than him. He told the interpreter one day that he wanted to get a military haircut so he'd look like a soldier. A few of us looked on as the cooks set up an impromptu barbershop outside the mess hall. Steve-O sat on a stool while his "stylist" snipped away at his dark, shaggy hair. At first, there was a lot of teasing and joking from the soldiers gathered around. But as his hair was shaved away, the ugly scars and gashes on his head were exposed.

Things got quiet. Steve-O looked up at us, wondering about the sudden silence. He read our expressions. A shadow of embarrassment passed over his boyish face. Then through sheer force of will, Steve-O worked up a smile, gestured at his shaved head and then at our similar nuggets, as if to say, *See, now I look just like you!*

Shortly after that, I was surprised to hear that Steve-O was telling the interpreter that he wanted to go home. He said he wanted to check on his family. I didn't want to hold him against his will. But I hated to turn loose an informant who had so much valuable information at his fingertips. I was concerned for his safety as well. If anyone among the insurgents suspected that he had been talking to us, he wouldn't last a second outside our protection. Really, it was his decision. I could hardly blame him for wanting to see his family. I offered to give him some money to help them out, but once again, he refused it.

"I don't want your money," he told the interpreter. He added that he had not helped us for the money. He only wanted to be protected from his father and the insurgency. I told Steve-O that I wanted him to come back once he knew his family was safe. I told him we needed to talk more. He promised to return.

When he walked out the door, I had a sick feeling that I'd never see him again.

HOME THREAT

Two days later, when Steve-O left the American camp, he did not feel endangered or exposed. He felt relief. His father and his henchmen had slowly been pulling the family in a direction that would only lead to the death of them all. Now his father was locked away. It would be better now.

He made his way along the dirt alleys, passing the long lines at the gas station just outside the entrance to the border checkpoint. It was easy to slip past unnoticed. The people in line were focused on cutting ahead of as many cars as possible, which always led to shouting matches and more often than not a brawl of some kind that resulted in more delays and caused more people to try to cut ahead of as many cars as possible. Chaos ruled as usual in Husaybah. Two men holding their empty gas cans got into a shouting match as he scooted past and headed toward the market area.

He ran through his plans again and again. He had taken every precaution because he knew the price of failure. It had worked; his father had been captured. He would no longer be forced to join the insurgency, and his family would no longer endure the violent beatings. Once he reached the market, he easily slipped into the flow of shoppers and traders. Still, this was not a place where he could relax his guard. He knew all too well what went on there. He had heard of people surrounded by a mob in the market, stabbed, or knocked unconscious and never seen again. The mujahideen hid in plain sight in the throngs that frequented the market. It allowed them to observe the American soldiers without being noticed themselves. From the marketplace, they could also see which Iraqis were trading with the Americans or offering them information in exchange for money. They saw everything that happened at the border checkpoint.

Steve-O flitted through the crowds, trying to blend in with the streams of other children, moving quickly, changing his pace, crisscrossing and zigzagging to avoid being followed. His neck hurt because he was constantly scanning back and forth for signs of his father's henchmen. No familiar faces appeared, and that worried him as much as anything. If no muj were on the streets, it likely meant they were gathered together, plotting an ambush.

He reached his house, pushed open the door, and immediately sensed trouble. His mother did not rush to greet him. Instead, she dropped her head and covered her face. Something was wrong, very wrong. His brothers and sisters looked at him like a stranger who had entered their home uninvited. They were oddly quiet as his mother moved toward him. She had something in her hands. He had planned to talk about his return from working in Syria, but he realized it was not necessary. Whatever had happened, his mother knew where he had really been.

When Tahira got closer, he saw the bruises on her face and arms. She whispered to him, her face inches from his: "Sayed and his men were here this morning, and they were looking for you. They said you were a traitor. They blamed you for your father's arrest. They gave me a week to turn you over to them. They said they would kill me if I did not do it. The Syrian was released by the Americans. He told Sayed everything. They know it was you."

Jamil could not draw air into his lungs. He felt light-headed and weak-kneed. He dropped into a chair, his head sagging. He could not find words. He had gone to the Americans to protect his family. He had been so careful. But now he and his family were marked. They would likely all be killed by Sayed. His mother pulled his hands into hers. "You must go with the Americans now; that is your path. You cannot stay here. It is not safe for you or the other children. Sayed will be back. His spies are everywhere."

She pressed several of his favorite music tapes into his hands, pointing to one that was from her own small collection. "This is for you to play and remember, always." He knew it well. They had listened to it together on several occasions. It was a song in which a mother offers words of encouragement to her child: *You must fly on your own, down a different path and away from me, but that is how it must be.* He understood what she was saying. She was giving him permission, her blessing, to leave them.

They both knew he could not stay and survive more than a few days. And once Sayed's men started killing, they would likely kill everyone in the house. He had to get back to the Americans and send them to help his family. He told his mother that he would be back, but she did not believe him. He hugged her, not wanting to let go. He stepped out the door, and it hit him that now he really was alone.

HUNTING THE HUNTER

To my surprise, Steve-O was back at the front gate in an hour. He was frantic. They brought him to me with an interpreter.

"They know!" he said.

"Steve-O, there's no way. Your father is still in custody here," I said.

"But the Syrian isn't. They let him go. He told my mother that the Americans told him about me helping them! And Sayed came to our house. He is a leader of the insurgency and very dangerous. He is a killer. He beat my mother and told her that she had a week to turn me over or he would kill her and my brothers and sisters!"

I could not believe what he was saying. Why would any of our guys give up the name of a valuable informant, especially a kid? This was insane—what the hell was going on? I tried to calm Steve-O down, but he was a wreck. "We will protect you and your family," I said. "You can stay here with us until we catch this guy." He looked at me with the kind of expression that said I'd let him down and then turned to the interpreter and asked to go back to his previous room.

The guys from ODA—the Special Forces team in charge of intelligence gathering—came looking for Dragon Company before I could go looking for them. It wasn't a coincidence; they had come to talk to me about my operational summary on Steve-O. The first question they asked me was about Sayed. What the hell? Every time I turned around, someone was mentioning this guy's name, and now Special Forces was bringing him up?

The first time I'd heard about Sayed was from Steve-O and his mother. She had claimed that he was responsible for burying the weapons cache in their yard. She said he was their neighbor and part of the insurgency. We had not believed her at the time. And I still thought Steve-O's father knew about the weapons. But I had noted the mention of Sayed's name in the operational summary, and it seemed to have set off alarms with the Special Forces intelligence unit.

I told them what had transpired since Steve-O's father was arrested, including the threats and assault on his mother by

Killer Troop, Second Platoon, at the Al Taqaddum Airfield making final preparations for first mission in Iraq, April 30, 2003

Second Platoon rolls out of FOB Eden (north of Hīt) to conduct searches of one hundred homes, May 29, 2003. (Staff Sergeant Gill is pictured in the back of the Humvee.)

Second Platoon conducts first dismounted mission on the banks of the Euphrates from FOB Eden, April 8, 2003

First Sergeant Hendrex overlooks the Euphrates, September 28, 2003, as he conducts a search of the farmland near Rawa (and the ambush site of the Dragon convoy, September 23, 2003).

Searching the groves after a mortar attack on FOB Eden in Hīt, Iraq, May 30, 2003

Tripod of leadership for Dragon Company on the Al Qadisayah Dam. *From left to right:* First Sergeant Hendrex (company first sergeant), Captain Roehrman (company commander), Lieutenant Sands (company executive officer)

View from the balcony of First Sergeant Hendrex's room at the Al Qadisayah Dam in Haditha, Iraq, July 5, 2005

Baghdad International Airport, Saddam's hunting and fishing palace, August 2, 2003. (Taken from atop the main palace, photo pictures one of the many smaller palaces surrounding the central one)

First Sergeant Hendrex during the only amphibious assault by a Heavy Tank Company in Rawa, Iraq, August 29, 2003

First Sergeant Hendrex standing in an ancient aqueduct on the banks of the Euphrates outside Hīt, Iraq, May 2003

Specialist Marquez after loading the boat found at Saddam's palace on the road from Baghdad International Airport to the dam in Haditha, Iraq, August 2, 2003

Tiger Squadron at FOB Tiger in Al Qaim just prior to the completion of the deployment. Dragon is one of five companies within the squadron. February 2, 2004

Almost three years after First Sergeant Hendrex's tank was destroyed in a mock battle at Fort Polk, Louisiana, he survived this explosion and catastrophic loss of a tank in the northwest region of Iraq during his return in the summer of 2005.

Dragon Bottom's (later renamed *Drift Wood*) maiden voyage on August 22, 2003. *From left to right:* Sergeant Moon, Sergeant Anderson, Private Ragle

The Dragon crew and Steve-O after the hospital mission with Special Forces, January 26, 2004

Steve-O on his first tank ride with Sergeant Moon at the border checkpoint in Husaybah, Iraq, January 6, 2004

First Sergeant
Hendrex with
Steve-O outside
Dragon's quarters
on FOB Tiger in
Al Qaim, Iraq,
March 7, 2004

Steve-O

You're an incredible kid!

Stay safe while we do

everything we can to get

you out of Al Qaim.

1SG Hendrex

A copy of the letter that Daniel gave Steve-O the day he left FOB Tiger on March 12, 2003;
Steve-O still carries the original in his wallet today.

Daniel and Christina Hendrex
in Florida on their wedding
day, May 10, 1997

Steve-O's first full day
in the United States—
Colorado Springs,
Colorado, on top of
Pikes Peak with First
Sergeant Hendrex

Sayed and his goons. The ODA captain didn't mince words: "If Sayed said he is going to come back in a week and kill her, then he will be back in a week to kill her."

It was usually rare for Special Forces guys to share intelligence, but we had a good relationship with them in Husaybah. We'd developed some good information on our own and shared it with them and had the firepower to back them up, so they were willing to work with us for our mutual benefit. They'd seen us in action on raids and responding to ambushes, and they'd called upon us a couple times to support their operations. In return, they supplied us with local intelligence acquired through their network. They always had great intelligence.

The Special Forces captain quickly filled me in on Sayed, whose full name was Sayed Atta Ali. He was considered to be a major link between the local jihadists and their international leadership. He was a conduit for foreign fighters, weapons, and money and a high value target of Special Forces intelligence operations in our area. The captain described Sayed as a vicious killer who tortured collaborators and helped bring foreign fighters into Iraq. It was believed that he was responsible for the planning and execution of numerous attacks on coalition forces and for the systematic terrorizing and slaying of key Iraqi officials, policemen, informants, and coalition sympathizers.

I began to fully understand Steve-O's concerns about his family. If Sayed was threatening them, they were in real danger. I also began to appreciate his courage even more. He clearly knew that in stepping into our camp, he was making himself a target for this killer. That is why he had planned it so carefully. He was a little boy dealing with very dangerous men, and his actions had dire consequences. In a town of killers, he had been thrown into a crowd of the worst and most sadistic.

Sayed was a shadow, a ghost, and a killer of his own people. Word on the street was that people who crossed him simply disappeared. And often, their entire families were killed. Steve-O and his family would never again be able to walk freely on the streets of Husaybah. His mission had failed terribly in that regard.

Nobody could say for sure how the insurgent leader found out that the boy had given us information. The Syrian who'd been taken into custody with Steve-O's father was released because they had nothing solid to hold him on. Steve-O's father was still being held. He had reportedly given up information on Sayed. Maybe the Syrian overheard somebody talking about Steve-O while he was in custody. Maybe one of the father's henchmen saw Steve-O during the weapons search and figured out who he was, even with the hood over his head. We also knew that the insurgency had its own spies and informants working in and around the border checkpoint. They might have spotted him coming and going.

Whatever had happened, the boy and his entire family were now in imminent danger. I talked to Capt. Roehrman. We agreed that we had to keep Steve-O under wraps. And we had to do something for his family. We also wanted to get to Sayed before he got to them, or at least to keep him on the run. So we put together a mission. Its stated purpose was to raid Sayed's home on the river. Steve-O said he could take us directly to it. With so much information, I felt confident that before the night's activities were over, we would have Sayed in handcuffs. We had to get him off the streets; otherwise, this boy and his family faced certain death.

Special Forces knew that Sayed owned a hideaway on the river, but they did not know its exact location. Steve-O told them that it was one of five houses owned by Sayed's extended family. One of the others was right across the street from the boy's own family home. On December 5, 2003, we led the raid on foot through four of the homes. From his hiding place in our convoy, Steve-O identified several of Sayed's relatives as we took them captive. But there was no sign of the leader himself. We did find family photo albums, but Steve-O said the photos of Sayed had been removed. And it was no coincidence that the phones were ringing in two of the four homes as our raiders entered.

We saved Sayed's river house for last. It was approximately five hundred meters from the others, separated by large irrigated fields that butted up against the Euphrates River. It was a good hideout. There were numerous escape routes if the occupants had to flee quickly. We went in on foot patrol to maintain the element of surprise. The farm fields were drenched and muddy. Every step took a massive effort. The 500-meter trek to the river house seemed like 500 miles. We stopped to rest briefly, and then we hit it. As we entered the house, we found five women, three children, and a teenage male. They didn't seem all that surprised to see us. We took digital photos of them and showed them to Steve-O in his hiding place. He identified Sayed's wife and son. Once again, the telephone started ringing. As we searched, we found several torn-up photographs. Others had the faces scratched out or cut out. In one of the children's bedrooms, we found an unusual plaything: an optical sighting system for mortars.

Steve-O, who seemed to know everyone and his brother— literally—in the area, suggested that we raid the house next door, as it belonged to a brother of Sayed's father-in-law. There, we found a photograph that appeared to have Sayed's image cut out. In all the homes raided, we had questioned twenty-two people. Only one admitted to knowing who Sayed was. It appeared that all photographs of him had been removed from all of the homes.

Sayed was obviously not a typical insurgent foot soldier. He'd set up an elaborate telephone alert system, and he had taken great pains to conceal his identity from us by shredding and cutting up photographs. As our search wound down, the sun appeared on the horizon. I was drenched in sweat, and the day was just beginning. Worse, after six hours of exhausting work, we were no closer to catching Sayed. I had a bad feeling. He was living up to his reputation as a phantom figure. This guy had gone to great lengths and efforts to ensure he could not be identified. Except for Steve-O's descriptions, we didn't know what he looked like. The Iraqi boy was proving to be a real asset to our soldiers. I tried to maintain a skeptical attitude, but he was winning me over too.

Our efforts were also benefiting from the fact that the boy was not the only informant coming through for us in Husaybah. Barney Fife had just told us of another weapons cache in the area. We were asked to accompany Special Forces on this raid due to the location. It was in a nest of vipers, directly behind the police station and a few hundred feet from Ambush Wadi. Barney Fife couldn't make this raid, so we took Steve-O instead.

We hit the place fast and furious, but after an extensive search, we came up empty-handed. We were wondering if we even had the right house when one of our team members discovered a hiding place beneath a staircase packed with the equivalent of a small war starter kit. Crazy Legs found two more of the infamous rockets, a mortar tube, two tank mines, three rocket-propelled grenade boosters, a five-pound bag of gunpowder, three 160-millimeter mortar charges, two RPGs, one mortar sight, one hand grenade, one pound of explosives, and ten 60-millimeter mortar charges. We'd heard that the Iraqis had looted their own military weapons depots after the successful overthrow of Saddam's government. I was ecstatic about taking all that artillery off the street, but it was scary to think about how much firepower the insurgents had in stashes like this all over town.

JOURNAL ENTRY: DECEMBER 13, 2003
The ghost finally has a face. Not as smart as he thinks.
Raided his home again this morning. Our man wasn't in,

but we finally got a picture. Reported to be wearing suicide vest. Fastest raid yet. All persons still asleep.

We staged another raid on the extended Sayed family and a couple of their homes and hideaways. Sayed himself was nowhere to be seen, but we did find our first photograph of him—a passport-size snapshot that had somehow escaped his team of shredders and snippers. I was ecstatic and knew our friends in Special Forces intelligence would be pleased too. But, truth be told, Sayed wasn't the main thing on my mind that night. I was much more interested in making contact with Steve-O's mother, who lived next door to his primary residence.

I took a small team and broke away from the raid there while the tanks and Humvees were rolling around outside Sayed's house, intentionally making a lot of noise to draw attention away from us. It was around two a.m. when we had to bang on the door of Steve-O's house to wake up his mother, frightening her and his siblings, who huddled around their mother as she stood in the doorway. I could still see the bruises on her face and hands.

Through our interpreter, I quickly explained who I was and that her son was safe. She seemed relieved and began talking very rapidly. She told us of the beating and of Sayed's demands that she turn her son over to him. I asked if she had a passport. She did. I then gave her four hundred dollars in cash from our fund for informants and told her she must leave immediately. She said she could go to the home of relatives in Fallujah. We were aware of the upcoming offensive in Fallujah and didn't want her going there. I told her it had become a war zone worse than Husaybah at that point.

"Where else can you go?" I asked her.

She said she had brothers in Baghdad. I felt better about that. It wasn't exactly a peaceful place either, but at least there was a possibility that we could arrange for her to be protected there. I told her to get the children's things together and to leave as quickly as possible. I even offered to escort her taxi out of town. She said that there was no need, that she would be leaving at first light. Then she asked how her son was doing. I could tell that she was torn about leaving him, even though she knew that it was important for her to protect herself and her other children.

From what he'd told me, I knew that Steve-O was very close to his mother. They shared their fears and their secrets with each other. I assured her that I would not let any harm come to him. "Do not return to Husaybah until you get word that we have captured Sayed," I told her.

When we returned to the border checkpoint that night, I told Steve-O that his mother was going to Baghdad with his brothers and sisters. He was sad, but he was relieved that they would be out of danger. He asked me a million questions. Was she okay? Did his brothers and sisters ask about him? Were any of the neighbors around? He resented his father mostly for placing his mother and siblings in harm's way. And now his cover was blown. His parents were out of the picture, and he had nowhere else to go.

17

A BOY AMONG MEN

For all of the inroads we were making, it seemed the insurgency was somehow growing in numbers and in strength. Paid mercenaries, religious zealots, and other foreign fighters were pouring into Iraq. These outsiders pulled the strings of the local insurgents, supplying them with money and weapons. The foreign fighters also brought expertise in guerrilla and urban warfare.

In the early days of our time in Husaybah, we weren't fighting a well-trained enemy. The skilled foreign fighters were rarely caught in the line of fire themselves, but they trained the insurgents in making and handling explosive devices and weapons. I'm sure they also guided their choice of targets and points of attack. More recently, though, we were facing fire from more experienced foreign fighters, and they weren't all from the Middle East. We had intelligence that two Russian fighters from Chechnya were operating in our little slice of heaven.

The most dangerous of our foes were the religious maniacs, the jihadists who were prepared to die for the opportunity to kill us. They were well trained and experienced in this type of warfare. They had tactics and strategies and advanced weaponry—

and they were not above using women and children as cover or as suicide bombers.

But that wasn't the worst of it. The increased American military presence in Husaybah had apparently incited Sayed and his henchmen to crack down on local Iraqis to maintain their control. They were ruthless. They had a group of eight to ten black bag operations guys, probably trained by Steve-O's father. They'd go into the homes of Iraqis, single out the father or mother or a child, and torture or kill them in front of the others to make the point that they would not tolerate American sympathizers. Women and girls were raped. They also used these techniques to force men and boys to fight for them, to plant bombs, or to gain access to the homes they needed as safe houses or weapons caches, lookouts, or ambush sites.

At first, it was hard for me and the other American soldiers to understand why most Iraqi citizens did not respond to our efforts to help them. But it became clear that until we rid them of the predators in their own neighborhoods, the Iraqi people would never be able to embrace the freedom they were being offered. They'd tell us: "You aren't here when the mujahideen come at night. You can't protect us from them around-the-clock. If you can't protect our families, how can we trust you or help you?"

COOKING CAMP

As the end of the year approached and the insurgency stepped up its attacks, I was relieved that we'd gotten Steve-O's family out of town two weeks before. He seemed to feel better about it too. The kid sure was resilient. With all that had happened to him, you'd think he'd hardly be able to lift his head. Yet, in the month that Steve-O had been with us at the border checkpoint, he seemed to thrive. We had him live with the cooks, helping them clean, cook, and take out trash. We put him in that job deliberately, so we could keep an eye on him at all times. There was no denying his value to us. Still, we monitored him day and night.

His charisma was irresistible, which made it all the more important to stay on the alert. That's not to say people walked circles around him. In truth, Steve-O quickly became a major personality at the border checkpoint. With all of the craziness and tension that surrounded our daily lives, this boy among us let us feel like boys ourselves in the calmer moments in our camp. He helped give us insight into the Iraqi people. He gave some of us the sense that our mission might at least benefit the innocents in Iraq, and he gave us hope for a country that seemed to have little hope for itself.

Our time living in, guarding, and conducting patrols from Husaybah's border checkpoint tested the training and experience of Dragon Company and the mettle of its members. I never felt closer to death. Any given minute of any given day could easily have been my last. Pick your poison: Mortar attacks. Rocket-propelled grenades. Land mines. Snipers. Ambushes. Suicide bombers. Car bombs. Crazed and drunken Iraqis. Religious zealots. Imminent danger lurked around every corner, in any car, within the folds of every cloak.

Our squadron commander recognized the intense nature and dangers of duty at the border checkpoint. The plan was to keep rotating companies and troops from there back to the relative— very relative—safety of Tiger Base just outside town. The normal rotation was in and out every two weeks. But Dragon Company's success in the assignment won us the dubious honor of an extension. Our first two-week tour was stretched to six weeks, which seemed an eternity. Yet, it is strange what you can get used to and how you learn to find comfort, even enjoyable moments, in the most stressful of situations.

Some of my best memories of Iraq arose from corners of our little border checkpoint enclave, even though it was surrounded by razor wire amid openly hostile people who did their daily best to terrorize or kill us. One of those moments came during an early-morning visit to the tactical operations center. As I entered, I was nearly knocked to my knees by the unfamiliar, overpowering scent of freshly scrambled eggs, with tomatoes and onions. My stomach started grumbling before I tracked down the source. Fresh-cooked anything was rare in those quarters. It was winter in Iraq. Even in the desert, it gets very cold, because the sand holds little heat at night. A 25- or 30-degree temperature drop puts a definite chill in your bones after your body has adjusted to 120-degree days.

With the arrival of much cooler weather, we'd purchased an Iraqi cooking stove that we put in a corner to keep the chill out of the operations center. The stove had inspired Chef Steve-O to spring into action with skillet in hand. He'd worked in an uncle's restaurant before the war and loved to cook. The previous day, the boy had gone around and begged and bartered for fresh produce from one vehicle to the next among the hundreds that passed through the border checkpoint each day. That morning, he put his culinary talents to work, transforming fresh zucchini, potatoes, eggs, tomatoes, onions, and cucumbers into a breakfast buffet. I joined the long line in Steve-O's impromptu mess hall.

We taught him American dishes, starting with the basic but ever-popular grilled cheese sandwich. Several burned loaves later, we took it up a notch with the grilled ham and cheese sandwich. That warm, sweet-smelling corner of the TOC became a rare place of comfort during those high-stress days. Steve-O was host and chef. He had unusual confidence and skill around the cooking fire.

Early one morning, I went to his cookstove corner with a pair of cold-weather gloves that Christina had sent me for the winter. These were a prized possession of mine: leather and yellow, the military color for the armored division. As insurance against theft or loss, I decided to "brand" them by heating up the metal crossed sabers on my Stetson cavalry hat—another trademark of our unit—and making a distinctive imprint on the gloves. (It's a cavalry thing.)

I had taken the crossed sabers off my Stetson and was standing in front of the stove trying to figure out the best way to heat them when Steve-O confidently cranked up the flame and took the sabers from me. The interpreter was not around, and I was hesitant to put this mission in the hands of the boy. You get only one shot to get branding right. There is no Wite-Out for mistakes made by burning leather. But Steve-O's display of confidence dispelled my doubts. He pulled a coat hanger out of the air, transformed it into a tool for holding the sabers over the flame, and started heating them to a bright orange glow. I couldn't help but admire his steady hands and his assurance. He then used pliers to place the red-hot sabers against the leather as he neatly branded the imprint onto both of my gloves exactly as I had envisioned. His eyes showed the pride he took in helping me.

Our extended stay at the border checkpoint meant that we had remained in the hot zone for Thanksgiving, which was pushed back a couple of weeks. But there was some respite. In a show of force aimed at stanching the flow of foreign fighters into Iraq, the Pentagon poured resources, soldiers, and weaponry into our region for a brief stretch. It meant more people around the Thanksgiving table, but it also offered us a measure of peace at a very welcome time. And we weren't forced to sit around platters of grilled cheese sandwiches posing as a holiday feast. The Pentagon stocked the kitchen, too. I dispatched three Humvees to Tiger Base for turkey and fixings. I returned with a meal to make the Pilgrims proud. We had freshly cooked whole turkeys, huge spiral hams, fresh jumbo shrimp, a large assortment of steamed vegetables, pumpkin pie, apple cobbler, and so on. For a final topping, I arranged to bring in satellite phones so that every soldier was able to touch base with family and loved ones for at least a few precious minutes.

We celebrated the distinctly American holiday on our razor-wrapped oasis in a decidedly hostile desert. Yet, it was an Iraqi native son who seemed to enjoy it the most. Steve-O walked through the festive mess hall spilling food in his wake. I was sure that there was more weight on his plate than on his bony body. He was everybody's little brother that day. Someone joked that our official greeter spoke very little English. He didn't need it. His smile and engaging manner lit up the joint. And more than a few of us counted him among the very few things we were thankful for in Iraq.

BACK TO BASE

After Thanksgiving, we finally came up for a rotation back to Tiger Base, where we were lucky enough to spend the next holiday. Without hesitation, we opted to take Steve-O with us. Sayed was still on the loose. We felt responsible for the boy's safety, and we didn't want to leave him with soldiers who were not aware of his value. Steve-O had adapted well to life at the border checkpoint, but I wondered how he would do within the larger confines of Tiger Base, where he was not so well known, farther from the familiar territory of his own town and its culture, and totally in the realm of American troops.

Once again, the boy surprised me by not only adapting to his new surroundings, but by becoming an integral part of life at Tiger Base. Truth be told, I had to brief more than one soldier whose alarms were triggered at the sight of an Iraqi boy strolling toward him in an American camp. We had the squadron make up a special identification tag for him that was easily spotted and then made sure Steve-O wore it every day. But it didn't take long before you'd see him slapping hands and taking pats on the back. He was our celebrity guest star and the source of no small amount of entertainment.

One relatively quiet morning at Tiger Base, I took advantage of the lull to roust the Iraqi boy living among our soldiers.

"Rise and shine! Don't just lie there stealing everyone's oxygen; it's a beautiful day in this fine, sand-filled, dust-covered, sun-baked country of yours. You need to get your ass up and join the rest of civilization."

Steve-O pulled back his covers, stretched, forced a smile, and gave me a cheery but heavily accented "Good morning, First Sergeant!"

I had a mission of a different sort for him that morning. I announced that I was going to teach him how to throw a football.

Steve-O's English was still very rudimentary, so the only thing he got out of that sentence was "football," which meant an entirely different sport to him than to an American kid. He grabbed his soccer ball. But I waved it off and held up my pigskin instead.

"Football, Steve-O! This is an American football. You can put that ball away!"

I gave him a quick lesson on how to hold the football, and then I threw him his first pass. He didn't catch it because his damaged eye skewed his depth perception. But he didn't complain or offer an excuse. He just picked it up and prepared to throw it back.

"First Sergeant!" he yelled.

He hadn't learned to say "catch" in English yet, so he just motioned with his hands to show that he was going to throw the ball.

This ought to be funny, I thought.

I never knew what to expect from him. So I was prepared to have a good laugh when the scrawny kid made his first attempt at throwing the oblong ball that looked like a watermelon in his small hands.

I moved in about thirty feet to make sure his first try would reach me. "Do you think you can throw it this far? I can get closer," I teased.

He flashed a smile to let me know that he got the joke. "Uh-huh, okay, First Sergeant, you will see."

Before I realized he had thrown it, the ball came whistling past my head like it had been blasted out of a tank's main gun.

This kid with chicken wings for arms whipped a perfect spiral that flew another thirty yards past me.

"Not bad, Steve-O, not bad."

He raised himself to his full height and puffed out his chest. "Uh-huh, I told you! I told you!" he said.

Steve-O had game. No doubt about that.

Capt. Roehrman, SFC Ross, and I were walking to the mess hall one afternoon with Steve-O in tow like a little brother tagging along. Ross, a platoon sergeant with a vividly raw vocabulary, noted that the guys had been helping Steve-O with his English.

I took the bait and asked the boy for a sampling. He smiled proudly, stuck out his chest, and clearly announced: "Bumble Bee tuna, your balls are showing!"

Steve-O's entourage doubled over in laughter. They'd taught him a silly catchphrase from *Ace Ventura,* the Jim Carey movie about a pet detective. Not exactly the King's English, or the Queen's. I tried to keep a straight face but failed. And Steve-O loved that he got me. It soon became his signature line, and you could catch him delivering it all over the camp, with his audiences roaring.

Of course, little brothers can annoy the shit out of big brothers too, and Steve-O was certainly capable of that. But often, it was an accidental annoyance or the result of an unexpected culture clash. One of Steve-O's favorite partners in crime was Spec. Rayo, a small but wiry guy of about the same stature as Steve-O, who shared his passion for soccer. I had seen them kicking a ball around and having a good time on several occasions. But one day at Tiger Base, Rayo came storming up to me in our living quarters. He was more agitated than I'd ever seen him.

"Keep that damn kid away from me! If he comes near me again, Top, I swear I am going to beat his ass!"

He walked off muttering, slamming the door on his way out. I had no idea what had set him off. Then Sergeant Strout came in through the same door. He was laughing so hard, he could hardly speak. Finally, he took a breath and blurted out, "Steve-O kissed Rayo!"

It took a while to get Rayo calmed down enough so that he could give us the details. He and Steve-O had just finished playing soccer. Feeling brotherly, Rayo had presented Steve-O with a gift—a CD player. The boy was so excited, he forgot that he was embedded in an entirely different culture. He did what Iraqi men often do to express manly affection with close friends and family members. He slid over, placed his hand on top of Rayo's, and planted a kiss on his cheek.

The problem was that Rayo comes out of a very macho Hispanic culture. He had no clue as to why Steve-O would be inclined to kiss him. And he went ballistic. He screamed in Spanish while Steve-O tried to explain in Arabic. Meanwhile, the guys in the peanut gallery were laughing hysterically and taunting them both. That's what sent Rayo marching off. Rayo was furious. Steve-O was hurt and confused. I convinced him to put that particular custom on hold for the rest of his stay among the American soldiers. But he did pick up some American male rituals to compensate.

Our soldiers relaxed by teaching him board and video games and pumping him up in the weight room. Within a few weeks, he packed solid muscle on to his lanky frame. The stronger he got, of course, the cockier he got. And that was dangerous in a camp full of men. Being the youngest and smallest had made him the target of a lot of teasing. There wasn't all that much age difference between him and the youngest guys, and sometimes the size difference wasn't all that great either. Male camaraderie can get rough, and as he muscled up, Steve-O rose to the challenge.

We put together a festive Christmas party at Tiger Base. Everyone was feeling feisty as we gathered in an area of the base quartered in a former Iraqi train depot. It was a cavernous old maintenance bay, an open concrete structure that had become our home when we were not operating out of the border checkpoint. The troops had set up a Christmas tree surrounded by gifts sent from home. The squadron cooks put together another big dinner. Afterward, there were groups playing video games, having a lively card tournament, and lining up to call home. We weren't quite nestled all snug in our beds, but it was as peaceful a setting as we'd had in a long time. The entire company was kicking back. Steve-O was playing Halo, an Xbox sci-fi combat game, with Specialist Schwartz, who was master of the universe when it came to that particular video game. Poor Steve-O went down in flames with about twenty guys watching, so he took a fair amount of taunting and a good bit of crowing from Schwartz.

Steve-O bided his time. Then, when Schwartz got up and walked across the room, the teen sneaked up behind him, tripped him, and threw him to the ground. Steve-O had gotten strong. But he was not in Schwartz's league—either in Xbox or in physical strength. Schwartz is a man—six feet tall, lean, and muscular. And he did not take well to being "punked" by some kid.

He popped up with murder in his eyes. Steve-O knew that he had roused a sleeping giant and took off running before Schwartz could clean his clock. They had a lot of room to run in the old train station bay. It looked a bit like an Alfred Hitchcock movie, with the big soldier chasing the much smaller boy through the station. Steve-O headed toward an area where wooden partitions had been set up to divide the platoons' sleeping areas. Even as quick as Steve-O was, Schwartz was gaining ground on him. He was reaching out for Steve-O's neck just as the kid stepped through an open door and slammed it shut behind him. Schwartz was going full speed when he hit the closed door, broke right through it, and went sprawling on the ground for a second time at the hands of Steve-O.

From Steve-O's initial prank to the horrendous crash into the door, the scene was witnessed by the entire company of nearly one hundred men. They were roaring with laughter. After picking up his glasses, rubbing the knot on his forehead, and dusting himself off, there was nothing Schwartz could do but join in the laughter—and bide his time for the payback. Steve-O missed that part of the show. He was still running in the desert, afraid to look back.

That Christmas Day provided a brief interlude for Dragon Company. It was one that we all needed. Late that night, we heard radio reports that our replacements back at the border checkpoint were spending their Christmas under a mortar bombardment from the insurgents. Our party fell silent as the report came in over the radio. We counted sixteen mortars, one after the other, as we heard them hit. There were no casualties, fortunately, other than our holiday mood.

INTO THE FIRE

Three days later, we returned to duty at the border checkpoint. Up to then, we'd worked our own outer security. Upon our return after Christmas, it had been taken over by the Iraqi Civil Defense Corps. They were not as corrupt as the police, but there were still questions that made us cautious around them. Some things changed; others proceeded like clockwork.

The Muslim evening prayer time—when Arabic music was broadcast from the mosques while mortars were loaded by the insurgents—was always special at the border checkpoint. It was a time to reflect, then run for cover. Amen. *Ka-boom!* It was the one daily event you could always set your watch to in Husaybah. Those Iraqi mortar madmen operated like Swiss clocks. And their publishing division came up with some pretty interesting holiday greetings too.

On New Year's Eve, a Special Forces intelligence officer brought me a leaflet plucked from hundreds that had been thrown from the train that runs near Tiger Base. The muj had even been so kind as to have it translated into English:

> Final warning to the crusade troops: You should know, invaders, we used traditional weapons to dismiss you away from our territories along the past period, but you became more stubborn. Therefore, we give you the last opportunity up to the Christmas, the New Year, to celebrate this occasion with your families. After that if you don't respond to this warning you would be annihilated using new weapons of a single affect as the groups of grasshoppers are annihilated.
>
> The Military Wing of
> The Vanguard of the Islamic Resistance

JOURNAL ENTRY: JANUARY 3, 2004
Latest intel update: Twelve rounds of 120-millimeter mortars with chemical warheads were moved into Husaybah. This was reported by OGA [Other Governmental Agency] through a HUMINT source. The credibility is unclear, but it adds another dimension to this wonderful place called Iraq.

One evening after the mosque music had faded, SFC Evans was a little slow on the postprayer takeoff. He and Steve-O were caught outside when the music stopped—a more deadly version of musical chairs. *Thump . . . thump . . . thump* came the ominous sound of mortar rounds being fired from their tubes. SFC Evans realized what was coming. He got a head start as they sprinted for the nearest building, but Steve-O—the skilled survivor—quickly closed the distance, nearly knocking over the soldier as they both sought cover. All around the border checkpoint, soldiers scrambled to safety. Tank commanders closed their steel hatches. Everyone moved inside, donned Kevlar helmets and body armor. The potential of chemical agents riding in on the mortars added strong incentive to find shelter while keeping protective gear close by. Chemical weapons were like a round of horseshoes—close was good enough.

A SPY IN OUR MIDST

One afternoon, I was near the southern gate of the border checkpoint, overlooking the large parking area where Iraqi cars wait for clearance into Syria. I saw Steve-O come out of the tactical operations center and stop suddenly. I watched with concern as he froze for several seconds. Then he broke into a run and darted back toward the TOC. He reached an armored personnel carrier and crouched behind it, peeking around a corner. He was hiding and watching something or someone out of my line of sight. I walked toward him, and when he saw me come from behind him, the boy started jabbering in Arabic and pulling at my sleeve. He pointed at an Iraqi worker twenty-five yards away. The guy, who had not seen us, was running electrical wires from the border checkpoint into our adjoining camp, supervised by an armed soldier. But Steve-O was worked up about him for some reason. I called for an interpreter. When he arrived, Steve-O jabbered at him. I picked out one key word as he pointed at the guy: "mujahideen"!

"He says the guy is a very bad mujahideen who worked in his father's cell and participated in attacks on coalition forces," the interpreter said.

I ordered a soldier to take the "electrician" into custody. Steve-O gave us the name of the spy. It matched with his Iraqi ID. Steve-O said this guy had been part of an insurgent mortar team that had attacked coalition forces in October. As he provided that information, it hit me that our friendly neighborhood electrician may have been pacing off distances inside our camp while pretending to be running electrical wire. It was not a stretch to figure that he could have been giving that info to the insurgents who were firing mortars and grenades into our camp. In Iraq, the good or the bad, black or white, always seemed to fade into various shades of gray. It was proof enough to me that this guy made Steve-O damn nervous. We had him arrested and escorted to headquarters to see if the intelligence guys had anything on him. Obviously, this spy had been gathering information within the interior confines of our camp, so we wanted to check him out thoroughly. Yet, even after we took him out of action, things heated up considerably.

JOURNAL ENTRY: JANUARY 8, 2004
I don't think this town will ever quiet down. It's the gateway for foreign fighters, starting point for illegal arms, and home to smugglers, thieves, and extremists. That combination does not equal success for peacekeeping operations.

First Sergeant Reiss from Bandit Troop was parked in a Bradley Fighting Vehicle high on the cliffs north of the Euphrates River one night when he got an expansive view of the volcanic nature of Husaybah. When he'd first stopped while checking on his scout platoon's observation point, the city had looked inviting enough in the cool darkness. The lights along Market Street and Route Raw and the illumination of the three mosques provided an almost holiday-type atmosphere to the town laid out in a near-perfect square grid.

Suddenly, Husaybah erupted. Explosions flashed followed seconds later by the sound blasts. Reiss's radio crackled with the report that the border checkpoint below was taking heavy mortar fire. Then came another report that a tank patrol—mine—was taking fire in town.

"Dragon X-ray, this is White Two. I am backing out of position and displacing farther south. I have mortars landing all around my vehicle. Damn, that was close!"

"Dragon X-ray, this is Dragon Seven. I am taking the QRF [Quick Reaction Force] to the eastern corner of Route Raw and Train to identify the mortar firing positions. We have four tanks and are clear of the BCP. . . . Dragon X-ray, CONTACT RPGs OUT."

The view of the erupting city was mesmerizing. White flashes, red tracers, the spark tails of rocket-propelled grenades, and the orange blaze of burning buildings lit up the night sky. Violence of some kind reigned in every quadrant of the city. On the east end of town, near Ambush Wadi, a huge explosion turned night into day. Then the entire planet seemed to shake with the roar of a tank's main gun being fired.

Down below, the border checkpoint took seventeen mortars that night. Several landed within a few feet of Sgt. Anderson's tank. We crouched, waiting for a call for help, a report of someone being hit, or a whiff of lethal chemicals. Somehow, none of those things occurred. Somehow, no one was hurt. Sometimes, it was pure luck. Other times, I was damn glad to be part of Dragon!

S.Sgt. Guetschow, who would lead the league in near-death experiences for this deployment, had one RPG whiz by his tank as it made the turn onto Route Raw in the city that night. He sprang into action, firing his machine gun in the direction of the flash. Incredibly, his spray hit the insurgent attacker just as he prepared to fire another RPG that went firing wildly up into the sky.

We received more small-arms fire as we pushed to the next corner. We then caught sight of several insurgents firing at us from within buildings. Our tank's lethal main gun had an even greater effect than intended. It hit the building and apparently blew up a cache of ammunition and fuel inside it. Later, we learned that a large number of insurgents had been wounded or killed. We took no casualties. But we knew our luck could not hold out forever.

It was time to get even more proactive. We needed to meet the insurgency's energy with our much greater firepower. We put together a plan and enacted it over the next few weeks. We began working the intelligence and hitting the insurgency at home, literally. We went door to door and, sometimes, through door after door. We were tired of reacting. Our goal was to put the enemy on the defensive. And we had a hometown boy who was determined to identify the man who had beaten his mother.

Steve-O was living in our camp, and he hated the nightly mortar attacks as much as we did. He was determined to find Sayed. "First Sergeant, you know I am the only one who knows what he looks like!" The kid had a point. So whenever Sayed was a primary target for one of our night raids, we took Steve-O along. We went after the terrorist with manpower and weapons, but also with one of his own favorite motivational tools: money. We had that small photo of him, so we made up a Wanted poster that offered a reward for his hide: six hundred dollars for his capture or his corpse—a small fortune in the local economy. We were sure it would produce some results, or at least make Sayed squirm. After all, there is no honor in a smuggler's town. And he had terrorized, maimed, and murdered so many people that some would probably pay us an equal amount to see him dragged away.

The official reason for hunting Sayed was that he was a major player in the insurgency, with links to its foreign financiers. The unstated reason was that even with Steve-O's father in custody and his mother and siblings gone from town, Sayed still posed a threat to Steve-O. So we made regular visits to his homes and hideouts. We wanted everyone to know that we were stalking him and that we were openly challenging the insurgents for control of the region. We made another unannounced visit to Mr. Sayed's home on January 8, our last official night controlling the border checkpoint before rotating back to Tiger Base for the final portion of our deployment.

Unfortunately, the man who had threatened Steve-O's family was not in to welcome us. Just to be sure that he knew of our eagerness to make his acquaintance, we left his relatives one of the new flyers. During our visit, SFC Evans and SFC Callahan, the two old men on the block, were in tanks screening Ambush Wadi for obvious reasons. Their efforts were rewarded with two rocket-propelled grenades, both of which landed directly between them. Their thermal sights easily picked up their attackers and made quick work of them and the cinder-block wall they thought they were hiding behind.

Our last night at the border checkpoint was a long one. With the start of a new year and our final move back to Tiger Base, we were nearing the end of our time in Iraq, and each of us knew the danger of that. In one month, we'd hit our one-year mark, which meant it would finally be our turn to go home. The enemy did not care that we were short-timers, of course. They were still eager to send us home in body bags. Something else struck us as we were packing up: We hadn't had a single informant show up in a couple weeks. We'd been so busy, we'd hardly noticed, but it made us uneasy when we realized that even the "regulars" who came to trade information for money or food hadn't been around.

Dragon moved back to Tiger Base and began the initial preparations for redeployment. Our lighter duty included security and force protection at the base. We kept up on things in Husaybah from other troops, including the intelligence guys from Special Forces and the OGA. They would stop by and give us the latest on the search for Sayed. We made them promise to include us if they ever thought they'd found him. We knew he was still in the area because his barbaric handiwork was still very much in evidence.

In early February, we learned what had happened to our flow

of informants. A mass grave was discovered in a dusty wadi just outside a small town ten kilometers east of Husaybah. Several of those found in it had been informants for us. This appeared to confirm our long-held suspicion that there were insurgent spies within the Iraqi Civil Defense Corps unit supposedly working with us at the border checkpoint. Their members would have seen informants come and go. They were better than the completely corrupt police, but we suspected there were insurgents among them. Steve-O was not a big fan of their outfit either, and it worried me that their spies had probably tagged him as a target early on. This town was a nightmare for Steve-O, and we were beginning to realize that even if we were able to catch Sayed, Steve-O would have a very, very slim chance of surviving outside the confines of U.S. protection. More and more, I felt the driving need to get Sayed off the streets, and I cared less and less whether it was in a body bag.

Our hopes of capturing him were elevated when Special Forces intelligence contacted us and said they'd had several reports that the Husaybah hospital was being used as a safe house for insurgency personnel and their equipment. There were indications that the hospital, which was in a very strategic location near the main entrance to Husaybah along Highway 12, not far from the marketplace, might also be a hideout for Sayed and some of his black bag henchmen. It was also just across the street from the neighborhood where Steve-O's family and many of the insurgents lived, with the notorious Ambush Wadi right next to it.

Because Dragon already had men and vehicles redeploying, we pulled together a twelve-man team from three different platoons. This seemed like our best opportunity to get Sayed. Then again, this would not be your ordinary raid. I'd never seen so many spooks, covert operators, and men with no names, ranks, or serial numbers. Every special operation branch of the U.S. government appeared to be involved in this one—and there were a few no one seemed to have heard of before. All together, it was a seventy-man team, and at least fifty-eight of them weren't officially there, or anywhere else on the books. "Spook World" was a completely different culture. No one wore name tags. Their "uniforms" were shabby sheik. First names and nicknames only were used in conversation. No straight answers were given.

We were glad to be there among the shaggy-haired, baggy-pants elite. We figured Sayed was our man, and we were determined to bag him and tag him for Steve-O and his mother. In fact, we took the boy along on the raid in case we needed to identify Sayed or his body. I woke Steve-O up at four in the morning and told him it was time. At first, he couldn't shake off the drowsiness. He was disoriented and confused. He sat up, and he lay back down. He had told me the day before that he was eager to go along on the raid if it meant capturing his nemesis. I leaned over him and said just one word that drew him out of bed and to his feet: "Sayed."

He got dressed quickly and joined us as we moved out. It was so dark out that our convoy drivers were using night-vision goggles to see the roads. Steve-O sat in the back of the Humvee. He'd picked up the digital camera we used to show him photos of people we captured. Then he accidentally triggered the camera, sending a bright white flash into the darkness. That set off the entire convoy, throwing everyone into combat mode as radio reports of small-arms fire and an ambush went out. I had to get on the radio pronto and calm everyone down so they didn't start firing at shadows and blow the mission because of a fidgety kid with a flash camera.

Dragon Company hit the hospital complex at seven a.m., targeting four buildings on the east side of the campus. There was no resistance and, unfortunately, no evidence of Sayed, his henchmen, or the weapons cache that had been reported. This was becoming all too familiar. Once again, we were two steps behind him. Steve-O stayed bundled up in the Humvee, wearing a U.S. military uniform with a hood over his head. We rounded up a group of Iraqis in the raid and wanted to see if Steve-O recognized any of them. So we lined them up, then shone high-power flashlights to blind them while Steve-O checked them out from behind the lights in the Humvee. He noted that we'd rounded up men that he knew well, but they were not mujahideen.

The morning sun was reaching for the horizon as we continued the search for weapons. Vendors appeared, opening their stands and shops along Market Street. I saw a butcher slit the throat of a goat. He began skinning it in the open air, drawing hardly any notice from the crowd that had gathered across the street from the hospital's main entrance, drawn by all of our military vehicles, the helicopters, and the early-morning activity. I had Sergeant Vanovermeer move the Humvee, positioning it so Steve-O could remain concealed while checking out the crowd for any hostile faces. After just a few minutes, Vanovermeer waved me over to the Humvee. Steve-O was agitated, doing his "muj dance" as he pointed at the crowd. He unleashed a torrent of Arabic. I understood little of it other than that key phrase again: "mujahideen."

While our heavy-hitting party of special ops spooks was coming up empty-handed inside the hospital grounds, Steve-O had spotted two insurgents strolling the sidewalks nearby. The first, a large man in a black dishdasha, was standing against the corner of the building. He pretended to be bored. Steve-O identified him as a financial source for the insurgency. Then he tagged a second person as one of Sayed's close associates, who'd participated in ambushes on coalition forces.

I rounded up a team to go into the crowd. They moved slowly toward the front of the hospital, trying not to alert their quarry. I briefed the Special Forces captain who was with us. I gave him the names Steve-O had provided for the two people he'd spotted in the crowd. Bingo! Our first hit, the man in black, was on their intelligence hit list as the brother of one of the primary financiers in the city—a top-level target. By the time our two suspects figured out what was going on, they were surrounded. We nabbed them both. In about two seconds, the brother of their black list target gave up his brother's location upstairs in the very same building he'd been leaning against. Within minutes, we'd captured that primary target, who lived up to his billing as a major financier for foreign fighters.

Thanks to Steve-O, our presunrise service was not a bust. He'd helped us capture three insurgents, including a high-value target who had been feeling very smug while watching us search the hospital grounds from his "safe" vantage point across the street. It was a very impressive performance on Steve-O's part— one that drew raves from the special ops troops with us.

BOY BAND

Steve-O's big role in making the hospital raid successful inspired a new series of special missions with him around Husaybah, often with Special Forces intelligence units. These cruising trips were built solely upon Steve-O's ability to pick out insurgents in crowds. We called them "Dragon Drive-Bys" and "Old-School Missions." It was a very simple approach but highly effective. The guerrilla fighters had gotten cocky because they thought we couldn't recognize them on the streets. But Steve-O could. The primary target was always Sayed, but Steve-O had shown that there were other insurgents to watch out for in Husaybah.

Still, even with Steve-O on board, these daytime missions were nerve-racking. There were hundreds of people on the streets, and you never knew who had a weapon beneath a robe or under a table. Normally, the local Iraqi insurgents would not start a firefight in a crowded place and risk getting innocents killed. But we'd seen a major influx of foreign fighters and hired mercenaries who weren't all that concerned about the local population.

The theme music from *Cops* played over and over again through my mind on these drive-bys.

Steve-O wore a protective vest and sat behind ballistic reinforced windows, scanning the crowds for mujahideen. When he spotted a suspect, he'd give us a name that we cross-checked with our target list. If we made a match, we'd send out a team to snag the suspect right off the street. It was a precision strike—the quicker and cleaner the better. Usually, it happened so quickly, there was not enough time for any other Iraqis to react, let alone to put up a fight. Our tactics worked so well that the intelligence forces adopted them.

In early February, we conducted a series of drive-bys and raids that netted some big fish, including more Syrians suspected of financing the insurgency. In one afternoon, we nabbed six high-value targets, including a Sudanese guy with connections to Saudi Arabia, Syria, and Jordan. He was suspected of being a financier for foreign fighters. He would set them up with cash and weapons and then send them to regions around the country.

Another target taken that night was the head of a Husaybah mujahideen cell, who led us to a big weapons cache. We went after that cache a few nights later and found that most of it had been moved, but we did find nine hand grenades and six fuses nearby. We questioned three people at the scene and found out that there were two bodies at the hospital we'd recently raided. We went there and found two of our informants, who had been tortured and killed. While at the hospital, Steve-O identified a jihadist leader connected to Sayed. We took him into custody and turned him over to military intelligence.

It had become almost routine, having this boy around who could see what we could not. At such times, he seemed almost like our good luck charm. Then, at others, he was very much a boy—one who spoke very little English. A female linguist, Sergeant Perkins, had been working with Steve-O, and one of our interpreters, Specialist Habib, was also helping him. But part of the problem was that Steve-O's father had forced him to quit school at a young age. He couldn't read or write in his own language, which hindered his efforts to learn ours.

As it turned out, Steve-O probably learned as much from watching DVDs with me and Capt. Roehrman while we did our paperwork or cleaned our weapons in our living quarters. It became a ritual for Steve-O to join us. With the craziness that we saw outside the wire on a daily basis, it felt good to share some downtime at Tiger Base.

We had a number of movies, but one of our favorite DVDs held a year's worth of episodes of our favorite television show, *24*. It's hard enough to follow all of the plot turns and twists in English, but Steve-O sat with us, enjoying the action scenes. He couldn't understand most of the conversations, but one night, he lit up as a character playing a Middle Eastern terrorist started shouting in Arabic. Steve-O jumped out of his chair in delight.

"I know what he said! I know what he said!"

18

FINGERS AND TOES

Our mission was nearly completed. We were within days of being out of there. On March 11, the U.S. Marines officially were to take over responsibility for Tiger Base, the border checkpoint, and the entire Al Qaim region. During the transition period, the marines asked us to show them the hot spots around Husaybah. We didn't want to push our good luck by exposing ourselves to the insurgents any more than necessary in those final days, but we knew our replacements were in for some rough times. The marines had been given bad information. They'd been told that their role in Husaybah would largely be a peacekeeping mission. We let them know that the only way they'd get any peace was to keep the pressure on the insurgents.

Our raids and patrols had given us an intimate knowledge of the neighborhoods where they hid out and stashed their weapons. Passing on a few tips was the least we could do. Still, it was tough to get back in our vehicles and go out there one more time, knowing that every trip through Husaybah could very easily be our last.

We agreed to accompany them in part because it was a Friday, which is generally the Iraqi version of a Sunday—a day for religious services, peace (or as close to it as Husaybah could get), and relaxation. Yet, I had an uneasy feeling. It isn't wise to tempt fate, and we'd certainly been lucky during our official tour of duty.

We rolled out at one p.m. on Route Penthouse, Highway 12, with two tanks and two Humvees; Steve-O rode with me, looking for another opportunity to catch Sayed by surprise. Spec. Schwartz was aboard as gunner, and Sgt. Betances was the driver. We had the marine company commander and gunnery sergeant in the backseat as observers. As we drove through the city, we pointed out every corner and trash pile where we'd encountered an improvised explosive device, every alley that had served as an ambush site, and every hole in a wall that had been created by rockets that, lucky for us, had missed their mark. We noted the dangers lurking in every landmark of our violent and exhausting tour: Ambush Wadi, the border checkpoint, the old Baath Party headquarters building (what was left of it), and the police station. The marines could only shake their heads in disbelief as we told of all that had gone on in and around Husaybah.

When we passed the hospital and the road to Steve-O's house, I noticed two Iraqi civilians talking and walking arm and arm toward us, totally unaware of our presence. We hadn't seen many people on the street that day, so I was keeping an eye on them. Suddenly, there was a deafening roar. The world erupted around us. I saw one of the two Iraqis in the street come flying directly at us, propelled with his arms and legs sprawled at weird angles. The other Iraqi was launched straight up into the air. I didn't see where either of them landed because our Humvee also was thrown up in the air and hurled backward a couple feet. A shock wave slammed my head back, wrenching my neck and rattling my brain. It felt like a bomb had gone off inside my head.

Crazy Legs was in the tank directly in front of our Humvee. He felt the blast and turned to see our Humvee engulfed in the explosion. He saw two bodies on the ground next to the Humvee and thought it was two of Dragon's soldiers down.

A 155-millimeter IED had been set off ten feet in front of us, right where the two Iraqis were walking. The shock wave of shrapnel, dust, smoke, and debris that had hit us inside our vehicle destroyed the antennae and the vehicle's communications system. After the initial blast, I turned to pull in Spec. Schwartz. I yelled to check on the others as I grabbed at him, but I wasn't sure they heard me. At that point, I could not hear myself because my ears were buzzing so loudly from the explosion. It was like watching TV with the mute button on. All I could hear was the static.

I was seriously worried about Schwartz, who was partially exposed to the blast because he was manning the machine gun atop the Humvee. I couldn't tell if he was even conscious when I looked up at his slumped torso. I dreaded what I might find. I had to get him down inside the vehicle in case the IED was just the first phase of an ambush. I prepared myself to be horrified because he'd taken the blast at close range with little protection. I feared that I might be pulling in a dead man, or at the very least, a severely maimed one.

I was shocked but damn glad to find Schwartz intact. He was stunned and bleeding from shrapnel in his arm, but he was otherwise okay. Still, he was shaken up, and he was not a pretty sight, either. His face was covered with grime from the explosion, and his eyes were bugged out like a cartoon character. But he hadn't had the fight knocked out of him. His instincts kicked in despite the blast he'd taken.

"I gotta get up and shoot," he said as I held him by his shirt.

All he wanted to do was get behind that .50 caliber gun and start shooting. But I kept him inside because the smoke and dust still engulfed us. I next tried to check on the others in the vehicle. The two marines were behind me. One of them had glass fragments in his face and arm, but neither had serious injuries. Our driver, Sgt. Betances, had slammed his head hard against the door of the Humvee and got a concussion, but he came out okay too.

Steve-O grabbed my shoulder. My hearing was on, off, on, off, as if someone were playing with the mute button. I was picking up staccato parts of frantic, high-pitched, streaming Arabic phrases from Steve-O. I asked him if he was hurt. He was so hyper, rocking back and forth in his seat. He didn't respond. I grabbed him by the shoulders and made him look me in the eyes. He finally stopped rocking and screaming. He leaned forward, stuck out his bottom lip, and put his index finger on it to show me a small cut where his mouth had hit the radio on the dash. It was bleeding slightly.

"You're fine. It's a small cut." He looked as if he was going to cry, and I realized: *He is not a soldier, you idiot. He's just a fourteen-year-old boy.* I put my hand on his shoulder and let him know he was okay. But just then, there was a burst of machine-gun fire that seemed to envelop our battered vehicle. That sent Steve-O back over the top. He was about to completely lose it. He had survived the improvised explosive device. But he thought he was going to die in an ambush instead. Smoke and dust still clouded our vision inside the Humvee, but my hearing had cleared up enough for me to recognize the sound of American-made .50 caliber machine guns. It was music to my ears.

"Da baba, Steve-O, *da baba. Da baba coolie zein."* ("Tank, tank. Tank very good.")

I used my fractured Arabic to try to tell him that the machine-gun fire was a good thing. It was the sound of our tanks protecting us from any further ambush. They had seen the remnants of the 155 shell's smoky trail fly in between the vehicles and slam into a building on the north side of the road. They thought they'd spotted the point of origin of an RPG attack. So they were directing their fire at that area. I signaled Steve-O to sit tight. He got the message and calmed down as I tried to make radio contact. But my hearing was still messed up. The armored vehicle had a dozen new air vents and a bulletproof windshield tested to its limits, but Steve-O and I escaped unscathed. If we'd been in a light-skinned Humvee without protective armor, the blast would have killed us all.

The next thirty seconds seemed like an eternity. I told everyone to stay in the Humvee until we could see. My hearing kept going in and out, but I caught the burst of heavy-caliber machine-gun fire. No one else realized that we'd been hit by a homemade bomb of some kind. They'd called it into headquarters as a rocket-propelled grenade attack, so they were blanketing the area to secure it.

I looked to the south next to the outer hospital wall. Two Iraqi civilians were lying in the road, one faceup. That generally was not a good sign, because even seriously wounded people roll over or onto their side to protect their stomachs. The instinct is to cover up your exposed internal organs. The other Iraqi was sprawled facedown. It appeared that they were innocent victims, two friends out for a stroll who were sacrificed by their own people in an effort to kill us.

As soon as we regained our senses after the explosion, we joined the other members of our patrol in responding to the attack. Once the perimeter seemed secure, we did a quick survey and moved north to the buildings that would serve as likely hiding places for whoever had set off the remote-controlled explosives. When we didn't see any signs of our attackers, we took the two civilian Iraqis to the hospital nearby. One was already dead. The second died at the hospital.

The Humvee had two shredded tires, a broken windshield, a punctured radiator, severed oil lines, and shrapnel holes all over the hood. The front windshield, made of three inches of reinforced bulletproof glass, was nearly penetrated by a big piece of shrapnel—

the glass warped four inches into the passenger compartment—that would have likely killed us if the windshield hadn't held.

Steve-O was back to being agitated, and he was driving me nuts. He jabbered at me incomprehensibly on the thirty-minute trip back to the base. Schwartz said he'd been trying to tell him something while we had gone to check the perimeter, but he couldn't understand him and we didn't have an interpreter with us. Once we were back at Tiger Base, Steve-O disappeared for a few minutes and then came running back with an interpreter.

"He saw one of his father's men, Wahid Hamzah, running after the IED exploded," the interpreter said. "He was carrying a battery! He's been trying to tell you!"

I looked in disbelief at the interpreter and Steve-O. We had some unfinished business to attend to.

We'd gone out that fateful day to help the marines get their bearings. Everyone knew that we had tempted fate and cheated death. Especially Schwartz. More than half of his body, his entire upper torso, was exposed to a violent blast that had killed two Iraqis and peppered the armored Humvee with nearly a dozen shrapnel holes. We got a better look at the damage in the maintenance bay at Tiger Base. There was shrapnel damage on the Humvee to the right, left, and just below the machine gunner's position.

I walked back to our living quarters thinking that Schwartz might spend the rest of his life wondering how he dodged death that day. A soldier who has faced death can be paralyzed by the emotional aftershock unless he focuses on the next fight. I didn't want Schwartz to leave Iraq with that near-death experience tainting his memories and weighing on his mind. He deserved better than that. We all deserved better than that. The slumped shoulders and hung heads indicated that this "unnecessary" final patrol could take a heavy toll on the spirits of our men. We'd done our jobs well. Yet, this attack could not go unanswered. We were not going to leave with our tail between our legs. We were going after the person who'd tried to kill us. Though we had walked away relatively unscathed, the next U.S. forces he attacked may not be so lucky. We were not going to leave bloodied and bruised with our ears ringing and our heads hanging. It was demoralizing to get sucker punched like that on the way out the door. Steve-O had handed us the name of the insurgent who triggered the bomb. We had to go after him.

I went straight to Capt. Roehrman. "We cannot let this mujahideen get away with attempted murder just because we are leaving," I told him.

Steve-O knew the triggerman's name, Wahid, and he knew where he lived. He was a major part of the local insurgency. I wanted to bring him in dead or alive. If Schwartz had been killed, there would have been no hesitation. We would have tracked Wahid across the continent. This was personal.

Capt. Roehrman agreed with me. Some of our guys thought we'd left our brains in our helmets, but we convinced them that this was something we had to do. We outlined our plan and gave them four hours to prepare themselves for the midnight mission. I asked SFC Callahan to assign Schwartz to my Humvee. I wanted him to face his fears, and I wanted him to be part of capturing the man who had almost killed him.

When he showed up to start prepping the Humvee, I slapped him on the back. There wasn't a need to talk. He understood why he was there. Steve-O came too. We needed him, and, as always, he wanted to be there. The kid had guts. He'd been scared in the IED explosion. We all had. Yet, he went out with us again without hesitation. We rolled out at two a.m. on February 28. Steve-O led us to the home where Wahid Hamzah lived with his parents. It was just a kilometer south of the explosion site. We came calling with two tanks and two armored Humvees.

Inside, we found a couple of women and five children, along with two men whom Steve-O tentatively identified as Wahid's father and a nephew. We separated them, and I questioned the father through an interpreter. Since we weren't one hundred percent sure this was Wahid's father, I didn't want him to know what we were up to right away. I just asked him to identify all of the children in the house and to tell me about all of his own children. He didn't mention Wahid in his response. Either he was covering for him, or we had the wrong house. Steve-O seemed a little uncertain himself, so that planted some doubts in my mind, too.

The father provided me information that I then leveraged with the nephew. I asked about the other family members by name, giving him the sense that I was well acquainted with the family. It loosened him up. He began offering more information about each family member. Reading from my notepad, I tossed question after question, name after name, to keep him talking. He was going a mile a minute when I threw out that I hadn't seen Wahid or the older sister in the house. He fell for it. He volunteered without thinking that an older sister lived with her husband and that Wahid was staying with his grandfather, Yusif.

I played it cool because I didn't want to give away that Wahid was our primary target. I questioned him first about the sister's husband and kept him chattering for a while until I asked for general directions to Yusif's house. I feared he might be in another city somewhere, but it turned out that the grandfather lived near the Husaybah police station. Bingo! I had tricked the nephew, but I didn't think he would be dim-witted enough to take us directly there. I was banking on Steve-O, who seemed to know everyone in town and their distant relatives. The interpreter and I went to the boy waiting in the back of the Humvee. I told him what we had learned. Once again, Steve-O came through for us.

"Do you mean Yusif—he is very old with three wives, uses a small wooden cane to walk around? I know exactly where he lives."

I went back to the father and asked him again to name all of his kids. He rattled off a few without naming Wahid. I asked why he hadn't included him. The father said he hadn't seen him for more than a year. We knew that was a lie. We packed up the father and nephew, confiscated their house phones, and took them for a ride.

The grandfather's house was just a few minutes away. We went into stealth mode, turning off the engines of our vehicles as we approached. We launched Sgt. Huegerich over the wall. He cleared with a foot to spare. He landed intact, popped up, and unlocked the gate from the inside. Our team swept into the house.

Second Lieutenant O'Halloran was holding a man to the ground when he called me over. I shone my flashlight in his face, and since it was attached to the business end of my M4 carbine, he paid attention when I demanded to know his name.

"Wahid Hamzah," he said.

Got him! I wanted to sing the "Hallelujah Chorus." We'd caught the bastard without losing a man. Now we could go home with our heads held high, knowing that he was going to be locked up for good. I got on the radio and briefed Capt. Roehrman, who was in a tank in the outer cordon: "We got him!"

Our guys went through the roof. The radio exploded with the cheers of the other soldiers. It was better than I had hoped. We caught the guy who'd nearly killed us, and we did it because Steve-O laid eyes on him hightailing it away from the ambush. Steve-O had moved into the gunner's hatch on the Humvee; his mask covered his face, but his eyes were smiling. I looked up at the boy, gave him a high five, and thought: *He does not know the impact he has had on these men. He has become a vital part of this team. He has brought us together and helped us define the insurgency and remove some key players from the streets.*

I felt we owed Steve-O an enormous debt. It had taken me a while to trust him, certainly. In the beginning, I wrote him off as another Iraqi street hustler, a little kid who just wanted a few dollars. I thought he might help us take a few weapons off the streets, but I had no idea that he would play such an important role in our mission in Husaybah. I respected his cunning and powerful survival instincts. He had foresight. He could analyze situations better than many adults I'd known. And he could charm people even when there were huge language and cultural barriers.

But what was this kid capable of? Could the insurgency have planted him with us? They were certainly not above sacrificing some of their own people to get to us. There were times when I wondered if Steve-O was the Iraqi version of a Trojan horse.

It took a long time for him to win me over. He didn't want money, which removed him from the street-hustler category. He was willing to identify insurgents at random, on the street, from computer files, within our own encampment. And he knew all of them, from street fighters to the imams and financiers. If we were being set up by this kid, the insurgents were certainly willing to pay a steep price.

When he'd gone home to check on his family and came back within hours, frantic for our help, it was then that I began to see that Steve-O had been driven to us because we represented the only safe harbor in the violent world he inhabited. He saw through the hypocrisy of his father's actions versus his words. Steve-O had heard his father boast of torturing and beating his fellow Muslims just as he had beaten the boy and his mother. His father continued to place their family in harm's way, and the boy felt his reckless acts would be the death of them all. To understand that was to understand how this son could turn in this father. There was no bond of trust or love between them, only fear and violence.

Steve-O came to us to escape certain death, and he guided us safely through three months of daily violence, ambushes, and attacks. He gave us a much greater understanding of the insurgency, which gave us far greater confidence and made us such an effective force.

My feelings toward Steve-O slowly evolved from an almost hostile suspicion and distrust into a grudging appreciation of his value as an informant and weapon against our enemy. And then it got more personal as I saw the price he and his family paid. The more thoughtful soldiers in our camp came to see Steve-O as a symbol of Iraq itself—a nation at war with itself more than with any outside force.

As a company of soldiers, we had gone through our own process of evolution. As Dragon Company came together, adapted, and took control of its operations in this violent place, Steve-O became a personal reason for our involvement. If this little boy could stand up to the brutality of the insurgency, then there was a sliver of hope that others would too. He was our starting point for winning the bigger battle. He gave us direction and information. He gave us a purpose amid the chaos. He gave us hope that our presence in this tormented country might have a positive impact on the lives of its good and innocent people.

19

A SOLDIER LEFT BEHIND

JOURNAL ENTRY: MARCH 4, 2004
*One of the toughest days I have dealt with since I have been
in this godforsaken country.*

This being Husaybah, our victory celebration over the capture of
Wahid was not an extended affair. We got back to Tiger Base at
five a.m., and I think I was already asleep as I walked to my cot
and collapsed. Two hours later, two huge explosions rocked us
out of our cots. A pair of 107-millimeter rockets hit just four hundred meters from our building. The insurgents had intelligence of
their own. They knew that we were not at full force because several of our units had already moved out for home. Most of our
marine replacements would not arrive for a couple more days.

Steve-O told me that he'd picked up on some Iraqis talking
about this at a pizza joint by the base where he sometimes went
to hang out. They didn't know him there, so he was able to pick
up local gossip and other information. He'd heard that the insurgents had *mu zein* ("no good") spies within the base camp and at
the border checkpoint. They were aware that the squadron's air

support, our attack helicopters, had already been shipped home. We were without continuous air coverage in the vast expanse of the desert between Tiger Base and the numerous cities along Highway 12 in Al Qaim. The insurgents were emboldened by our vulnerability. There would be no winding-down time. The remainder of Dragon Company would have to fight our way to the very end of our deployment here.

The next couple nights of combat patrols attracted no ambushes or attacks. We took advantage of the calm to plan one final raid before we shipped out. As our marine replacements began operations in Al Qaim, I made sure they understood what Steve-O had done for the American forces here and how important it was that he was protected even after Dragon Company shipped out. They got it. But I still wanted to make one final run at the guy who had put a bounty on his head: Sayed.

At two o'clock in the morning on March 4, 2004, we conducted a combat patrol with two tanks and two Humvees along Highway 12, then veered off into the residential area toward Sayed's main residence. Steve-O rode in my Humvee and stayed in the vehicle when we hit the house.

Sayed was nowhere to be found, but we did nab another guy in the house. We photographed him and took the camera to Steve-O, who identified him as Sayed's brother Qadir. Steve-O said Qadir was active in anticoalition efforts in the area. Qadir told the interpreter that he'd just gotten out of the Baghdad prison. He wore a wristband that seemed to confirm that, but it later turned out that he was a high-value target. Qadir had been let go because there was not enough evidence against him. Steve-O once again changed all of that. He named times, places, events, and attacks that Qadir had been involved in, ensuring that he would be making a return trip to our prison for insurgents.

We had finished checking around Sayed's house and were preparing to head back to Tiger Base when Steve-O asked if we could stop by his house first. It was just next door. He wanted to check it out and grab some family photos and any of his clothes that were still there. He also mentioned that his father had hidden a weapon under the floorboards that might still be there. I didn't think it was a good idea to send him in. I asked SFC Evans and S.Sgt. Guetschow to go check it out first. We didn't want any surprises facing Steve-O when he entered his house.

I was standing in the door of my Humvee, radioing my report on the capture of Sayed's brother. My vehicle was parked outside Steve-O's house, and I could see the team entering from the back. I saw the inside light come on and then watched their outlines pass slowly in front of the windows. In the stillness of the night, I heard SFC Evans yell from inside the house, "Top, you need to come see this!"

I had worked with SFC Evans long enough to know that he was not an easily excitable man. His tone made my heart race. I didn't want to go into Steve-O's house for fear of what might have happened. *Please don't let it be what I think it is!*

I had a couple guys stay with Steve-O while I walked into the house. It was a mess. A stench hit me as soon as I walked inside. I feared the worst, but it turned out to be coming from food rotting in the open refrigerator. There was mold everywhere—on the food, the counters, the stove. It didn't look like Steve-O's mother and siblings had packed up and taken off. It looked like someone had come in while they were still there and interrupted a meal being prepared. I had a bad feeling about what had happened. Every room was torn apart. There were holes punched in the walls. Furniture was upended and thrown around. Something or someone had come in and halted the family's preparations.

I remembered the mother's words to me months before. She said they were leaving as soon as they packed their bags. I'd given her money to pay for their journey. Why didn't she leave? It was a small fortune by Iraqi standards, enough to easily sustain her and her children in Baghdad for six months to a year. That was in December. It was now March. From the state of the house, it looked like they never got out of Husaybah. For over two months, I'd thought they were safe. I'd been relieved that they'd gotten out of town. I had to find out what happened to them.

When I returned to the Humvee, I tried not to let Steve-O see my fears. I went to him with the interpreter and asked him if he had any relatives living nearby. He said an uncle lived right behind his house. Leaving Steve-O, I took SFC Evans and S.Sgt. Guetschow and the interpreter to the uncle's house. We were pretty upset about what we'd seen. Our adrenaline was flowing. This was not a part of town where you just walked around in the middle of the night knocking on doors and asking questions. We didn't know if the uncle was from the mother's or the father's side, so we didn't know his level of involvement with the insurgency. So we dispensed with the niceties.

Guetschow stepped back and kicked the door, but he kicked it so hard, his leg went right through the wood and got stuck there. Evans stepped up and kicked the door too, with Guetschow's foot still lodged in it. This time, it flew open, and Guetschow went sprawling. It wasn't the cleanest forcible entry on military record. But we did find the uncle inside and took him outdoors for questioning.

Through our interpreter, he relayed the events that had transpired after our departure that morning in December. My fears were confirmed. Sayed and his men had come to the boy's house a few hours after we'd left. The uncle's story was hard to decipher, even with an interpreter, but one thing was clear: Sayed had beaten and tortured Steve-O's mother again and then shot her in the stomach. The uncle had heard that she later died, but he could not confirm it.

I felt nauseous. I glanced over at my Humvee, where Steve-O remained hidden. The pain ripped through me. How the hell was

I going to tell this little kid that his mother had been mortally shot by Sayed? According to the uncle, Steve-O's brothers and sisters had been taken by relatives to live with their grandfather in Fallujah. His story seemed shaky. I asked the interpreter to keep grilling him. He admitted that he had heard some recent rumors that the mother might still be alive, but no one seemed to know where she might be. My gut was churning so badly, I could hardly stand. I turned toward the Humvee, dreading the implications of what I'd learned. On the best days, it is difficult to sort out the truth in Iraq. But it appeared that there was little chance that Steve-O's mother was alive.

It would have been hard to believe the uncle's account, except for the condition of the house. As I walked to the Humvee, my nausea was giving way to anger. I was angry at myself for allowing this to happen, angry at the mother for not leaving when I told her to, and angry about feeling so helpless.

Steve-O seemed to sense something was wrong. But when I got back to the Humvee, I told him that his family was in Fallujah and that he couldn't go into the house because of possible booby traps left by Sayed. Downtown Husaybah was not the place for telling a boy such news. There were too many spies watching, too many places for Steve-O to run and hide if he lost it. I didn't know how he would react, so I had to protect him from the worst of it for now.

Back at Tiger Base, I let Steve-O get a few hours of sleep while I tossed and turned. I finally got up and dressed, with a heavy sadness weighing on me. I went to Steve-O's room and told him we needed to go to squadron headquarters. I had already told the interpreter that we would meet him there to discuss what we'd found at the house. In a year full of tough situations, this was one of the hardest things I had to do. Steve-O is a sharp, sensitive kid. I knew he would realize that his mother's death, if she was really dead, was the direct result of his coming to us.

I explained to Steve-O that we hadn't been able to find Sayed and that there were reports that he had gotten to his mother. I told him we weren't sure exactly what had happened to her because of varying reports, but there was a strong chance she'd been shot. I couldn't bring myself to tell him the rest because I really didn't know what was true myself. I did tell him that his brothers and sisters were reportedly living with his grandfather in Fallujah.

Steve-O looked away from me as the interpreter relayed what I had said. He stared off into the desert, and I could see tears rolling down his cheeks. He was quiet for a long stretch. I could tell that he was letting this news sink in. His arms began to shake. He crossed them to maintain his composure while he stared off into the desert. His face was stoic, though his tears gave away his feelings. They were so big, I could see them trailing down his arms. I had no concept of the emotional turmoil he was going through, but I would have given anything to take it away from him at that moment.

He finally turned his head toward me and matter-of-factly said, "I'm going to go and find Sayed myself and kill him."

His voice was strong, the determination fierce. I believed that given the chance, he would kill Sayed. But I couldn't let him leave. I told him to leave Sayed to us. I promised that he would go on any missions that targeted him. I hugged him and felt him stifle a sob.

"Steve-O, I have never kept anything from you, even this. I will get you out of Husaybah and Iraq. I don't know how yet, but I promise I will. If you try to find Sayed, I won't be able to protect you. Do you understand that?" He nodded. "You have to trust me."

I told him I was determined to do whatever it took to help him. He got up and said he wanted to be alone, but I ordered two soldiers not to let him out of their sight, to make sure he didn't go after Sayed. He was an incredibly resourceful kid and more resilient than anyone I'd ever known. *No fourteen-year-old should have to go through what he's endured,* I thought. It struck me that even though I didn't have a son, I was feeling the sort of emotions a father must feel. It was an overpowering sensation, beyond even the protective instincts I had developed for the soldiers in my charge.

After speaking with Steve-O, I was more determined than ever to get him out of there. At squadron headquarters, I called anyone and everyone who might be of help, including the Special Forces chaplain, our CIA contact to the Coalition Provisional Authority in Baghdad, everyone in my chain of command, and even some of the media contacts I'd made. I also searched the Internet for information on adoption, political asylum, and other avenues that might help me to get Steve-O out.

A few days later, as the sun was setting, I saw Steve-O and another young Iraqi boy kicking a soccer ball back and forth at the base camp. They were darting in and out, trying to catch each other, and running around like they didn't have a care in the world. It was a rare glimpse of Steve-O as a young teenager, doing what kids his age in any country should be doing. I knew just how deceptive that vision of normalcy was. Steve-O saw me and waved good-bye to the other kid, kicking the soccer ball as he jogged over. When he got to me, he flashed his warm smile, but I could see the pain still lingering in his eyes. It had been only forty-eight hours since I had told him about his mother.

I pulled him close to me and said, "You are an amazing kid, Steve-O. I hope you know that. Don't let the craziness of this place ever break your spirit!"

As I ruffled his hair, I knew he couldn't understand a word I was saying. He just looked up at me, smiled, and we walked back to the tactical operations center with my arm around his shoulder.

FAMILY DECISION

That night, I called Christina and told her that it looked like Steve-O's mother had been killed in retaliation for turning his father in to coalition forces. As always, she cut right to the heart of the matter: "You have to get him out of there. He can't ever go back. They'll kill him, too," she said.

This was a new type of battle for me. I wasn't sure where to begin. I didn't know whom to target. So I sent this report to Christina and anyone and everyone who might be able to help me get Steve-O out of Iraq.

> **Report on Jamil**
>
> On December 3, 2003, an Iraqi boy who came to be known as informant "Steve-O," age fourteen, walked into the Husaybah border checkpoint and alerted Dragon Company, Tiger Squadron, Third Armored Cavalry Regiment, that his father was going to kill him because he wanted to help coalition forces. Steve-O said his father was connected to mujahideen and a prior Iraqi army major. Steve-O stated that his dad had buried multiple RPGs, explosives, and weapons in his yard and that coalition forces missed the weapons during the search of his house. Steve-O also said he knew the names of forty mujahideen fighters in the region.
>
> The information was acted upon, and Dragon Company found a weapons cache of rockets, RPGs, and hand grenades. The father and a mujahideen fighter were detained and sent to FOB [Forward Operating Base] Tiger. The father had links to other black listed personnel, one of whom is Sayed Atta Ali, a cell leader and primary player in attacks on

coalition forces within the Al Qaim region.

After the detention of Steve-O's father, Sayed threatened his mother as to his whereabouts and physically beat her. Sayed knows that Steve-O helped coalition forces and will kill him if given the chance. If Steve-O were to go back to Husaybah or the Al Qaim region, he would be killed. Steve-O has been very helpful as a secondary source on Husaybah mujahideen and has currently helped identify over thirty by name and their actions against coalition forces.

As Third Armored Cavalry Regiment prepares for redeployment to CONUS [the continental United States], we want to ensure there is a solid plan for Steve-O and his relocation. We are trying to get information on relocation within a different region or province of Iraq and also the possibility of relocating him to the United States. Steve-O has stated he would go to the U.S. Any and all information as to the process of relocation, or agencies that could assist, would be helpful and greatly appreciated. Steve-O has made moral decisions that most of us can't fathom making at any age, much less at thirteen or fourteen. We have been inspired by his actions and want to ensure that the Third Armored Cavalry Regiment does everything within its power to help this boy succeed in a very tough situation.

Update: Dragon conducted final raid to locate Sayed in March 2004 and confirmed through Steve-O's relatives that his mother had been shot and killed by Sayed.

Everywhere I turned, whether it was the Pentagon, the Department of Homeland Security, or the State Department, people were sympathetic to, even inspired by, Steve-O's story. But each and every one of them also said that there were formidable obstacles to relocating an Iraqi boy to the United States, especially a Muslim child with at least one parent still alive. There just was not a process for doing such a thing. His situation was unlike anything the bureaucracy had ever encountered. No one had a clue as to how to begin.

Technically, he was not an orphan, which limited our options considerably. Adoption by an American couple was out of the question due to strong laws in the Arab world that prohibit Westerners from adopting Muslim children. Besides, Steve-O's father was still alive, and there was no confirmation of his mother's death. My deployment was rapidly coming to an end. I was excited about returning home to my beautiful wife and a place where I wouldn't have to fear for my life every minute and every hour of the day. Yet, there was this ache in my chest every time I thought about leaving Steve-O.

I sat down with Capt. Roehrman, and we talked over our options for getting Steve-O to safety. We ultimately came to the decision that our only realistic option was to take him at least to Kuwait. We didn't think we could get him on a military airplane because of the paperwork involved in asking permission to put an Iraqi boy on a government flight. So I decided to take him out of Husaybah by Humvee convoy.

Capt. Roehrman and I knew this wasn't an ideal option, but there didn't appear to be any alternatives. We couldn't think of a way to do it through approved channels. We thought if we could get him into Kuwait, we could talk to the State Department at the Kuwait embassy. We were hoping to either find a way to get him to the United States or put him in a protective situation with our soldiers in Kuwait. Still, there were major concerns with that plan.

For one thing, Kuwaitis are not huge fans of Iraqis of any age group, and neither the captain nor I had personal contacts among military personnel stationed long term in Kuwait. So there was no guarantee we would find someone there to take responsibility for his safety. The legality was shaky, to say the least. We were putting ourselves on the line. There's nothing like triggering an international incident to put a kink in one's military career. We simply knew that we could not leave Steve-O in Iraq. If we did, he would be killed.

A few days after my discouraging talk with Capt. Roehrman, a more viable solution presented itself. Lieutenant Colonel Lopez and Command Sergeant Major Huff of 3–7 Infantry Battalion, First Marine Division, formed the command leadership of the marine infantry battalion replacing our unit. I was in the open-bay living area when they walked in with First Sergeant Gowdy from Tiger Squadron. He was giving them the grand tour of their new digs. Gowdy had helped me get Steve-O's story to the media. Part of his job was to supervise the visits of the news media in the region, so he had been very good about hooking me up with a lot of them.

To my everlasting gratitude, 1st Sgt. Gowdy introduced me to the marines: "This is First Sergeant Hendrex. He has been taking care of Steve-O, the Iraqi boy I was telling you about."

Lt. Col. Lopez looked at me intently, the way colonels tend to do. Then, to my surprise, he said that he'd heard a lot of amazing things about Steve-O and the assistance he'd given Dragon Company. He complimented us on all that we'd done in a very difficult situation. "I read his story, and First Sergeant Gowdy has filled us in on the details of what you are trying to do to get him out of here. If you need to, my sergeant major and I will take care of him while you do what you need to do to get him out. This is a return visit for many of us, and we still have several connections with Iraqis whom we worked with in Najaf. They are now very close and personal friends."

My instincts told me Lt. Col. Lopez was a man of his word. This gave me a little breathing room to work on a long-term solution that would keep me and Capt. Roehrman out of jail. As I shook his hand and took him up on his offer, I felt hopeful for the first time that this might actually work out.

It was mid-afternoon at Tiger Base on March 9, 2004. We were just two days from our departure date. The marines took a huge burden off my shoulders when Lt. Col. Lopez said they would be glad to protect and care for Steve-O until I could work out a way to get him safely out of Iraq and, hopefully, into the United States. I could tell he was sincere. He understood what Steve-O meant to our guys. He felt that Steve-O could be of value to his men, too. I still had not a clue as to how I was going to get Steve-O out of Iraq, but it was a great relief to know that he would be safe with Lt. Col. Lopez's men.

LEAVING STEVE-O

Our marine replacements were packed eight to the room—twice the number we'd had—in the barracks at Tiger Base on the outskirts of Husaybah. At six thirty a.m. on March 11, First Sergeant Francois led me through the maze of bunks and cots and wood partitions to Steve-O's bed. I pushed aside a plastic poncho that had been draped over the door to block the hall light. There were eight cots inside. Seven men and one boy. Steve-O looked tiny and fragile in his cot, surrounded by huge, snoring men with arms bigger than Steve-O's whole body. I shook his shoulder gently, and he looked up as I told him, "I have to go, buddy."

He turned and sat up with his back to me, rubbing his eyes and stretching to clear his head. Leaving my old platoon at the dam in Haditha had been tough. Telling this boy that his mother had been shot and was probably dead was heart-wrenching. And now saying good-bye was ripping me to the core. I played up the fact that this was just a temporary separation, but I had no idea what the future had in store for this kid who had come to mean so much to me and all the guys in Dragon Company. Every time I'd had to say good-bye to Christina, I knew that as long as nothing killed me, we would be reunited. I didn't have any such assurances with Steve-O. So far, all I had encountered was red tape and brick walls and people who wished they could help but were unable to.

Steve-O wasn't much for staring into anyone's eyes. He was too self-conscious about his damaged pupil. He looked down and kicked his feet in the air. His English was coming along, but it was still very rudimentary. My Arabic was limited to barked orders and curt questions. I'm not sure either one of us would have known what to say if we could have communicated in depth. As it was, I squeezed his shoulder and felt my throat tighten as I handed him a picture of us together.

"Steve-O, I promise to get you out of here," I said, looking him in the eye. "I promise. I even wrote it down on this piece of paper for you. See here? It says: 'You're an incredible kid! Stay safe while we do everything we can to get you out of here.'"

It was difficult to get the words out as I handed him my IOU. I'd never had such paternal feelings and emotions, and even though I'd practiced this farewell, I was choking up badly. I was about to turn and go when I remembered that I had one more gift for Steve-O. He always liked to swipe my floppy desert hat with my name stitched on it and then strut around wearing it. I'd had to chase him down more than once to get it back. Now, struggling with my emotions, I handed it to him and told him that I expected him to return it to me in good shape the next time I saw him.

He held the hat in his hand, stood up, and then fell against me, shaking, as I gave him one last hug with tears welling up in my eyes. "Remember, Steve-O," I said, bending down to squeeze his other hand as he clutched my note, "I promise." After one last pat on the head, I left him beside his cot.

Sgt. Johnson was waiting for me in a Humvee outside. I was so torn up, I couldn't speak. I just stared ahead. Sgt. Johnson kindly left me to my thoughts. I was struggling to keep it together as we drove off. The enormity of all that had occurred in that year hit me in a wave of emotion. Images rolled through my mind. I swear I relived every ambush, explosion, and intense moment of the deployment before we'd driven three miles into the desert.

I felt miserable leaving Steve-O behind. He'd lived up to his promises. I'd failed to live up to mine. I was leaving. He was still in danger. Initially, I'd been relieved that the marines were going to look after him. But it hit me even as we were pulling out that they were going to have their hands full in Husaybah. The insurgents would quickly figure out that they had neither heavy armor nor tanks. Then all hell would break loose. How long would the marines be able to protect Steve-O under those circumstances?

Every first sergeant focuses on bringing his soldiers home. Steve-O had become a valuable part of Dragon Company: He'd helped to define us and our mission; he'd given us our only hope that we might be accomplishing something through all of our sacrifices; he had helped us see the human side of Iraq and the suffering of the innocent people in it. In return, he'd lost his family. We were his family now; the men of Dragon Company were his new family. And there we were, abandoning him.

I was leaving a man behind—something I had vowed that I would never do.

20

UNFINISHED BUSINESS

JOURNAL ENTRY: MARCH 14, 2004
The first thing I did in Kuwait: used the satellite phone while on Highway 80 to call the one person who makes this all worth while. Christina, I love you.

When the last of Dragon Company reached the border and crossed into Kuwait on March 14 at 9:25 a.m., waves of relief swept over all of us. It was not just a psychological thing. It was definitely physical, too. In all of my deployments, I've never seen it so openly and universally expressed. Grown men were hugging each other and laughing. We'd survived! Each of us felt the burden lifting, the easing of tension, the unknotting of muscles. It seemed like we'd awakened from a long, tormented sleep to discover that the world was still there, and, remarkably, we still had family, friends, and lives to enjoy.

It was pure torture to spend the last two days of a deployment traveling through five hundred miles of the most treacherous territory in light-skinned Humvees. We had to pass through a series of hostile hellholes. The insurgents were well aware of our comings and goings. It wouldn't take much for them to realize how vulnerable we were on this two-day scramble across the desert.

Sixty percent of our company had already flown back, so we were not at full strength. Our tanks had been taken south for shipping. We were traveling in vehicles that we had not dared to drive in Husaybah because of all the mines and ambushes. In Husaybah, it would have been considered suicide. I hadn't been in a light-skinned Humvee in more than six months. For this journey, we lined them with bulletproof Kevlar blankets, then we put double-layered sandbags on the floorboards and taped old flak vests (Vietnam style) and chicken vests (tank crewman Kevlar) to the plastic doors. We also attached quarter-inch plates of steel to the frames in critical areas. I could barely see the driver behind me because he was almost completely wrapped up in a large Kevlar blanket. It would have been comical except that the danger was very real. We looked like remnants of some postapocalyptic army, a Mad Max convoy through the badlands.

It was a long, strange journey, like traveling backward through time. We passed through places that we hadn't seen since early in our deployment. I later told Christina that at first I couldn't believe that a year had gone by so quickly; but then when we started seeing these familiar landmarks and towns in the desert—places where we'd had these incredibly intense experiences—I suddenly felt like I'd been gone ten years or more. I had to fight off waves of disorientation and emotions related to the intense physical and mental stress that we'd gone through for the past year.

It's odd, the things that struck me. As we got farther south and away from the areas racked by violence, I couldn't get over the fact that soldiers were moving around so carefree in single vehicle convoys. Here, light-skinned Humvees seemed the norm. Soldiers wore very little protective gear. It began to hit me hard that our Iraq experience was far different from that of many other

American soldiers at that point. At the border, we'd taken the full brunt of the insurgency's brewing storm as it grew stronger day by day, fed by fresh bands of foreign fighters and weaponry.

Even after we reached Kuwait, we were not out of danger. Redeployment—the limbolike stage in which you are moving on to the next assignment—can be a very dangerous period. Soldiers can easily get injured or killed because they've dropped their guard or neglected to follow their training as things wind down. We tried to keep that in mind during our two weeks of preparations for the final leg of our journey. It seemed like time slowed down just to torment us as we cleaned and loaded our tanks, auxiliary equipment, weapons, and personal gear. It was very tough to keep everyone focused as they looked ahead to reuniting with loved ones, family, and friends.

Capt. Roehrman and I took time away from our preparations to visit the U.S. embassy in search of a way to get Steve-O out of Iraq. The people there gave us information on things like adoption, humanitarian parole, political asylum, and refugee status, but they didn't offer much hope that any of those routes would work out. One official cautioned me that if the press learned that I was trying to get Steve-O out for his safety, they might play it up as a sign of weakness or fear. We didn't want this to be interpreted as an indication that our military was so uncertain of its control of Iraq that it couldn't protect a fourteen-year-old boy from his own people. The embassy official made her point. My mission to help Steve-O could have international repercussions if I wasn't careful. Point taken.

I drove away from the U.S. embassy feeling like we'd lost ground in our efforts to get Steve-O to safety. How naive could I have been? I actually thought that I could get the U.S. Marines to fly him to Kuwait so he could join the members of Dragon Company for our homecoming in Colorado Springs. Getting my men out of Iraq without a casualty was hard, and getting Steve-O to safety was proving just as difficult.

Back at home, Christina went to work on behalf of Steve-O even before we were out of the Middle East. She and her mother contacted the offices of congresspeople, network television shows, and local affiliates, trying to drum up interest in our mission to get Steve-O out of Iraq. They, too, kept hearing how difficult a task it would be. After two weeks of working on his case while in Kuwait, I had to concede that I was not going to get Steve-O out before I returned home.

On March 29, 2004, we boarded a 747 civilian chartered flight to America. We had one layover—three hours in Prague in the Czech Republic. Upon our arrival in Prague, Lieutenant Colonel Reilly arranged to have an airport bar sectioned off for all 270 of our soldiers. It had been a very tough year. This was our first contact with alcohol. As I walked into the bar, it was pandemonium. Off to the right, three very attractive eastern European women were tending the bar. After a year of being around primarily men, the sight of females was welcome. The bar was surrounded by a ten-man front line going four deep. All of them were vying to get the attention of the three bartenders, who earned more in tips during those few hours than they had all month. There were also a few marriage proposals thrown their way.

An hour and a half into our party in Prague, with many dark Czech ales polished off, we began to truly relax for the first time in a long time. Finally, we felt free to talk about what we'd accomplished in Husaybah without fear of jinxing anything. The alcohol allowed the stories, laughter, and tears to flow. It was an amazing two hours. The emotions were overwhelming. The one universal feeling was that Dragon Company had been blessed. We'd survived and accomplished a great deal under relentless attacks and ambushes from October 2003 to February 2004. We were all amazed that we had not sustained any serious casualties in an environment of daily violence.

Stories came pouring out of the soldiers, and many were

about Steve-O. The boy was part of each soldier's experience in Iraq and at the heart of our success. Hope is a dangerous companion in a setting as violent and hostile as Iraq. But at that point, it was okay to think once again about holding Christina and returning to a "normal" life. And so I allowed myself that happiness for the first time in a year of putting survival first. Still, the image of a dark-haired boy kept coming into my mind.

HOMECOMING

As our military plane pulled away from Prague, I closed my eyes and slept easily for the first time in a long, long time. I woke up just before we touched down in Colorado Springs. It was the shortest ten-hour flight I had ever been on. We cheered, yelled, and laughed as we landed and taxied in at three a.m.

With all of my deployments around the world, I'd never really experienced a big, public welcome home ceremony. I'd returned to my home base in Germany after Operation Desert Storm, so it wasn't exactly a real homecoming. Christina and I had generally celebrated these returns from deployment quietly, which was fine with me. But Fort Carson went all out for our return from Operation Iraqi Freedom. Christina had written to me about similar ceremonies held for troops around the country. She said the military was making certain that returning soldiers knew they were appreciated. Our welcome home ceremony was at five a.m., so I knew Christina would be up before dawn to get ready, and then she would probably have to drive 100 mph to get there on time.

The mountain air left me gasping when we got off the plane and boarded buses for the final, short leg of our journey. I couldn't get enough in my lungs, but it was a wonderful feeling to breathe in clean, crisp air, free of sand, for a change. We saw the traffic jam of arriving families as our buses pulled into the base, and it struck me—as it would again and again in the coming weeks—just how lucky we were to be bringing everyone home safely.

I couldn't wait to see Christina and to hold her again. The Special Events Center was packed. Patriotic songs blasted from speakers as we marched in. The screams and cheering shattered any attempt to control emotions, unleashing a gloriously messy, blubbering sob-fest. It was all I could do to restrain myself from bolting from the formation, sweeping up Christina, and hauling ass out of there. The ceremony seemed to go on for an eternity. It was nice to be honored and welcomed and appreciated, but all we really wanted was to grab our loved ones and go home. It was time to return to civilian life. We wanted to be regular people for a while. Not soldiers. Not Americans. Not targets. Not enforcers. Not peacekeepers. Just people.

I spotted Christina just as we were dismissed, amid the ensuing chaos. Families and soldiers rushed at each other. People intertwined in a mass of uniforms and colors. I waded through the crowd, trying to keep my eyes on the top of her head. Still, it was hard to ignore the dramatic reunions of husbands and wives, sons with parents, fathers with children they'd never seen.

And then, in a moment, there she was! Christina, standing in front of me, in the flesh. Not in a dream. Suddenly, the world was right again. It was perhaps the most intense, emotional moment we've ever shared—with the possible exception of the birth of our daughter, Sydney, which would take place almost three hours and nine months later.

21

A NEW MISSION

Christina still teases me that the first thing I did after we pulled into the driveway of our house was grab the garbage cans and bring them in from the curb. But doing something so normal seemed important to me at the time. It was like reclaiming my true identity. The days that followed were blissful. It always takes a while to get reoriented to a world where no one is attempting to shoot, ambush, or blow you up every few hours.

But as soon as I was back with Christina, we fell into a nice routine almost immediately: Waking up in a comfortable bed (a bed with sheets, a comforter, and pillows!), having a cup of coffee on the back porch, walking barefoot on soft carpet, daily chores, going to the store—it all fell into place so easily. We prolonged our honeymoon and took a long vacation in a convertible, cruising the Pacific Coast Highway from Portland, Oregon, to Los Angeles, California.

Two weeks later, I returned to Fort Carson in Colorado Springs, to a desk job. The routine was comforting and welcomed, but being back in a military setting reminded me that I still had one big bit of unfinished business awaiting me in Iraq. I had made a promise to Steve-O and to myself, and I was sure as hell going to keep it.

Other soldiers were moving back into their everyday lives with their families too. Most did their best not to think about what we'd been through in Iraq, let alone what was going on there in our absence. As great as it was to be home, that was tough to deal with emotionally. I would catch myself wondering if the entire thing had just been a dream—the hardships, the heat, the mortars, the IEDs, the small-arms fire, the RPGs, the land mines, the raids . . . It all began to feel like a very distant memory, almost like it never happened.

I had told Christina very little about what Dragon Company actually did in Iraq. Like I said earlier, I hadn't lied; I had just given her the PG-13 version of my deployment. But keeping a journal allowed me to help her understand the year that I'd had, and it helped me deal with what had happened over there too. As soon as I started reading through it, the memories came flooding back with Technicolor clarity, which, believe it or not, was a good thing. Framing emotional events that could easily be mixed and confused chronologically kept me from thinking that I was going crazy. I would have never been able to explain the operations and my feelings logically if not for that journal. It also left nothing to hide, detailing every contact with the enemy and every mission we conducted. I think it scared the hell out of Christina the first time she read it.

Returning as a unit also has a major positive effect. Being able to talk with or have a beer (or two or three) with those who had just suffered the same hardships and emotions is a great way of healing. Only those who were with you can truly understand.

Reintegration into civilian life was a little tougher. At first, I found large crowds at the mall or in a store nerve-racking. Too many people moving in too many directions and way too damn close to me. It was hard to keep my eyes on them all. Loud, unexpected noises were the worst. The backfire of a car in a parking lot, the slam of a door, the clang of an object hitting the ground—these were things that sent a jolt of electricity through my nervous system, made every muscle in my body tense, and had me scanning the surroundings for cover. (The most ironic fact of all is that I am now not a big fan of huge fireworks on the Fourth of July.)

Oddly enough, driving was one of the biggest adjustments. In Iraq, we owned the road. We waved oncoming traffic over (due to vehicle bomb threats) and ensured that civilian cars maintained their distance from our convoys and patrols. A car getting too close to your convoy in Iraq would put you in a heightened state of awareness and a hair trigger away from contact. After a year of driving down the middle of the highway and forcing all civilian vehicles off the road, I feared my own road rage in making a simple trip to Blockbuster to rent a movie.

For the most part, though, returning to the United States had a really calming effect on me. I had felt no attachment to Iraq or to its people after the Gulf War. I accepted my second deployment as my duty and returned feeling nothing for the nation. I knew people had suffered under Saddam Hussein's dictatorship, just as others had suffered in Somalia and Bosnia, and I felt what humans usually feel for the victims of oppression and cruelty. Still, somehow, I did not relate to the Iraqis.

In the first several months of my second deployment there, I found little to change that. Steve-O was the first Iraqi for whom I felt anything. It was the same for most of the members of Dragon Company and for the other soldiers in Husaybah. We knew him and his family. For many of us, Steve-O represented our hopes for Iraq. He had rejected his father's hatred of Americans. He'd seen how our soldiers treated people on the streets, and Steve-O had decided that we could be trusted. He represented a first step on a bridge over a wide cultural chasm.

In the tribal culture of his country, revenge and retribution are passed down like dark family heirlooms from generation to generation. I did not need a reminder of that, but I got one anyway. I learned that shortly after we'd left, these twin eight-year-old boys who'd become regulars around the border checkpoint were hanged from a two-story balcony by the insurgents. The boys and their father had been tortured and killed because they'd sold sodas to our soldiers. Without a doubt, Steve-O would never be able to walk out of the camp without being seized and killed.

With his mother and siblings gone from Husaybah and their fates unknown—and his father still in an American military prison—Steve-O really had no home. As a fourteen-year-old boy, he'd made a decision that the American soldiers were his only hope to escape death. Now fate had placed his continued survival in my hands.

Christina shared my sense of responsibility and jumped into action. As I mentioned, she'd contacted the offices and aides of several members of Congress. Her mother did the same from Florida. Once I got home, I tried to stir up interest in Steve-O's case by e-mailing information to the Web sites of network news and talk shows. I also explored the legalities of bringing him to the United States and serving as his guardian. From the start, we were told that adoption was still not an option. His father was not likely to give his consent, and even if he did, Muslim laws prohibit children of their faith from being adopted by non-Muslims.

Steve-O seemed to be a natural candidate to apply for refugee status or political asylum. Millions of people are admitted to the United States each year through these processes. But his case was complicated by the fact that he was a minor, his father was a U.S. prisoner of war, his mother's fate was uncertain, and there were many known adult relatives still living in Iraq. His relatives were primarily Sunni Muslim and heavily involved in the insurgency. His grandfather lived in Fallujah. None of his relatives would look kindly upon his actions, regardless of the circumstances. If they didn't kill Steve-O themselves, he would have been quickly handed over to Sayed or some other cutthroat.

It was also true that Steve-O didn't exactly fit neatly into any one category. A refugee is generally someone living outside his or her homeland who can't or doesn't want to return because of fear of persecution. Political asylum is generally applied for by someone already living in the United States, even if the person is an illegal resident. Again, Steve-O's unique situation and the potentially volatile issues of his age, religion, and his parents' status greatly complicated matters. Most of all, we didn't want to set off an international political controversy that could result in him being sent back to a certain death in Iraq. I kept having this recurring thought of some official demanding to know why American forces in Iraq couldn't offer adequate protection to a fourteen-year-old boy.

Looming over our efforts and further complicating them was the memory of the Elian Gonzales controversy. That long-running fiasco and the news photographs of the Cuban child being snatched away from his Miami relatives at rifle point was still fresh in the minds of many of the politicians and bureaucrats we contacted. The five-year-old boy was rescued in the Atlantic Ocean while floating in an inner tube in 1999 after his mother and ten others died attempting to escape Cuba. He became the subject of an international custody battle and a massive political tug-of-war when his father, backed by Cuban dictator Fidel Castro, began demanding his return. After five months of wrangling, federal agents with rifles seized the boy from his relatives in Miami and returned him to his father in Cuba.

Nobody wanted to be dragged into another situation like that. So we were constantly dealing with politicians, who passed us on to the bureaucracy, where the bureaucrats passed us on to one agency, then another. Officials in the State Department said that it was a matter for Homeland Security, and officials there said it would have to go through the Coalition Provisional Authority in Baghdad. I grew so frustrated with government avenues, I began to think I'd have to find some sort of private charity or relief organization.

Three months had passed since I'd left Iraq, and with all the effort and time I put into trying to get Steve-O out of there, I had nothing to show for it. Days turned into weeks, then into months, and my options were decreasing. I'd kept track of Steve-O through our marine replacements, who were now looking after him. Then, in May 2004, I received Steve-O's first e-mail. The marines were continuing his English lessons, and it was heartwarming to receive something directly from him:

> To: 1SG Hendrex
> How are you doing? I miss you and all my friends from Dragon Company and the army. I hope you are all doing well. The marines are nice and are treating me good. I have made some new friends so I am happy. I called you a while ago and your wife answered the phone. She could not understand me unfortunately, so I e-mailed you, did you get it?
>   Well, please say hello to everyone for me and I will never forget what you all did for me, especially you, 1SG Hendrex. I really miss all of you and I hope to see you all again someday soon.
>   Thank you again.
>   Love,
>   Steve-O

BACK TO THE FRONT

The U.S. Marines from the Seventh Marine Regiment, First Marine Division, I Marine Expeditionary Force, were taking care of the soldier I left behind. Husaybah had become so volatile that they could no longer allow Steve-O to leave Tiger Base even with heavy security. This group of marines, who'd had only about five months' rest in the United States before returning to Iraq and Husaybah, began taking casualties within their first twenty-four hours there. They'd been told that this would be mostly a peace-keeping assignment in which they'd be building water treatment plants, schools, and police stations. They did all that, but they also dealt with some of the most intense fighting since the war had "officially" ended. They encountered the same things we'd been dealing with—roadside bombs, mortar attacks, ambushes, snipers, land mines, and sporadic firefights—but in even greater intensity.

Dragon Company had manned Tiger Base and the border checkpoint in Husaybah as part of a heavily armored cavalry regiment with a lethal arsenal that included tanks, Bradleys, artillery, and scout and attack helicopters. Our versatile firepower had allowed us to take a very aggressive approach—and even then, the insurgent forces had given us all we could handle. They attacked, bombarded, and ambushed us at every opportunity, but we'd managed to cut back their opportunities substantially.

The insurgents had been bold enough to take on Dragon Company's firepower, but they paid a heavy toll. They were probably thanking Allah when the marines came in because even though they were great fighters, they simply did not have the same weapons and protection at their disposal. They were basically boots on the ground. The insurgents picked up on that and took full advantage. The mood on the streets, which wasn't exactly hospitable when we were there, turned even more con-frontational.

In their first weeks in Husaybah, the marines took heavy losses and the insurgents hardly let up. In their seven months of duty there, fifteen marines, one Special Forces soldier, and one Iraqi-American interpreter were killed. One of the worst days occurred shortly after we left. Five marines were killed and ten wounded on April 17, 2004, in a fourteen-hour street fight with as many as three hundred insurgents. Marine Captain Rick Gannon was among those killed in block-to-block, house-to-house fighting. Near the end of the battle, he was trying to lead a rescue effort for two of his sniper squads trapped on a city rooftop. While moving to the rooftop, his unit came under intense rocket-propelled grenade, machine-gun, and small-arms fire. He entered an Iraqi house and encountered nine mujahideen fighters who opened fire and killed him. The border checkpoint was renamed Camp Gannon to honor him. He was also posthumously awarded a Silver Star.

THE FACE OF AN ENEMY

Steve-O still contributed to the military effort, even though he no longer went out on missions. Whenever insurgents or suspected anticoalition force members were detained, the marine intelligence officers would have Steve-O secretly look them over to see if he could identify any of them. And that is how, in a rather anticlimactic way, my young friend helped the marines capture someone we'd been trying to nab for a long, long time.

The marines had continued to conduct raids in response to the increasing attacks and ambushes. In a raid on Market Street a couple months after Dragon Company left, they captured a group of ten veteran foreign fighters, including some Chechnyans and Syrians who were obviously training the local insurgents in guerrilla tactics. This was a very tough, well-trained bunch, the sort who would never give up a fight.

The marines were mostly interested in the foreign fighters whom they regarded as "Tier One," or top-priority, detainees. They brought them back to Tiger Base, photographed them, and then took the photos to Steve-O. He identified those who were definitely not from Husaybah, confirming the marines' suspicions that they were foreign fighters and great catches. But then Steve-O began to get highly animated as he looked at a group photograph from the place where the insurgents were captured. He pointed to one of the pictures and simply said, "Sayed!"

Steve-O could not believe his eyes. He was staring at the man believed to have killed his mother. At first, the marines with him had no idea what was upsetting him. He kept yelling at them that he wanted to see this guy in person. He asked for a weapon, saying he wanted to shoot this guy. The marine captain asked through an interpreter, "Who is Sayed?"

Frustrated, Steve-O screamed at him: "You know. You know. First Sergeant Hendrex told you! He's the man who killed my mother! You have his picture and the number of attacks against coalition forces. It is on First Sergeant Francois's computer. I will show you!"

Then the marine captain followed him, and Steve-O showed him the operational summary on the computer. There was a photograph of Sayed with it and my list of all of his activities and suspected activities with the insurgents. Only then did the marines realize whom they had captured along with the foreign fighters.

Based on Steve-O's identification, Special Forces intelligence, and my reports on Sayed, they immediately took him in for interrogation. I imagined he was more than a little surprised. He'd probably figured he could blend into the background since the marines had initially focused on the foreign fighters. Sayed might well have slipped out of U.S. custody as easily as the Syrian fighter who was captured with Steve-O's father.

With the material I'd left them and Steve-O's intimate knowledge of his former neighbor, the marines were able to hit Sayed with very specific questions. He played the innocent Iraqi to perfection: just a man with the wrong crowd. He was deep into his concocted story. He was glad the Americans were here helping Iraqis. He just wanted a safe place for his family to live. He didn't even know the other men he was captured with, he was just a local farmer who had walked into the store on Market Street when the marines came busting in the front door. He was terrified that he would be killed in all the commotion. He was thankful to the marines for rescuing him.

The interrogator and interpreter listened intently to Sayed's story. As he finished his long-winded series of lies, the interrogator finally spoke. "Did you watch her die?"

That took Sayed by surprise. What was this man saying to him? Maybe the interpreter got it wrong, so he asked him to repeat it.

This time, the interrogator inserted the name of Steve-O's mother in his question, along with specifics about where she'd been shot.

Sayed was visibly shaken. More specific questions followed. He realized we were onto him. The interrogator knew he had Sayed when he asked for a cigarette. He needed it to stop the hand tremors. Within a short period, he admitted to the shooting of Steve-O's mother, attacks on coalition forces, bringing in foreign fighters, and the mass grave found outside of Husaybah. He was amazed by the amount of information they had on him. The marines were stunned too. They had not realized what a critical catch this guy was until Steve-O clued them in and they pulled his files.

As happy as he was about Sayed's capture, Steve-O told me in an e-mail that he cried himself to sleep that night. The last shred of hope he'd been holding on to was wiped out with Sayed's admission of guilt to the marines. It had been a tough week. Just a few days earlier while watching CNN, he had been stunned to see footage of a devastated area near a prominent bridge in Fallujah. His grandfather lived next to that bridge. Steve-O, his brothers, and sisters had played there when they visited their grandfather. The CNN report was on the major coalition offensive in Fallujah. Steve-O listened and broke down in tears when the news report said that everything around the bridge had been obliterated. He nearly collapsed on the floor when film footage showed that his grandfather's house had been reduced to a large pile of rock, rebar, and debris.

Steve-O had never felt so alone, or so lost. He had no idea what he would do now. His mother was confirmed dead, and the likelihood that his grandfather and siblings had also been killed now weighed on his mind. If they were there when the bombs landed, there was little chance that they survived. His hopes for them were all but crushed. He went to his cot that night believing that he would never get out of Iraq and that he, too, would most likely be killed.

22

A PROMISE KEPT

Nothing was working. I couldn't figure out what else to do to get Steve-O out of Iraq. Husaybah was rapidly sliding toward anarchy and self-destruction. The marines were scheduled to pull out soon. And I felt hog-tied to my desk at Fort Carson in Colorado Springs. There, I was pushing paper, going through my daily routine, while he was hanging in limbo. I was getting desperate.

And then I picked up on something that appeared to be a great lead. I was watching a late-night show on television and saw an interview with Gary Sinise, star of *CSI: NY.* He was talking about Operation Iraqi Children, the organization he'd founded with author Laura Hillenbrand, who wrote the bestseller *Seabiscuit.* The organization collects and ships school supplies and toys to Iraq for distribution by U.S. troops. Sinise said he'd been to Iraq twice for USO shows, and he'd decided to do something to help the future of Iraq, the children.

I quickly sent an e-mail to Operation Iraqi Children's Web page and relayed Steve-O's story. A couple of weeks passed before I heard back, but their response was very positive. They had good contacts in the media that they were willing to share to get Steve-O's story more attention. But by the time I heard back from Operation Iraqi Children, I had to tell them that we'd picked up momentum from an entirely unexpected source.

I was in our kitchen in Colorado Springs when the phone rang. The voice on the other end was barely audible. But the crackle of the international connection was all too familiar. "I am calling to speak with First Sergeant Hendrex. I am Michael Phillips, a reporter with the *Wall Street Journal*."

I had been expecting this call from Iraq. A few days earlier, CSM Huff from the marines in Husaybah had e-mailed me that a *WSJ* reporter was at our former Tiger Base in the Al Qaim region. He said they were going to try to link him up with Steve-O. It was another in a long line of leads that had promise. But I hadn't held out much hope until this conversation. I could tell from his voice that Phillips thought this was a great story—if any of it was true.

"I have just had a long and interesting conversation, through an interpreter, with a boy nicknamed Steve-O, and I would like to confirm with you what he told me. The kid had several stories that were hard to believe."

I asked what Steve-O had told him.

"He claimed he'd turned in his own father and helped U.S. soldiers capture more than forty other insurgents. He said that his mother had been killed because of his assistance to the coalition forces. That he'd ridden on patrols and raids. And that he had been in several firefights," Phillips said.

He was very skeptical of Steve-O's claims. But I set him straight. I told him that everything the boy had said was true. Our conversation lasted about twenty minutes. Phillips kept asking questions, and I kept answering, "Yes, it's true."

I offered to show him operational summaries from Dragon Company's missions with Steve-O. The reporter was still cautious, but I could tell he saw the potential for a great story. I told him that he could talk to our company commander, Capt. Roehrman, and my squadron commander, Lt. Col. Reilly, for further verification, and he agreed to do that and get back to me. I could hardly blame him for being skeptical. Steve-O usually got so animated while telling his stories that it was hard to believe he wasn't making them up as he went along. But after Phillips checked and double-checked everything, he wrote a story and filed it with his editors.

Before Michael Phillips left Al Qaim, he called me again on his satellite phone. He said his editors had liked the story and that it would hit the paper soon. Then, to my surprise, he put Steve-O on the line, and he hit me with his first true, nonprofane English sentence: "First Sergeant Hendrex, how are you doing? It is nice to talk to you again."

It had been more than three months since I had told him good-bye, but I could tell that he had been working hard on his English. He had almost no accent. One of the marine intelligence officers had been working with him on his pronunciation. He'd even helped him with spelling and numbers, which was remarkable given that Steve-O was illiterate even in his own language. He had improved dramatically, and it was damn nice to hear his voice. He told me that the marines were taking good care of him. I told him to sit tight and that I was hoping the *Wall Street Journal* story would help get him out of Al Qaim.

The newspaper story broke on June 14, 2004. It ran all over the country, and I gained a real appreciation for the positive aspects of the power of the press. Michael Phillips made the point right away that Steve-O had paid a very steep price for his decision to walk into our camp and assist us against the insurgency:

> U.S. officials say he has provided a wealth of military intelligence, allowing them to capture numerous insurgents in Iraq over the past six months. But the teenager's decision to turn on his father, who he says beat him, has cost him his family and his freedom.

The *Wall Street Journal* article also placed Steve-O's story within the framework of Iraq's volatile environment. It noted that he was a marked man in his own nation and that we were desperately working to find a way to get him out of Iraq and to a safer place. Phillips wrote about the many obstacles we had to overcome if we were to get the boy out of the country. He noted that there was the danger of setting off an international controversy if it wasn't handled carefully.

The story documented Steve-O's role in helping us fight back. It noted correctly that for a time, we put the insurgents on the defensive through our raids and patrols and through our willingness to respond to their ambushes with all of the weapons at our disposal. And it ended with Steve-O, in his typical straightforward manner, saying that he often woke up crying about his mother's death; he admitted that he felt he would definitely be killed if we left him behind unprotected.

The story opened doors all over, including some to very influential folks in the Pentagon. The initial telephone call I received started out on a very good note:

"This is Robert Reilly. I work in the Office of the Secretary of Defense at the Pentagon. You and your boys did an amazing job in Iraq, and I am going to help you get Steve-O out of there."

It sounded too good to be true, but Mr. Reilly had read the story in the *Wall Street Journal* and then verified it. He wasn't playing games. After I briefly reviewed for him what I had tried to do so far to get Steve-O out of Iraq, he assured me that I would soon be hearing from someone with the contacts, skills, and knowledge to accomplish that mission.

Three weeks later, I was contacted via e-mail by Colonel Fred Gerber, the special projects officer for the Office of the Army Surgeon General in Washington, DC. Col. Gerber was no bureaucrat. He'd been a battalion commander in Operation Just Cause in Panama and in Operation Desert Storm. He told me that he had recently returned from deployment to the Coalition Provisional Authority in Baghdad as the chief of operations for the Ministry of Health. Col. Gerber, who is now a civilian involved in Operation Hope in Iraq, was very skilled at navigating—and, if necessary, circumnavigating—the bureaucracy and getting things done.

More than most people, he was aware of the dangers that Steve-O faced. While Col. Gerber was in Baghdad, an Iraqi boy was caught in a cross fire and accidentally shot by American forces. His father brought the wounded boy into the ministry hospital. Col. Gerber made sure the boy received the surgery he needed to save a badly torn-up leg. The boy's grateful father later invited Col. Gerber to dinner with his family. As he was leaving their home that night, the colonel was shot in the head in an ambush. He easily could have been killed, but the bullet just grazed his skull.

Since his redeployment and in his new role in DC, he had assisted several Iraqis in coming to the United States for training, health care, and the like. Fortunately for me, and for Steve-O, the Office of the Secretary of Defense felt this was right up the colonel's alley.

Col. Gerber was a whirlwind. In his e-mail, he said: *I am going to get started to assist this young man who assisted you in Iraq. I am going to do everything I can to help you accomplish getting him to CONUS.* That first e-mail was about five pages long, full of direct questions pertaining to Steve-O and what it would take to get him out of Iraq. He was straight up: *I need no-shit accurate information on exactly what he did; give me the hard facts and give it to me with no sugar!* How could you not like this guy?

Does he have a passport, Iraqi ID card?
Need information on Steve-O's brothers, sisters, mother,
    father, and relatives.

Who has he been living with for the past six months?
Is the father still in prison and is he scheduled to get out?
I need the details on what he did to assist coalition forces.
Where is the boy living now?
Is his life still in danger? Need documentation.
Does he have medical needs?
When we get him back to CONUS, where's he going to live?
Who will take care of him when he gets here? Food,
    clothing, expenses.
I will need an escort to fly him back to Fort Carson.

Five pages later, he ended his e-mail simply: *Okay, Top, that's it for now. Looking forward to working with you on this project.*

Luckily, I had been working on this since before my departure from Iraq, so it didn't take long to send the colonel my dissertation, with the "hard facts without sugar." Our first step was to get approval for Steve-O to come to the States, without worrying about how long a stay it would be. Col. Gerber told me that the eye injury Steve-O received from being kicked in the head by his uncle could serve as his ticket out of Iraq.

"It sounds like a serious injury that can't be treated in Iraq. They don't have the medical facilities, so we can get him temporary public benefit parole to get him back to the States for medical assistance through the Department of Homeland Security," he said. "I've done it before. He is allowed to come over on a temporary visa. It doesn't get him here permanently, but it gets him here."

I liked the way Col. Gerber thought. He said that even with all the support, it could be a lengthy process, and he was right. We spent several weeks putting together all of the required information, which was a major task in itself. It was submitted as a "temporary special public benefit parole request." And it had to get approved through the Department of Homeland Security. The big hurdle, since Steve-O was a minor, was that we had to find a family member who would provide a signed statement authorizing Steve-O to leave Iraq and come to the United States. That was a huge challenge because Nassir was in prison, Tahira was dead, and every other relative whom Steve-O had talked about was involved with the insurgency. Still, we needed a close relative in Iraq who would give permission.

I'd met the uncle who lived directly behind Steve-O's house. He was the one who'd told us that Tahira had been killed. He seemed like our best and only choice, so I directed our efforts at contacting him via the marines in Husaybah. The other major challenge was that Steve-O would need a passport, or at a bare minimum, an Iraqi ID, to get out of his country. But that wouldn't be easy since he came from a tribal village where public records were not kept. He didn't even have a birth certificate.

I had contacted CSM Huff and the marines and told them that their interviews with Michael Phillips had really helped get things rolling. Steve-O was on the fast track, one with a few obstacles on it, but at that point, it looked like we were going to pull it off. I told CSM Huff about Steve-O's uncle, the need for a passport or an Iraqi ID, and the requirement that he had to get a physical before they'd let him into the United States. He agreed to take care of those major details since I couldn't do much from Colorado Springs. I sent him the information, sworn statements, intelligence reports, and operational summaries that validated Steve-O's story as much as possible.

Then it was a waiting game for me while the marines did the legwork thousands and thousands of miles away. Step by step, they pulled off what looked like mission impossible. CSM Huff managed to overcome one challenge by having a "special identification" made for Steve-O. It wasn't a passport or an official Iraqi ID. It didn't come from the Coalition Provisional Authority, the

Pentagon, or the Al Qaim Department of Motor Vehicles. But it sure looked official, and that apparently meant a lot. Col. Gerber felt it would meet the requirements. I had my doubts, but I trusted his ingenuity and resourcefulness. Just as we cleared that hurdle, another appeared.

I'd put all my hopes in Steve-O's uncle providing us the family authorization we needed. But the uncle had a little problem. He'd been detained by the marines for actions against coalition forces. It wasn't a minor infraction. He had taken part in direct attacks on U.S. Marines. They told me he was lucky to be alive. They had him locked up in an Iraqi prison, where he probably wasn't feeling like being helpful to our efforts with Steve-O. It made me think back to that night when we'd questioned him. The uncle had played nice then, but only because we didn't give him the opportunity to strike first.

We were left without someone in a position of authority to sign off on Steve-O's "temporary" exit to the United States. The marines told me that they weren't giving up. Still, it was an excruciating process, even with all the support and assistance I was receiving. Over a three-month period, Col. Gerber and I meticulously put together the information that was needed to get Steve-O out of Husaybah. That material included the claim that Steve-O, who was in the protective custody of the U.S. Marines, was in need of medical attention that could not be provided in his own country. The documentation also said that he'd been an intelligence source for us, that he was in need of continued U.S. protection, and that he was coming to the United States for an official debriefing.

The marines took care of Steve-O's medical screening. They got him the deluxe package. He was escorted to medical facilities at the U.S. air base in Al Asad. The first appointment was a dental exam, during which he had a couple cavities filled to protect the famous Steve-O smile. He wasn't thrilled with his first encounter with a dental drill. But he'd have chosen a root canal over the next stop—a complete physical, with immunization shots, administered by a female physician! It all went horribly wrong when she asked him to "stand up and drop your pants, then look to the left and cough."

"Nuuuh-*uuuh,* no way" he replied. "You must be *mesh-noon.*" (Arabic for "crazy.")

The woman doc called in the marines. They probably had to threaten him with deadly force before Steve-O caved. I would have loved to have seen the look on his face when the interpreter described exactly what the doctor wanted him to do.

Meanwhile, back in the maze of red tape, the marines at Tiger Base were working miracles. Lt. Col. Lopez and CSM Huff decided to go straight to the top by calling on the "ultimate" parental figure within the tribal community: the sheik of Steve-O's tribe. Steve-O's father was a member of one of Husaybah's two ruling—and often warring—tribes. Steve-O had told me about this sheik. The boy didn't trust him. But the marines trusted that the sheik would operate in his own best interests—and getting Steve-O out of Iraq was definitely in this guy's best interests.

Like many leaders in the region, he was suspected of playing both sides of the conflict by appearing to cooperate with the coalition forces while secretly supporting the insurgency. The tribal leader may have decided that as long as Steve-O was protected by the marines, the boy was a threat to the insurgency. So why wouldn't the sheik help send the Iraqi boy thousands of miles away, where he could no longer assist the U.S. effort in Al Qaim? Whatever his motives, the sheik signed on the dotted line, and the letter dated August 12, 2004, was sent to the commanding officer of the United States Marine Corps, Third Battalion, Seventh Marines, RCT-7, First Marine Division, Camp Al Qaim.

Subj: RELEASE OF PARENTAL AND TRIBAL RIGHTS

1. By virtue of this letter, the undersigned, the Tribal Sheik of ████████████ tribe, located in the Al Qaim region of Al Anbar Province, Iraq, hereby forever and absolutely releases any and all parental and tribal rights and interests in the fifteen-year-old boy commonly known as Steve-O.

2. Due to Steve-O's particular situation, it is in his best interest to leave Iraq permanently. His father is a criminal, detained in Abu Garayb prison, and his mother has been killed in retaliation for Steve-O's cooperation with the United States government's efforts to help rebuild Iraq. Therefore, Steve-O has no chance for a successful life in Iraq.

3. My wish for Steve-O is to make a better life for himself. The best way for him to do this is to go to the United States, obtain an education, and build a life for himself.

████████████████████████
████████████████ Tribal Sheik.

With the sheik's letter and Steve-O's new identification papers, our plans began coming together in September 2004. Col. Gerber marshaled the paperwork through and then forwarded the packet to the Department of Homeland Security. He'd proven to be one hard-nosed soldier, but one with a big heart. He greased the wheels with the bureaucracy, and the media kept us in the spotlight thanks to a round of follow-up stories inspired by the *Wall Street Journal* article. It hadn't escaped my attention that I'd be responsible for Steve-O's financial needs once he came to the United States, so I welcomed the opportunity to get his story out even more. In August 2004, reporter Heather Nauert, who was then with FOX News, contacted me about doing a story. She agreed to include information on a trust fund for Steve-O, and when her story ran, people responded generously.

Though we were doing all we thought possible to get Steve-O out of Iraq, I was getting nervous because we were running out of time. The marines who'd been protecting him were scheduled to pull out of Husaybah at the end of their tour. They would be gone by October 1, and I did not want Steve-O handed off to yet another outfit. The next group stationed in Husaybah might not be as interested in protecting an Iraqi boy. There were too many things that could go wrong; I kept envisioning Steve-O thrown out on the streets, where the insurgents were waiting like wolves.

CSM Huff assured me that if nothing else, they'd put the teenager in one of their uniforms and smuggle him out of the country. I appreciated his commitment, but I hoped that in a few days we'd find a solution that would keep everyone out of jail. Timing was critical. We'd set September 10 as the day for Steve-O's flight back to the States. That would give us a few weeks for the official approval to be completed. Col. Gerber hooked me up with his liaisons in the U.S. Air Force, who arranged for Steve-O's flights. We agreed that the best plan was to get the boy to an air force base in Balad, Iraq, and then on to a military flight to Germany, where I would meet him and accompany him to the States.

There was no standard procedure for what we were trying to pull off, and by the time we got it set up, Steve-O's itinerary seemed to include everything but a camel caravan across Kuwait. Finally, I received notification on September 1 that everything was officially set. But this was a military operation, so there were no guarantees. The Office of the Secretary of Defense had to approve "an exception to policy" to permit Steve-O to travel on a

U.S. military aircraft. Once that was arranged, Homeland Security had to approve the temporary special public benefit parole to be granted for a maximum period of no more than ninety days, so that Steve-O could be brought to the United States for medical evaluation and personal protection.

Our mission was further complicated by the fact that Col. Gerber wasn't the sort of soldier content to take on one challenge at a time. Steve-O had traveling companions. Col. Gerber also had arranged trips to the United States for his former interpreter and an Iraqi woman, both of whom had serious injuries requiring treatment. All three travelers under Col. Gerber's care were eventually to meet up in Balad and then fly together.

I had arranged for the marines in Husaybah to escort Steve-O to Balad Air Base. Steve-O's final approval documents would be forwarded to our contacts in the passenger terminal there. A female army captain was supposed to go to Balad and serve as the officer in charge of the joint missions, ensuring that all three people were allowed onto the military flight to Ramstein Air Base in Germany. I was to meet them in Germany and then escort the group to Baltimore, where we would hook up with Col. Gerber. I would then take Steve-O back to Colorado Springs and a new beginning. Of course, this being Iraq, nobody thought it would be easy.

On September 5, Steve-O left Al Qaim by Humvee. Lt. Col. Lopez had formed a special convoy just to get them the one hundred miles down the Euphrates to the Al Asad Air Base, where they would board a military helicopter for a quick flight to the bigger Balad Air Base on the Tigris River, seventy miles north of Baghdad. They assembled at the marines battalion headquarters building, the same one where Steve-O had learned the tragic news about his mother.

Steve-O lugged a huge packet filled with his medical and dental examination papers, his new identification, and all of the other documentation that Col. Gerber had ordered. The boy felt like he was walking in a dream. Steve-O never lacked for imagination, but this was beyond anything he could have invented. He was leaving the only place he'd ever known for a place he had difficulty accepting as real. He said good-bye, hugged his friends, and posed for photographs with the marines who had served as his guardians. It was hard to say good-bye, but he was eager to find a place where he did not have to constantly fear for his life.

LEAVING HUSAYBAH

As always in Iraq, the first leg of the journey called for a long drive through the desert. Yet, Steve-O was far from bored. He felt as though his head and heart might burst from all the thoughts and images and emotions that accompanied each mile traveled. He felt safe with these soldiers, but he realized he was not one of them. He was leaving the place where he truly belonged, but it had become a place where he could no longer survive on his own. His family had been torn apart, the fate of his brothers and sisters was unknown. He had put his future in the hands of a group of Americans who were now promising him a new life in a part of the world that he knew only from images on television and in the movies and magazines. It did not seem real. None of this seemed real.

23

DANGER IN THE DESERT

Lt. Col. Lopez led the convoy with Corporal "Pinky" Virus as his driver. Steve-O took comfort in the presence of the lanky corporal whose nickname came from his red hair, fair skin, and perpetual sunburn. Pinky and Steve-O had bunked in a room with several other marines at Tiger Base, and they'd become an unlikely comical team known for their pranks on each other as well as on many innocent victims. Pinky tried to play the protective older brother role, but he was as much an instigator as Steve-O. The two of them nearly drove their bunkmates to madness after Pinky, for reasons unknown, taught Steve-O the *Mary Poppins* song "Supercalifragilisticexpialidocious." Of course, Steve-O thought the title itself was hilarious, and he would repeat it over and over again with his own Iraqi spin on it.

Steve-O tried to focus on those lighter moments as Pinky drove them through the desert on their hundred-mile journey, but his mind kept flashing back to images of his mother and his brothers and sisters. He fought off doubts and guilt and questions about his decision to inform on his own father and the insurgent cell by recalling their beatings, torture, and killing of other Iraqis.

He squeezed the door handle at the thought of Sayed and what he had done to his mother. He reminded himself that the insurgent leader would probably have killed him, too, if he had not sought the protection of the Americans now escorting him.

Steve-O still felt vulnerable, particularly when he noted how cautious the marines were being. They had decided to avoid travel on Highway 12, which was a frequent staging place for ambushes and improvised explosive devices, and chose an alternate path along an old supply route that Steve-O knew well. The rugged road ran through a tiny rural enclave that was the last outpost before entering the open desert. It had fewer than one hundred buildings, all of them primitive huts without electricity or running water. As the convoy approached trailing plumes of dust, children came begging for handouts. None of them recognized Steve-O, but he knew many of them, and he knew their suffering.

He had worked in this village known on American military maps as "T-1." The only industry in the outpost was a brick factory owned by one of Steve-O's uncles. His father had sent him there to work among other child laborers when he was only ten years old. Memories of the staggering heat and exhaustion swept over Steve-O as the vehicles crept through the village. Yet, he also felt a sense of pride because he had done such difficult work to earn money for his family at such a young age.

The convoy sped up after passing through the village and quickly reached Al Asad Air Base. Steve-O was still lost in thought, so Pinky shook him by the shoulder as they entered the base, reminding him of the strict instructions he'd been given by Lt. Col. Lopez: "The commander told me that I am supposed to escort you to Balad Air Base and not leave you until you are on the plane for Germany, and that's what I'm going to do, Steve-O."

A few hours later, Pinky and Steve-O were strapped aboard a roaring Sea Stallion military helicopter flying through the darkness to Balad. It was the teenager's first flight of any sort, and he felt both nervous and giddy. He was glad to have Pinky with him, especially when the chopper suddenly lurched to the side, dropped down, and reversed its course, throwing both of them around in their seats.

"Someone was shooting at us!" yelled Pinky, who'd spotted the red tracers coming up from the blackness below.

All those aboard were wearing earplugs to protect them from the roar of the helicopter's engines, but Steve-O gathered from Pinky's expression and the helicopter pilot's maneuvers that they were under attack. His stomach flip-flopped with the rapid change in altitude and direction. Pinky saw him go white and handed him an airsickness bag, but Steve-O fought off the nausea. The pilot had banked the helicopter hard after spotting their attackers through his night-vision goggles. He was a combat helicopter pilot, so he followed his instincts by counterattacking. Steve-O was shocked when the helicopter's guns roared to life and relieved when the pilot quickly finished the counterattack and returned to their course for Balad.

ON THE HOME FRONT

Halfway around the world, I was fighting another battle. The final approval for Steve-O's journey hit a snag when the Department of Homeland Security demanded that Steve-O be accompanied by an Iraqi adult into the United States. Fortunately, savvy Col. Gerber stepped in quickly and concocted a plan to cover this new requirement by presenting his former interpreter, Ali, as Steve-O's escort. Col. Gerber's friend had quite an amazing story himself. After the colonel left Iraq and went to work in the Pentagon, Ali had been ambushed by insurgents, who shot him seven times in the arms, chest, and legs. Left for dead, Ali crawled to a nearby hospital. Doctors there saved his life, but he still needed advanced surgery for an arm that had been shattered in three places. Col. Gerber had made it his mission to get Ali to the States for that surgery. He made the promise, in part, because he owed his life to Ali. When Col. Gerber was shot in the head by a sniper during his tour in Iraq, Ali had risked his own life to go to his aid.

I was glad to learn that Ali would be accompanying Steve-O on the flight to Germany, but just as our plan appeared to be coming together, yet another problem arose. Somewhere in the military bureaucracy, a bean counter was demanding to know who was paying for all the flights we'd arranged for our group. Both Col. Gerber and I had thought the tab was covered, but apparently not.

Fortunately, Steve-O had a fan in Colonel H. R. McMaster, the new regimental commander, who quickly approved payment for the teenager's military and commercial flights. Since Ali was Steve-O's escort, Col. McMaster agreed to pay his airfare too. Unfortunately, the good colonel wasn't able to clear up every aspect of this particular military SNAFU (Situation Normal, All Fucked Up). There was still the matter of payment for the injured Iraqi woman, which was the responsibility of the female army captain's commanding officers. Her commanding officers would not okay payment quickly enough for the Iraqi woman to be part of our group. This threw off our game plan because the captain was also supposed to serve as the officer in charge of our entire group of travelers at Balad. Without her, they were all cattle and no cowboys.

Col. Gerber was so riled up about this turn of events that I thought he might just hijack a military jet and go get the Iraqi woman himself. We'd been counting on the army captain. She knew the overall plan, which had been improvised on the run. Steve-O and Ali were en route, and they didn't have a clue. Steve-O didn't know that he needed an adult Iraqi escort, and he'd never heard of Ali. The former interpreter had no idea of his role in the boy's trip, either. This was looking like a disaster in the making.

We were three days away from Steve-O's planned arrival in the United States, and we had to come up with yet another plan to get our two travelers together. Col. Gerber hammered it together and fired off the paperwork, but when I tried to alert Steve-O, I couldn't find either him or Pinky.

I couldn't find anyone at the Balad Air Base who'd seen or heard of them. Frantic, I worked the phones and e-mail. I couldn't get through to the officer in charge of the base's passenger terminal, but I e-mailed him the approved travel papers for Steve-O and Ali. Hours later, I learned that I'd e-mailed everything to a soldier who'd been redeployed back to the United States. So I had to send the approval again after briefing his replacement. The September 10 flight out of Balad was in less than forty-eight hours. Steve-O and Ali were cleared for the flight, but we couldn't find them. No one in Balad had seen a young Iraqi boy with a marine escort, nor had they been contacted by Ali.

Fighting insurgents in the Al Anbar Province was starting to look like easy work. I was one frustrated soldier when I headed out for the Colorado Springs airport at five a.m. I was headed for Germany, even though I had no idea how Steve-O was going to make his flight to meet me there. I met Spec. Habib at the airport. He was traveling with me to serve as an interpreter with Steve-O when, and if, we hooked up. I continued to work the phones at the airport while waiting for my flight, but I still had no luck finding our missing travelers.

In frustration, I called Christina from the airport: "This may take a little longer than I planned, and I hope it is not all for nothing." I didn't tell her that I was determined to go all the way into Iraq and carry Steve-O out over my shoulder if that's what it took. I wasn't coming back without him. The search by phone continued after we landed in Baltimore for a two-hour layover. After several calls, broken connections, and maddening delays, I found someone in Balad who said he'd located the military paperwork for Steve-O and Ali's flight. But there was still no sign of them at the air base. "Call me back in an hour, and I'll keep trying to find them," he said.

I don't know how I kept from screaming every profanity I'd ever mastered. I'd just spent an entire year dealing with the most intense military experience of my life, and after surviving a dozen deadly battles or more, I was being slowly tortured by red tape and poor communication. Rather than hang myself by the pay-phone cord in the airport, I called Col. Gerber and shared my pain.

Once again, he had an answer. Col. Gerber had reached Ali and filled him in on the new plan. He told him to go to the gate of the Balad Air Base and hold his ground until he found Steve-O and Pinky. So I knew Ali would be in place. All I had to do now was get Steve-O there. I dialed my contact in Balad again. It was another horrible connection, like talking through a jet engine, but I got word that they'd had a Pinky spotting. He'd contacted the air base to check in, and they'd relayed his new instructions to hook up with Ali.

It was all in Pinky's hands now. There was nothing I could do until my flight touched down in Germany eight hours before Steve-O and Ali were scheduled to get there. I made good use of that time by fretting and stewing and dreaming up worst-case scenarios. It was a long, long flight, and as soon as our plane landed in Frankfurt, I bolted for the pay phones once again. I got through to the night-shift crew at the Balad Air Base, and, of course, the first person I talked to had not one fucking clue as to what was going on. My frustration meter was spinning out of control:

"Let me talk to someone in charge!" I barked into the phone.

The next voice I heard had a very welcome air of authority and control. It was the air force officer in charge with whom I'd talked an eternity earlier, and he had nothing but good news.

"They left this morning and should be arriving there in a few hours. You should thank that marine corporal. He put in a hell of a lot of effort to find the Iraqi at the gate." Pinky had come through like a four-star general. He got Steve-O and Ali together and on the plane. All I had to do was wait for them to show up in Germany.

MISSION ACCOMPLISHED

Eight hours later, the electric doors slid open at the arrival gate. I was one intent soldier. The first person to come up the ramp was Steve-O, trailed by an air force escort and Ali. It had been six months since I'd seen him. He looked like a typical American teen in a beige baseball cap, denim jeans, and a gray T-shirt picturing the head of an eagle on an American flag with the caption OPERATION IRAQI FREEDOM. I had forgotten the power of his familiar, broad smile. It lit up the terminal and brought everything into focus for me. All the scrambling and frustration was forgotten. Our boy was safe.

I couldn't stop smiling. I hugged him until he begged for air. He'd grown a couple of inches, and he'd muscled up. I put a Denver Broncos cap on his head, as requested by the other members of Dragon Company waiting for us back in Colorado. Steve-O then whipped off his backpack and reached for his wallet. He presented me with the note I'd written to him, promising that I would get him out of Iraq.

"I have kept it in my wallet ever since you left," he said.

We were both smiling so much, we couldn't speak. I signed papers acknowledging that I was taking custody of Steve-O, and then we headed for a room I'd reserved until it was time to board our flight. As we walked there, Steve-O filled me in on his journey, including the attack on his helicopter, with Ali and Spec. Habib taking turns translating.

When we got to the room, Steve-O pulled out a picture album he wanted to show me, triggering more stories about his time with the marines. He was laughing and lighthearted until he came to photographs of those soldiers who'd been killed in the last six months. It hit me again that both Steve-O and I could have been among those who died. Steve-O grew quiet too, but then he said he had something he wanted to tell me—in English.

"I don't know if I can say it correctly, First Sergeant. I want to thank you for everything you have done to get me to this point. I love you so much."

Oh man, that got to me, and to Steve-O, too. He paused, collected his thoughts, and then reached into his backpack once more to pull out my floppy desert hat.

"You don't need to say any more," I told him as he handed it to me.

We hugged each other with tears streaming down our faces, grinning like a couple of crazy loons.

24

A NEW LIFE

Christina picked us up at the Colorado Springs airport late on the night of September 10, 2004. Steve-O and I were wiped out. We walked through the quiet terminal and met a welcoming committee of about twenty soldiers from Dragon Company. They said they'd come to welcome the last of our men home.

Steve-O perked up when he saw the familiar faces. He hugged them all and thanked them. It helped him to know that he had so many friends in this unfamiliar place. Jet-lagged and weary, we drove the half hour home to Colorado Springs without a whole lot of conversation. Outside our house in the foothills overlooking the town, Steve-O stopped and gazed into the darkness. I figured he was studying the rows of pine trees or adjusting to the mountain air, which can seem unreal, especially for a boy who had known only the desert.

We showed him to his bedroom and said good night. I think he was asleep before his head hit the pillow. Christina and I had a plan in place for the next morning. I wanted Steve-O to remember his first day in the United States as something special, so right when he woke up, I announced that I was taking him on a quick trip. (Our interpreter, Spec. Habib, had spent the night to help with the language barrier, and he joined us.) I thought that there was no better place for Steve-O to view the greatness of his new surroundings than Pikes Peak, known as "America's Mountain." The views from 14,115 feet high along the Continental Divide had inspired the poet who wrote "America the Beautiful"; I figured they might inspire Steve-O, too.

The three of us took the scenic route, driving to the top of the mountain just outside Colorado Springs. Normally, I like to hike up, but it was going to take this desert boy a while to adjust to the altitude. I didn't want Steve-O to spend his first day in America gasping for oxygen.

The cloudless sky offered spectacular views that day. Colorado Springs was spread out directly below us. You could practically see all the way to Kansas City. Steve-O was in awe. He'd never seen mountains or snow, and I'm pretty sure he'd never gotten this grand a view in the desert. He sat on the rocks overlooking the Springs, soaking it all in and, I'm sure, contemplating what the future might bring.

I thought the light air might affect his energy level, but he ran around from one spot to the next, giddy with excitement. Eventually, though, the change in altitude drained his gas tank and he grew weak. So after a quick snack at the Summit House restaurant, we headed back down the mountain. Spec. Habib fell asleep immediately, and our young prankster took the opportunity to take close-up photographs of him drooling.

I had wanted Steve-O to get a sense of the beauty of our country, but our outing was also designed to give Christina and our friends time to prepare for a surprise party we'd planned for him. He realized something was up when he saw the cars lining both sides of the street around our block. When I opened the front door, we were greeted by applause and cheers. The ceiling was covered with red, white, and blue helium-filled balloons. Patriotic banners and streamers adorned every corner, crevice, and room in the house.

Dragon Company packed the house with a supporting force of spouses, girlfriends, and children. Everyone wanted to meet the famous Iraqi boy who'd helped us survive our most challenging deployment. People cheered, shook his hand, hugged him, clapped him on the back. The welcome left him fumbling for words even in his own language. He did manage to let us know that there were times when he thought he'd never see us again.

Steve-O clearly relished being the center of attention, even if he couldn't communicate very easily with everyone. At one point, there was a big commotion as kids and adults rushed to the front yard. They'd spotted a young bear that had wandered into the neighborhood from the surrounding woods. I thought Steve-O would be excited to see his first bear, but he hardly showed any interest. Christina thought that was strange, so she asked Spec. Habib to find out what Steve-O was thinking.

He told the interpreter that he had already seen the bear.

"Steve-O, what are you talking about?" Christina asked.

Steve-O shrugged when the interpreter relayed her question. Then he added an explanation.

"When he was getting out of the car last night, he saw the creature standing across the road, staring at him. He rubbed his eyes, but it was still there, and since you two didn't react, he figured it was just a normal thing," the interpreter said.

That's what Steve-O had been staring at in the darkness! Neither Christina nor I had seen the bear, and when we didn't react to it, Steve-O thought it was just an everyday thing.

"We're going to have to watch out for stuff like this," Christina told me.

One soldier's private presentation to Steve-O really summed up everyone's feelings and made the night even more special. Spec. "Schlo-Mo" Schwartz pulled Steve-O into a corner and quietly presented him with a memento of our shared experiences in Iraq. He gave Steve-O the Purple Heart medal he'd been awarded for his injuries from being sprayed by shrapnel by the improvised explosive device that had gone off right in front of our Humvee that day in Husaybah.

Schwartz had struggled emotionally after that near-death experience, so I knew the significance of what he was doing.

"Steve-O, I want you to have this," Schwartz said. "We wouldn't have caught the guy who tried to kill us if it wasn't for you. In fact, we all owe a lot to you. Some of us might not have made it home at all if it wasn't for you."

AMERICAN PASSAGE

A few weeks later, Steve-O underwent surgery to correct the damage that his uncle had done to his eye. The medical care was arranged through a generous Iraqi-American woman named Aȳzer. This incredible woman has lived in the United States for thirty years. She graciously helped us smooth Steve-O's transition into a new culture. She also introduced him to Beth and Randy Gradishar, the former NFL Pro Bowl linebacker for the Denver Broncos, who played during the fearsome days of the "Orange Crush" defense. The Gradishars took an interest in Steve-O's medical problems and hooked us up with an Englewood ophthalmologist, Dr. Robert King, who offered to perform the delicate operation. The surgeon and staff at Sky Ridge Medical Center, near Denver, provided their services for free to help Steve-O shed a painful reminder of his past.

He was terrified going into the operation because, in his experience, hospitals were places for suffering, not healing. As I'd learned in Iraq, the insurgents often used hospital operating rooms as torture chambers and interrogation rooms. Standard medical care there wasn't always painless either. Steve-O had never been to an American hospital, so I couldn't blame him for being apprehensive, especially after his first trip to the dentist and his first physical. The staff at the medical center eased his fears by walking him through their facilities and showing him the clean and modern operating room. The surgery straightened his damaged eye. He also received eyeglasses to help correct his vision.

When the bandage was removed, Steve-O's disposition changed immediately. He'd developed the habit of trying to hide his eyes beneath the bill of his caps, but he stopped doing that, and he no longer squinted in bright sunlight. When he looked in the mirror for the first time and checked out his eye, he was overjoyed. "It's straight!" he said.

The corrective eye surgery worked wonders for Steve-O's confidence, and it helped ease him into his new life as a teenager in this country. He's had his challenges, to be sure, but even I have difficulty picking him out of a crowd of high school kids these days. That fact became apparent on one particular chilly Friday night in autumn at a high school football game. The game on the field had ended. Amid all of the players in pads and helmets, there stood one short, wiry defensive lineman who'd led his team's defense that night, including eight quarterback sacks and two fumble recoveries. His opponents had sized him up at the beginning of the game and figured he wouldn't be much of a threat. Their opinions changed the first time he flew past his opponent on the line and nailed the quarterback.

After the game, his teammates patted him on the back and congratulated him. The coach told him that he hit harder than anybody on the team. Everyone seemed to marvel at this boy's fearless performance, with the exception of those aware of his exploits on another field, in another land.

FACING THE FATHER

I was home for only ten months when I was deployed back to Iraq for Operation Iraqi Freedom III. As sorry as I was to have to leave again so soon, my redeployment did provide me with an opportunity that I had not anticipated. In November 2005, I traveled by helicopter to Baghdad from Tal Afar in the Ninewa Province, where I'd been stationed. I'd been ordered to travel there to testify for the Central Criminal Court of Iraq in Baghdad. Saddam himself was on trial in the area, but I went to a different courtroom and faced a man of far greater interest to me. The defendant was Steve-O's father. He was facing charges that resulted from our raid and arrest of him two years earlier.

I first saw him outside the judge's office. He was wearing a yellow prisoner jumpsuit; his hands and ankles were shackled. I had anticipated that I'd feel anger or hatred, but I felt nothing. In fact, his appearance had changed, and I briefly doubted whether they'd brought the right guy. I walked over to him and, through an interpreter, asked: "What was your wife's name? When did you last see her?"

He did not recognize me. He seemed puzzled by the personal questions from an American. But he answered: "Her name is Tahira, and I haven't seen her in two years, since I was arrested."

I had hoped for some confirmation on Tahira's fate from him either way. Both Steve-O's uncle and Sayed himself had reported that she was dead, but the truth was always difficult to ascertain in Iraq. I'd held out hope that she was alive. It looked like I wasn't going to get any more information from the father. I left him and returned to the courtroom.

It was merely a preliminary hearing, so there was no sense of resolution. The judge simply heard the evidence of the weapons cache we'd found in the father's yard. The trial on the charges was scheduled for a month later in front of a three-judge panel. That very morning, a judge had been ambushed. Security guards surrounded our hearing. During the hearing, Steve-O's father sat on a couch across from the judge. I felt no shame for wishing that I'd been able to deal with him on the battlefield instead of in the courtroom.

I gave my testimony about the father's involvement with the

insurgency and his attacks on us, primarily the November 11 attack at the bridge over Ambush Wadi. I further testified to the father's ties to Sayed and foreign fighters coming into Iraq. As I spoke in the courtroom, I could see Nassir come to the realization that I was one of the soldiers who had befriended his son. I knew much more than he'd thought possible. Sweat began to form on his brow and his pose of confidence and indifference broke down as I laid out the details of his involvement with the insurgency. Under Iraqi law, Steve-O was not allowed to testify against his father, but SFC Evans and Sgt. Bandel also testified about the weapons we'd found in his yard. The evidence piled higher and higher as the father sank lower and lower in his seat.

The hearing ended without drama, but I requested permission to talk to the father afterward. I wanted to try one last time for Steve-O. I grilled him again about the fates of his other children and his wife. This time, he claimed that Steve-O's brothers and sisters were alive. The oldest sister had gotten married, he said. He seemed to be telling the truth about the children, but his accounts of his wife's status kept shifting. In this telling, he claimed he'd seen her two weeks earlier. It contradicted what he'd told me before the hearing. I had fully expected the bullshit answers I received, but my rage was growing by the second.

As I was leaving, I pulled a round from my pocket and handed it to the interpreter to give to Nassir. I asked him to translate for me: "This is a gift from me to you. It is a 5.56-millimeter bullet fired from a U.S. M4 rifle. Please keep it to remember me. If we ever meet again under the same circumstances as our first encounter, I will have another one to give you, except it will be going much faster." The startled JAG (Judge Advocate General) officer on the case stopped the interpreter from translating, but I think Nassir got my message.

AFTERWORD

As with all things in life, you try to make the best decisions you can under the circumstances presented to you. Steve-O began his new chapter in the United States by staying with me and Christina. But after eight months, it became clear that we were not going to be the best long-term care option for him. He has so much potential, but Steve-O needs a great deal of guidance to help him deal with his tumultuous past and the challenges of assimilating into Western culture. It was very difficult for me to admit that, as much as I love and care for him as a son, a younger brother, and even a soldier, I was not in a position to give him all that he needed.

The thing that brought us together—namely, my military career—ultimately posed the biggest obstacle for our hopes of becoming a family. Steve-O grew up in a male-dominated society, and he needs a strong male presence in his life every day, particularly in his teenage years. My redeployment to Iraq for another year took me out of the picture right when he would have needed me the most. Even upon my return from that tour, I am looking at long stretches of absence from home for training exercises and schooling.

I made a promise to Steve-O, and I will always be there for him. But I had to bow to the experts, including a child psychologist who advised me that Steve-O could begin his healing only by breaking with certain aspects of his past. I was too close and too much a part of some of the most traumatic incidents of his life in Iraq. The psychologist felt the boy needed to live apart from the military environment and in a more normal family setting. It is not the perfect ending I'd envisioned for us, but I truly believe this is what is best for him. We are still very close, and we keep in touch regularly now that I'm back home. We will always be a part of each other's lives.

There is no doubt that if Steve-O had stayed in Iraq, he would have been killed by his enemies in the insurgency. He is a survivor with powerful instincts, but they would have gotten to him eventually. Forgiveness is not part of the tribal code in his native village. While struggling to bring him to safety, I'd often flash to images of the mass grave that was discovered outside Husaybah or to the bodies of informants that were found hanging on Market Street. Those images kept me focused on living up to my promise to him because I knew he would suffer a similar fate if I failed in my mission to bring him to safety.

I am a veteran soldier, a professional, and I have learned to deal with the darker truths of the world I inhabit. But my feelings for Steve-O have been something of a surprise to me. I have asked myself why on many occasions: Why did I give a shit about this particular kid? Was he that much different from other Iraqi informants who put their lives on the line? What was it about him or his situation that provoked such a response from me and the other members of Dragon Company?

It has often struck me that if I'd found Steve-O hiding under the bridge with a weapon in hand during the Husaybah ambush by his father's insurgent cell on November 11, 2003, I might well have shot and killed him, thinking him a deadly threat to me and my soldiers. Now that I'm home with Christina and our daughter, Sydney, I have the luxury of hindsight to put such reflections into perspective. My second tour in Iraq also gave me some insight into Steve-O's situation. On that deployment, I saw young Iraqi men, boys only a few years older than Steve-O, joining the

U.S.-trained Iraqi police forces and Iraqi army in droves. Every one of them faced threats and attacks from the insurgency, but they signed up to fight for peace and democracy. They understand what Steve-O instinctively grasped when he made the decision to come into our camp.

For me and most of the soldiers in Dragon Company, Steve-O came to represent Iraq's best hope. His desire for freedom gave us validation and made us feel that we were not wasting our time or risking our lives for no good reason. So, consciously or otherwise, we came to think of Steve-O as our reason for carrying on. He represented a struggling country and all of the people in it who wanted a better life. There are thousands of heroic Iraqis who fought and continue to fight for freedom and security. Steve-O is just one of them, but he is the one who means the most to me and my soldiers in the most arduous year of our lives.

On April 19, 2005, I was two months into my second Iraq deployment when I read an article in the *Washington Post* titled "The Grim Reaper, Riding a Fire Truck in Iraq." I was mesmerized by the story, for it described a spectacular attack on a small marine base in, you guessed it, Husaybah. This was an all-out assault on Camp Gannon. What really caught my attention in the article was the description of the vehicle that was loaded with explosives and driven into the checkpoint compound by an insurgent suicide bomber. It was a bright red fire truck—the same one that we had used to haul water around Tiger Base during our time there. In our final weeks in Husaybah together, Steve-O had identified a mujahideen driving that fire truck on Tiger Base. We had him arrested immediately. If Steve-O hadn't spotted the spy in our camp, the now-legendary "Grim Reaper Attack" might have occurred on our watch.

Steve-O saved American lives, without a doubt. This country owes him its gratitude and support. I owe him much more, and I intend to fulfill the promise I made to him, and beyond. In the spring of 2005 with the pro-bono help of Jeff Joseph, Colorado's top immigration lawyer, Steve-O's political asylum was approved. He is now with a strong, supportive family, and he appears to be thriving with them. Together, we will make certain that he gets every opportunity to succeed in this country and in whatever he wants to do with his life. He lost all that he had when he stepped into our camp, yet he was a major reason that we returned home without losing a single soldier in Dragon Company. I will forever be grateful.

AFTERWORD BY STEVE-O

When I saw 1SG in the airport I felt happy and safe for the first time in a long time. I couldn't believe I got out of Husaybah—I thought I would be killed there. When 1SG left his hat and started calling me after he left Iraq, I started believing. I know he promised, but seeing him again made me the happiest I have ever been. I didn't know how to thank him.

I never thought America would be like it is. What I heard in Iraq was that America was bad, all the people in it were bad. I don't believe what people say in your ear or on TV. You need to see it with your own eyes. America gives you freedom and a lot of choices. The people are human beings just like Iraqi people.

It is very different here. In America they treat animals like they treat human beings. Girls' clothing and women in charge is very different. If you don't listen to the women, oh boy, it will be hell—you will get in big trouble. School is different. They don't hit you or make you do stuff you don't want to do, like cut your hair if it is too long or your nails if they grow too long. You can do what you want as long as you follow simple rules. I am learning to do the right thing. I am trying, but it is hard. It is still hard to follow rules sometimes, to learn to read and write English, to meet kids when they find out you are Iraqi. They say mean things, like, "You are a terrorist, ugly, gay." It is hard to walk away, but you have to. Even if they push you, you still have to walk away.

Soldiers of Dragon, I thank you for helping make me safe. You treated me like a brother and a fellow soldier. You helped me more than my own people. I am happy for the opportunity to come to America for a new life—not a lot of people have an opportunity like this. I am happy to survive Husaybah and get out with the help of the American soldiers. Seeing Dragon soldiers in America is different. They were very serious in Iraq doing their job. In America they are happy with their families, kids, and wives, and it was great to see them here.

Daniel/Christina: Thank you for bringing me to America and a new life. My own family didn't care for me like you do. Christina, thank you, you treated me like your own son and care about me a lot. I will never forget this. When 1SG Hendrex went back to Iraq I was very sad. . . . I cried a lot. I started thinking he was going to get hurt or killed. I wanted to go back with 1SG and Dragon to help and protect them. It was very hard not to be able to go back. My new family helps me learn the rules, teaches me how to treat people right, teaches me not to cuss and not to lie. I now understand, with another family, American rules and what is right and what is wrong.

I have three goals in my life: (1) learn to read and write English, (2) do something where I can help people, and (3) have a family of my own someday. I want to go into the military to repay them for bringing me here. I consider myself American. I want to help defend her.

ACKNOWLEDGMENTS

Many great officers, noncommissioned officers, and soldiers are at the roots of my success in the army. I am eternally grateful for their guidance, the experience that I have gained, and for the opportunities that I have been given.

As for this book, it was a collaboration that endured our being on separate continents while working under peculiar conditions (another trip to Iraq for me and a few tropical storms and Hurricane Katrina for Wes). I am glad we both survived to complete a book that I am very proud of. Wes, thank you!

And for the men of Dragon Company, my last words in the Dragon's Den-Redeployment Newsletter February–March 2004: I would like to express my gratitude and admiration for the finest group of soldiers, noncommissioned officers, and officers I have ever seen assembled. Upon reflection of the past year I am awed by the technical abilities, creativeness, and flexibility the men of this company have shown. They have expertly completed every mission assigned! Many times on short notice and outside their normal scope of operations, this company showed a resiliency that I have never before seen. Platoons cross-leveled with the ease and expertise of seasoned veterans, while the majority of soldiers displayed abilities well outside their military occupational skills. Several branches of the Armed Services relayed comments on the tactical abilities and professionalism of Dragon soldiers. Army Special Forces, Central Intelligence Agency, and the marines have all laid praise upon Dragon. All the accolades are due to the hard work of men who have gone well above and beyond. As that same focus is applied to our redeployment I would just like to say that I am truly grateful and honored to have been able to work with Dragon Company.

Your efforts and sacrifices were humbling!

—*SFC Daniel Hendrex*

FALLEN HEROES OF THE THIRD ARMORED CAVALRY REGIMENT

OPERATION IRAQI FREEDOM I

MARCH 2003–MARCH 2004

Spec. Spencer T. Karol	RHHT 3rd ACR
1st Lt. Michael Adams	ATroop, 1/3 ACR
Sgt. Michael E. Dooley	B Troop, 1/3 ACR
S.Sgt. Andrew Pokorny	ADA Battery, 3rd ACR
S.Sgt. Daniel Bader	ADA Battery, 3rd ACR
Spec. Brian H. Penisten	ADA Battery, 3rd ACR
PFC Vorn J. Mack	HHT 1/3 ACR
Spec. James A. Chance III	C 890th Engineers
S.Sgt. William T. Latham	E Troop, 2/3 ACR
Sgt. Thomas F. Broomhead	E Troop, 2/3 ACR
S.Sgt. Michael B. Quinn	E Troop, 2/3 ACR
PFC Justin W. Pollard	G Troop, 2/3 ACR
PFC Jesse A. Givens	H Company, 2/3 ACR
Capt. Joshua T. Byers	HHT 2/3 ACR
Spec. Stephen M. Scott	HHT 2/3 ACR
Spec. Darius T. Jennings	HWB 2/3 ACR
S.Sgt. Frederick L. Miller Jr.	K Troop, 3/3 ACR
PV2 Benjamin L. Freeman	K Troop, 3/3 ACR
PFC Armando Soriano	HWB 3/3 ACR
S.Sgt. Richard S. Eaton Jr.	B 323 MI 3/3 ACR

CW2 Mathew Laskowski	O Troop, 4/3 ACR
CW2 Stephen Wells	O Troop, 4/3 ACR
Sgt. Paul F. Fisher	F 106 AVN
1st Lt. Brian D. Slavenas	F 106 AVN
CW4 Bruce A. Smith	F 106 AVN
Sgt. Paul F. Velasqurez	F 106 AVN
CW3 Brian K. Van Dusen	571st MED
CW2 Hans N. Gukeisen	571st MED
Sgt. Richard A. Carl	571st MED
Spec. Michael A. Diraimondo	571st MED
CW2 Phillip A. Johnson	571st MED
Spec. Christopher A. Golby	571st MED
CW2 Ian D. Manuel	571st MED
Maj. Matthew E. Schram	HHT RSS 3 ACR
Sgt. Ernest G. Bucklew	HHT RSS 3 ACR
Sgt. Taft V. Williams	MAINT TRP/RSS 3 ACR
PFC David M. Kirchoff	2133d TRANS/RSS 3 ACR
Spec. Frances M. Vega	1–151 AG(POSTAL) RSS 3 ACR
S.Sgt. Stephen A. Bertolino	AVIM TRP/RSS 3 ACR
Spec. Aaron J. Sissel	2133d TRANS/RSS 3 ACR
Spec. Ryan C. Ferguson	S & T TRP/RSS 3 ACR
Sgt. Joel Perez	A BTRY 2–5 FA
S.Sgt. Joe N. Wilson	A BTRY 2–5 FA
Sgt. Keelan L. Moss	B BTRY 2–5 FA
Spec. Steven D. Conover	C BTRY 2–5 FA
Spec. Rafael L. Navea	C BTRY 2–5 FA
Sgt. Ross A. Pennanen	C BTRY 2–5 FA
PFC Karina S. Lau	B CO 16th SIG
PFC Anthony D. D'Agostino	D CO 16th SIG

OPERATION IRAQI FREEDOM III

MARCH 2005–FEBRUARY 2006

Maj. Michael R. Martinez	RHHT 3rd ACR
Maj. Douglas A. Labouff	RHHT 3rd ACR
PFC Joseph Labian Knott	RHHT 3rd ACR

2nd Lt. Charles R. Rubado	C Troop, 1/3 ACR
Spec. Joshua T. Brazee	HWB 1/3 ACR
Cpl. Stephen P. Saxton	ADA Battery, 3rd ACR
Cpl. Charles T. Wilkerson	ADA Battery, 3rd ACR
Cpl. Joseph L. Martinez	E Troop, 2/3 ACR
Sgt. Denis J. Gallardo	E Troop, 2/3 ACR
Sgt. Jacob M. Simpson	F Troop, 2/3 ACR
Sgt. Tyrone L. Chisholm	F Troop, 2/3 ACR
PV2 Robert W. Murray Jr.	G Troop, 2/3 ACR
PFC Ricky W. Rockholt	G Troop, 2/3 ACR
Spec. Hoby F. Bradfield	G Troop, 2/3 ACR
PFC Eric P. Woods	HHT 2/3 ACR
Spec. Robert C. Pope III	I Troop, 3/3 ACR
Spec. Jared W. Kubasak	I Troop, 3/3 ACR
S.Sgt. Brian L. Freeman	I Troop, 3/3 ACR
PFC Mario A. Reyes	I Troop, 3/3 ACR
SFC Christopher W. Phelps	I Troop, 3/3 ACR
1st Lt. Justin S. Smith	I Troop, 3/3 ACR
PFC Ramon A. Villatoro	K Troop, 3/3 ACR
Sgt. Milton M. Monzon	K Troop, 3/3 ACR
PFC Ernest W. Dallas Jr.	K Troop, 3/3 ACR
S.Sgt. Jason W. Montefering	K Troop, 3/3 ACR
Spec. Ronnie D. Williams	K Troop, 3/3 ACR
S.Sgt. Justin L. Vasquez	L Troop, 3/3 ACR
Cpl. Lyle J. Cambridge	L Troop, 3/3 ACR
PFC Brian S. Ulbrich	L Troop, 3/3 ACR
Spec. Eric J. Poelman	L Troop, 3/3 ACR
Sgt. Timothy J. Sutton	M Company, 3/3 ACR
SFC Eric P. Pearrow	M Company, 3/3 ACR
PFC Robert A. Swaney	HWB 3/3 ACR
S.Sgt. Scottie L. Bright	HWB 3/3 ACR
CW2 Dennis P. Hay	P Troop, 4/3 ACR
Cpl. Jeffrey A. Williams	MED Troop, RSS 3rd ACR
Sgt. Timothy R. Boyce	MAINT Troop, RSS 3rd ACR
S.Sgt. Jeremy A. Brown	66 MI CO, 3rd ACR

1st Lt. Joseph D. Demoors	66 MI CO, 3rd ACR
Sgt. Ivan V. Alarcon	473rd QTR MSTR CO, 142nd CSB
SFC Brett E. Walden	1st BN, 5th SF GROUP (A)
SFC Robert V. Derenda	98th DIV, Advisory Support Team
Lt. Col. Terrence K. Crowe	98th DIV, Advisory Support Team

Made in the USA
Lexington, KY
19 June 2014